Building a Successful 21st Century Music Career

Simon Cann

THOMSON

~TM

COURSE TECHNOLOGY

Professional ■ Technical ■ Reference

ISBN-10: 1-59863-370-8

ISBN-13: 978-1-59863-370-2

Library of Congress Catalog Card Number: 2006909692

Printed in the United States of America

07 08 09 10 11 TW 10 9 8 7 6 5 4 3 2 1

Publisher and General Manager, Thomson Course Technology PTR:
Stacy L. Hiquet

Associate Director of Marketing:
Sarah O'Donnell

Manager of Editorial Services:
Heather Talbot

Marketing Manager:
Mark Hughes

Acquisitions Editor:
Orren Merton

Marketing Assistant:
Adena Flitt

Project Editor/Copy Editor:
Cathleen D. Snyder

PTR Editorial Services Coordinator:
Erin Johnson

Interior Layout:
Shawn Morningstar

Cover Designer:
Mike Tanamachi

Indexer:
Larry Sweazy

Proofreader:
Gene Redding

THOMSON

━━━━★━━━━ ™

COURSE TECHNOLOGY

Professional ■ Technical ■ Reference

Thomson Course Technology PTR, a division of Thomson Learning Inc.
25 Thomson Place ■ Boston, MA 02210 ■ http://www.courseptr.com

Acknowledgments

I would like to thank everyone who has been involved in the writing of this book. There are a few people I would particularly like to single out.

- Lucy Jordache from Marillion and Derek Sivers from CD Baby, together with all of the other people I spoke to while writing this book.

- Cathleen Snyder, Orren Merton, and the good folks at Thomson. In addition, Shawn Morningstar for the layout, Mike Tanamachi for the artwork, and Gene Redding for proofreading and finding the mathematical errors.

- A book like this can't go without mentioning Richard Moody and the many conversations we've had over many years about building communities and constructing websites. And hi to Mrs. Moody and the little Moodys too!!

- David, Lisa, and Mae. You didn't do anything to help with the book, but it's always good to have you people around.

About the Author

Simon Cann is a musician and writer based in London.

He worked for more than 15 years as a management consultant, where his clients included global music industry/entertainment/broadcasting companies, as well as companies in the financial services, aeronautical, pharmaceutical, and chemical industries.

He is the author of *Cakewalk Synthesizers: From Presets to Power User* and *How to Make a Noise*, and he is co-author of *Sample This!*

You can contact Simon through his website: www.noisesculpture.com.

Contents

Part I Introduction

Part II The Fan Base

Part III The Product

Part IV The Nasty Commercial Bits

Chapter 9 Economics 101   189

Chapter 10 Building the Team around You   265

Chapter 11 Your Pay Packet   295

Part V Putting the Theory into Practice

Chapter 12 Putting All the Pieces Together   319

Chapter 13 Career Templates   371

Chapter 14 Tales from the Sharp End   401

Index   413

Introduction

 # Introduction

This book is about how you can proactively start and manage your own music career so that you can earn your living through making music—whether as a musician playing pop, rock, soul, R&B, classical, or any other style of music; as a songwriter; or as a composer. In particular, the book focuses on two aspects:

- Exploring the options available to you to develop your career.

- Developing a plan of action to proactively make your career happen. In other words, taking the range of options and making the right choices to ensure you succeed. Without a coherent, unified strategy, all you have are bits and pieces of dreams and hopes.

Once you have your plan of action, it's up to you to implement it and to keep refining this plan in light of experience.

In short, this is a "how to" book: I am assuming that you have the musical talent—or if you don't have the talent yet, that you are actively improving your skills.

Your Career Begins Today

If it hasn't already started, then your career in music begins today—even if you're still studying or you are not ready to turn professional at the moment, start your career today. All you have to do is decide to begin your career, and you're off. You don't need to wait for a record company to call and offer you a contract, because they won't. All you need to do is decide to start that career.

Then the hard work begins.

This book is a guide to the hard work: the practicalities of how you take the decision that you want a career in music and make it happen.

Even if your music career has already begun, this book is still for you. It is aimed at everyone who wants to be involved and earn a living in the music industry: musicians, including singers (of course), aspiring musicians, *American Idol/X Factor* (or your national equivalent) contestants, songwriters, beat creators, and music students, as well as people who either work or want to work within in the industry (whether for record companies, as managers, or in many of the other roles that are out there).

So what do you need to do to have a music career? The reality is quite straightforward (see Figure 1.1). All you need is an audience—in other words, someone to buy your records—and you're set. You really do need to get your head around the simplicity of what you need to survive.

Figure 1.1 The key to success is blindingly straightforward: All you need is an audience who will buy your music. No audience = no career.

You don't need a record company, you don't need a publishing contract, and you don't need a manager—all you need is an audience. At the end of the day, the audience, the fans, or whatever you want to call them are the only people who matter because they will be funding your career. Without an audience, you will not have any income and you will have no career.

As I said, this book is about the hard work needed to make your music career happen. In short, it is about the hard work that you need to undertake to acquire and keep an audience. Once you have the audience, you need to keep them happy and ensure they keep buying "product" from you so you can continue to have a source of income. This book looks at how to get your product to your audience so that you can continue to have an income.

Why the Emphasis on Being Proactive?
I Just Wanna Play Music!

If you would prefer to sit around and wait for some big record company executive to call you and offer you a deal, please feel free to stop reading now and put this book down. However, if you don't take control of your music career and make it happen, then it is almost certain never to come about.

There are many other compelling reasons for following the approach I am advocating here. First, and most significantly, it puts the relationship between you, the artist, and the fan at its heart. No one else but you, the artist, can have a relationship with your fans. No one else but you can create and maintain this relationship. You wouldn't expect to get married and then ask someone else to have a relationship with your husband/wife, so why is it acceptable for musicians to ignore the most important relationship in their professional lives?

If you ignore this relationship or leave it to someone else, then eventually your fan base (and remember, your fan base equals your income) will walk away feeling that they have had cash stolen out of their pockets.

Another reason for following the ideas in this book is that you keep control (see Figure 1.2).

Control is one of those vague terms that musicians usually waffle over without really having any idea about what it means, so let me list some of the areas where you get to have control:

- Artistic control. You can write the songs you want, you can record the songs you want to record, and then you can release the songs you want to release.

- Deals. You are in control of every deal. You don't need to sign away any rights. You won't hear your song used in a TV advertisement for hemorrhoid cream (unless, of course, you want to and you are being financially rewarded).

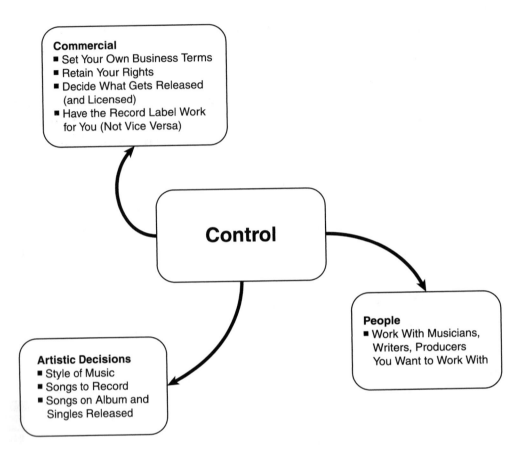

Figure 1.2
What is control? Why is it a good thing? In what areas might you want to have control?

- People. You can deal with the people you want to deal with (and when you want to deal with them). If there is a producer whom you have always wanted to work with, if you have control you can hire that person (provided he wants to work with you). Equally, if there is anyone with whom you wish to collaborate, you can—provided he is willing and the necessary arrangements can be made.

In short, control means you decide every who, what, where, when, and how in connection with your career. In particular, you decide when your career begins and how it is run.

The other great benefit of having control is that the chances of you getting ripped off are reduced. If you have control over all aspects of your business, then there will be far fewer opportunities for shady characters to take a slice of your income.

If you're looking for an insight into the ways that majors can work and how losing control can mess you up, then I suggest you check out *The Daily Adventures of Mixerman* by Mixerman (www.mixerman.net). At the time of writing, the book was unavailable but the web diaries were still accessible. This hilarious and—unfortunately for the band— true tale recounts the story of a newly signed band recording their first album.

How You Can Make It Happen

I will go into this in more detail throughout the book, but in short, the process you need to follow to have a music career will go something like this:

1. Decide to have a career in music and dedicate the necessary time and energy (in other words, all of your time and all of your energy) to making it happen. If you're one of those people who adopts a "work hard, play hard" attitude, then give up now. You work hard or fail. If you've got time to play (let alone play hard), then you're not working hard enough.

2. Create your "product," which could be anything from which you can generate income. (It could be a live performance, a CD, and so on.) Whatever you create, it needs to be the very best that it can be. I talk about products (in all their forms) in much greater detail in Chapter 8, "Creating and Developing the Product."

3. Find an audience. In other words, find someone who will buy your product. You then need to convert your audience into income. Translated into practical terms, you need to persuade your audience to buy, and keep buying, your product.

4. Once you have established your audience, keep your audience. It is so much easier to sell to an existing fan than to find a new fan to sell to.

5. Expand your audience. This will give you:
    - More people to buy your new products
    - A new source of people to buy your existing products

6. Develop new/updated products that you can sell to your expanding audience to generate increased revenue.

This book is not an all-or-nothing choice; instead, think of it as a smorgasbord of ideas. You can take some of the ideas from this book and apply them, but ignore other ideas. You're a creative person—figure out what is useful for you and how it applies to your situation. What matters is that you adopt ideas that work. What is not negotiable is that you should take control of your career rather than being a commodity to be played with by your manager and/or record company or, worse still, a commodity that is never bought.

Even if you don't like an idea I put forward, I would encourage you to reconsider and perhaps try it. If you keep doing the same things that you've always done, then you're likely to keep getting the same results. If you want to get different results (for instance, you want to change failure to success), then you'll have to do something different.

I will go further into the mechanics of making your career happen in Chapter 2, "Do You Really Want a Career in Music?"

The Commercial Imperative

Talking about the commercial aspects of the music business is not very rock and roll. But remember, what *is* very rock and roll is ending up heartbroken and busted with no money.

There are certain basic human necessities: food and shelter, to name two. In the Western world, you need money to procure food and shelter.

I therefore presume you are happy with the basic concept that you need to generate money from your musical endeavors if you are going to eat and pay for a roof over your head.

However, we need to go further than just accepting that you need money to buy food. If you're not going to pay attention to the business end of the business, then how are you going to know if/when you're being ripped off?

You also need to ensure that you (and your partners) are financially credible individuals—in other words, you're not blacklisted with credit agencies or bankrupt. If you lack credibility, then you will find it hard to deal with the banks, which in this wired-up world could be quite a challenge. You will find it hard to use cash or barter if you're trying to sell your CD to someone on the other side of the world.

You are also going to need a certain degree of financial credibility if you're going to borrow money or raise finances in other ways. (See the section "Other Sources of Finance" in Chapter 9, "Economics 101.") As an example, if you have no financial standing, then you're unlikely to be able to raise money to record your next CD or to finance a tour when you're starting out.

Adopting the Strategies Set Out in This Book

This book does not outline one single strategy. Indeed, there is no one way or magical formula to ensure a successful music career. Instead, this book sets out lots of separate ideas. It is up to you how you put these pieces together. How you do so will depend on what you want to achieve and your particular circumstances. You will see that the final part of this book (Part V, "Putting the Theory into Practice") is dedicated to looking at different ways that you can manage your career.

This flexibility is good news: It gives you many more chances to forge a successful career. However, the range of options also means that you have greater freedom to make mistakes. Although it might be unlikely that you will get anything wrong as such, you are far more likely to do things in the wrong order. We all know that you shouldn't learn to walk before you can crawl, and this principle applies equally here. For instance, you shouldn't release a CD until you have an audience ready to buy it.

As we progress through the book, you will see there are certain recurring themes. Often I will look at these themes from different angles so you can see how one idea can be applied in several different ways or in different situations.

There are, however, certain principles that are not negotiable. The principles I see as being set in stone are:

- Cut the expenses of doing business as far as you can (and in particular, cut your expenses).

- Cut out the middleman (or middlewoman) as far as possible, but do not ignore people who can make you more profitable.

- Make a living by generating income over a longer period. Don't look to make a million immediately and then walk away; instead, aim to generate income over your whole career.

This is unashamedly a book about business: My intention is that you will create an ethical, sustainable business. As part of this goal, I focus on how to foster organic growth of your business. I do look at some of the more "hard sell" tactics you can use, but over the longer term, I do not believe these tactics create a sustainable business, so I have given less importance to these aspects.

Getting the Most from This Book

As you will read in Chapter 3, "Influences for Change and the Opportunities These Changes Bring," there are many new opportunities for the musician to carve his or her own career. This book is not a guess about the future—it is about how you can make money and survive now. The book discusses a range of music business and general business principles. It brings forward a range of tried and tested working practices and combines them with the new opportunities and thinking that are available in the 21st century. The combination of tried and tested with new thinking will help you to be successful.

While reading this book, I suggest you keep a pen, a highlighter, and a supply of those little yellow sticky notes close by and mark any areas that are of interest to you. These notes should make it easier to refer back to this book when you are drawing up your own strategy. I would also suggest that you re-read this book (perhaps after 12 months) when you want to review or revise your strategy. You may find that ideas that didn't work earlier are now worth considering.

Before you start reading, let me offer you a few thoughts about the information in this book. If you are of an impatient nature, then skip over the rest of this chapter and start reading Chapter 2. However, if you skip ahead, please do come back and read some of these words of caution at a later date.

Each chapter in this book is intended to be freestanding. You don't need to read from the start to the end, although you will find the content does flow more logically if you do. There are five Parts, and you may find this book easier to digest if you take the chapters in each Part together.

Each of the five Parts has its own distinct focus.

- Part I: Introduction. This Part introduces the main themes and ideas that are then applied throughout the book.

- Part II: The Fan Base. This Part looks at your most important asset (your fan base) and considers how to nurture these people for your and their mutual benefit.

- Part III: The Product. This Part considers the things you do that make money and discusses how to do these so that (a) your fans are happy and (b) you make money.

- Part IV: The Nasty Commercial Bits. This Part looks at the whole money issue—in particular, what money you can make and where it comes from.

- Part V: Putting the Theory into Practice. This final Part takes all of the ideas discussed in the book and shows how you can mix and match the concepts to create your own successful music career. It also includes a case study of Marillion, a band that has already applied some of these principles in practice.

You will see that I have cross-referenced between chapters. I have also overlapped the content where this aids the understanding (or where the need for emphasis justifies the repetition).

There are a few other points I would like you to think about before you proceed.

Changing Times

It's always good to throw in a cliché as early as possible, so let me throw you my first....

We are now living in a time when the only constant is change, and as the world around us develops, this book will go out of date. This book was written at the end of 2006/start of 2007, and all examples quoted were current and relevant at that time. For instance, there is currently a healthy (albeit declining) market for CDs. I do not know where the CD market will be in one year's time, let alone five or ten years.

My hunch is the CD market will decline, and the download market will increase. However, my hunch about the future is irrelevant: Because most projections about the future turn out to be wrong, this book deals solely with the here and now. In reading this book and applying the principles, you need to consider changes that may have taken place since the book was written.

To give you an example of something that may change, look at the cost of CD reproduction. When CDs first came out, the reproduction costs were comparatively high. Today, the reproduction costs have fallen. My guess is the costs will continue to fall; however, that is a guess. If you are going to produce your own CD you need to find the costs that will apply to you. The price you will pay will depend on many factors, including the number of CDs to be produced, the printing (on the CD and the booklet), and the location of the reproduction plant (you will find that costs in different countries and different cities within a country vary enormously).

Regional Variations

I'm a Brit, and much of the data and many of the examples quoted in this book come from UK sources. Where I'm quoting UK sources, the principles can be applied globally. However, there will be times when I quote UK data in order to highlight regional variations, and in these situations I will note that I am highlighting the variation.

To give you an example of regional variations, think about touring. Mainland United Kingdom is a few hundred miles in each direction (roughly 400 miles wide and 600 miles high). Within that area there is a population of 60 million people. By contrast, Australia has a population of around 20 million people but is roughly 3,000 miles wide and 2,000 miles high. The implications for physically reaching an audience if you are touring make the UK a far more efficient location.

However, if you look at gasoline (petrol) costs and compare the UK and the US, then the US is a much better place if you're using road transport. At the moment (subject to regional variations within both countries), the price of gasoline in the US is around $2.20 per gallon. By contrast, the price for a liter of petrol in the UK is 88p. Converting liters to US gallons (1 liter = 0.2642 gallons) and pounds to dollars (at the rate of $1 = £0.52) petrol in the UK is equivalent to nearly $6.50 per gallon—in other words, around three times the price. This has implications for touring in the UK.

Although I will compare and contrast regional variations, I'm not going to look at all possible variations because that would really get to be tiresomely dull. Instead, I would suggest that you make sure you understand how each factor discussed in this book can be affected by your local market conditions.

I should also point out that laws vary by country (and state). Please ensure that you make yourself aware of any legal requirements that apply to you. In this context there are two books that I would recommend you check out:

- *All You Need to Know About the Music Business* (Free Press, 2006) by Donald S Passman

- *Music – The Business: The Essential Guide to the Law and the Deals* (Virgin Books, 2003) by Ann Harrison

Passman is based in the US, and Harrison is based in the UK. Each book focuses more heavily on its home market. That being said, they are both excellent books, and I recommend you read them both.

What This Book Does Not Cover

This book is about how to develop and maintain a successful career in music. I have assumed a certain level of understanding/knowledge and that you have the common sense to figure out how to make certain things happen. So for instance, this book does not explain:

- How to write a song

- How to sing in tune

- How to find gigs (although I will talk about ways to use gigs to increase the size of your fan base)

- How to get a CD pressed and the legal requirements associated with releasing a commercial recording

- How to commission artwork for a poster and the necessary copyrights you should obtain in order to use the artwork

I hope that the basic mechanics behind much of this stuff (such as how to get a CD pressed) are fairly straightforward for you. However, for the associated legal requirements, I would suggest you check out the two books mentioned in the previous section.

Things You Don't Understand

We shouldn't go any further without a word of caution: Be wary of things you don't understand.

For instance, I don't understand eBay. This is not a matter that I'm stupid—I can write a book, so I figure I must have a certain level of intelligence—however, I have never bought or sold anything on eBay, therefore I don't have the understanding that comes with experience of conducting a transaction on eBay. My perception, which is probably wrong and prejudiced, is that eBay is a place where other people sell their unwanted tat. I've got enough tat of my own without being taken in by my ignorance of the whole eBay process.

Now, I'm not suggesting you shouldn't do anything that you haven't done before. But rather, I am suggesting that you recognize the things you don't know (such as eBay for me), acknowledge this piece of learning that you still have to do, and proceed with caution (see Figure 1.3). If you're going to do something new, research it first. Once you've researched it, try it in a small-scale way. Once you have some experience, refine what you're doing in light of that experience, and then go for it in a big way.

Whatever you do, please don't risk your whole career and financial stability on something that only *sounds* like a good idea.

Scalability

It is common sense that you should start small. In that way you will be less likely to make disastrous financial mistakes. However, you should always be sufficiently flexible to grow. Sometimes your system may be able to grow with you, and sometimes you may have to completely change what you are doing.

For instance, you might start off by sending out CDs by hand. If you are sending 10 or 20 CDs a week, that is quite feasible. However, if you suddenly have to send out 10,000 CDs, then you may have difficulties (although having an order for 10,000 CDs does sound like a nice problem to have).

You should also remember that you don't have to employ only one solution for any problem. For instance, you can sell CDs at gigs but engage someone else (such as a fulfillment service, which I will discuss in Chapter 3) to send out your internet/mail orders.

Products and Services

Through this book I make reference to various products and services. The mentions I make are not endorsements. I only mention these to illustrate the range of products/services that are available. As always, you should undertake your own due diligence and choose a product/service only once you understand what you are taking on.

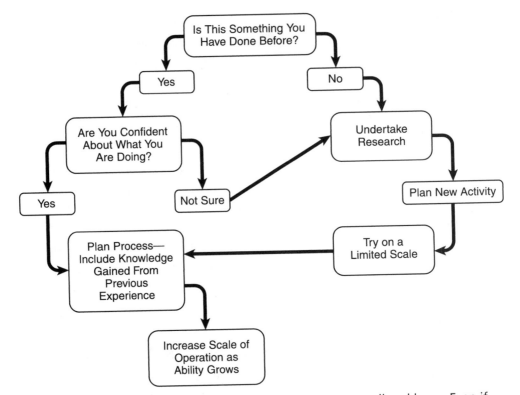

Figure 1.3 If you have never done something before, start small and learn. Even if you have done something before, always be sure to keep improving what you are doing as you gain experience.

Further Reading

I refer to a number of books that I think may be useful. All of the books mentioned in this book are listed on my website at www.noisesculpture .com/c21music.

Although there are other books available, I have only referenced books that I have read and that I feel I can recommend. From time to time I will add to this list of books, so if you see something on my website that isn't mentioned here, don't worry too much.

The Next Chapters

This chapter has introduced some of the main ideas that are discussed in this book. The remainder of the book fleshes out those ideas and looks at how you can implement them in a practical manner.

2 Do You Really Want a Career in Music?

I was watching *The X Factor* last night. *The X Factor* is the UK equivalent of *American Idol*: a talent show where all-comers have the chance of winning a £1,000,000 record deal. At the time of writing this chapter, the program was showing the initial public auditions.

One guy who turned up for an audition was interviewed outside the venue, where he proudly showed off his car. He obviously had spent a lot of time working on his car (or "pimping his ride," to use the vernacular that I'm sure would appeal to this guy). This interview led me to an obvious question: What is this guy's passion? Music or his car?

I suspect neither. I suspect his passion is for chasing women, and he sees his car and music as being two ways to achieve his aim.

Now, please do not misconstrue the point I am trying to make. I am not suggesting that chasing women (and/or men) is wrong. I am simply asking what the priority is in this guy's life: women, cars, or music? My suspicion is music comes third on his list. I think there are two easy tests for this guy to check out his commitment to a music career:

- Test 1: Compare how much money he has spent on his car to how much money he has spent on his music career.

- Test 2: Compare how much time he has invested in his car to how much time he has invested in his music career.

From the sound of his audition, he has never had a singing lesson in his life. I would also guess that he has never spent any of his cash getting inside a recording studio with a hot producer to lay down some tracks.

If I'm right, and music is third on this guy's list, then music is not a priority for him. Either music is a priority that comes at the top of the list, or it's not a priority. If it's not a priority, then a career in music is probably never going to happen.

So what matters to you—your music career or something else?

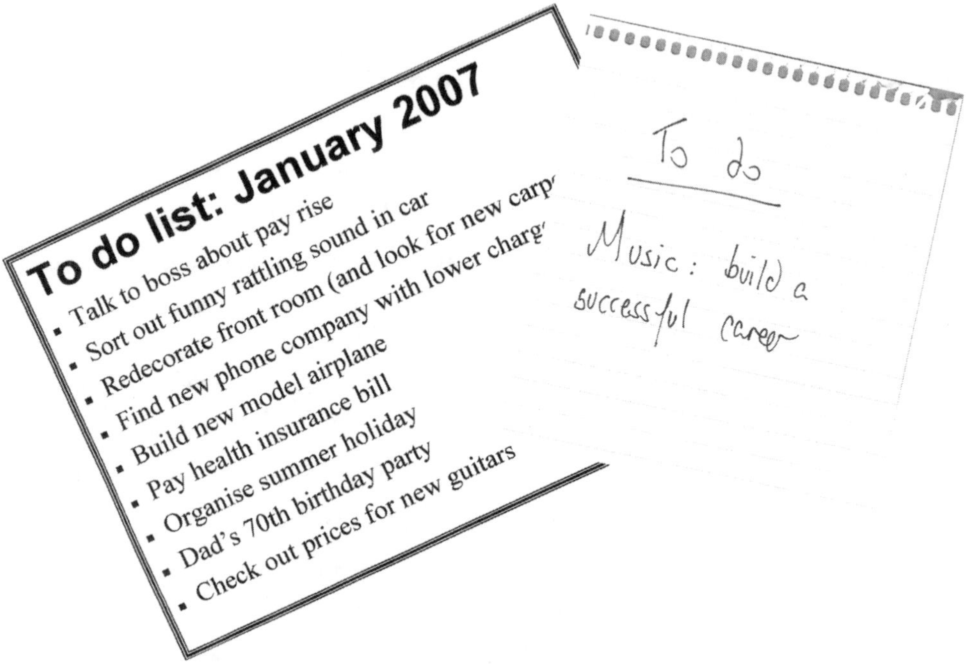

To do list: January 2007

- Talk to boss about pay rise
- Sort out funny rattling sound in car
- Redecorate front room (and look for new carp⸱
- Find new phone company with lower charg⸱
- Build new model airplane
- Pay health insurance bill
- Organise summer holiday
- Dad's 70th birthday party
- Check out prices for new guitars

To do
_____

Music: build a successful career

Figure 2.1
Which list is more likely to lead to a successful career in music?

Are you passionate about music? Are you committed to your music career? Or is music something that comes way down on the list after work, study, home, family, friends, and your other "hobbies"?

And when you actually get around to music, what are you doing then? Are you spending your time setting up your computer so that it runs your newest piece of software without a hitch? (And when it doesn't work, are you spending countless hours talking to several software developers, trying to get to the root of the problems and then testing new fixes?) Or are you getting out there and actually furthering your career?

As I've already said in the previous chapter, if you're one of those people who adopts a "work hard, play hard" attitude, then give up now. You work hard or fail. If you've got time to play (let alone play hard), then you're not working hard enough. The other great advantage of working hard is that you gain experience much more quickly. This makes you better sooner, and so you will be able to see the tangible results of your success at an earlier stage.

If music is something you do for fun, that's great. However, do not pretend you want it to be a career if it's just something you do for fun. Please carry on enjoying your music—you may even find you make some money from an activity that brings you pleasure—however, please do not kid yourself that you are trying to pursue a career in music if you are not prepared to make the commitment to sustain your livelihood.

If you are certain you want a career in music, you will need to deal with all areas of the business if you are to succeed. Realistically, you cannot spend every waking hour making music: Time not making music is time you will need to spend on business matters.

I would not expect you to have the same passion for the business aspects as you do for the music. However, you will need to have a similar level of commitment. If you can't commit to doing the business side or ensuring that there is someone to attend to the business side on your behalf, then your musical career will fail.

After this rather harsh introduction, I am going to ask what may seem an odd question: Do you really want a career in music? Take a moment and think about what it means and how you can achieve it. Now, are you really sure you want it?

If you are sure, then answer me a few questions:

- What is it you are passionate about? Do you have a passion to be a writer or a performer? Are you interested in the fame and the adulation, or are you just chasing the money and women/men?

- Can you live with the lack of security and especially the perilous state in which your finances are likely to be?

- Do you have a husband/wife/significant other? Do you have kids? What are their attitudes to this? Are they happy with the risks you want to take? How will your relationship with these people be affected by a career in music?

If you're still convinced that you want a career in music after you've thought about some of these issues, great. If you're not convinced, then get a proper job. It will give you far more financial security, as well as a pension and healthcare coverage (if you're lucky). If you're not 100% committed, then why would anyone else want to help you with your career (or risk his or her career on working with you)?

Kick-Starting Your Career

If you want a career in music, you have a simple choice to make: Either you take hold of your career and you make it happen for yourself, or you wait for someone else to find you and hope they take care of your career. If you've left your career to someone else, then I assume you won't be reading a music career book....

As I've already said, your music career starts whenever you decide it starts. You don't need to wait for Simon Cowell (or any other Mr. or Mrs. Big in the music industry) to sign you. In fact, if you sit around waiting for someone to find you, it's not going to happen for you.

There have been some significant changes in the music industry (and to business in general) over the last few years that I will discuss in Chapter 3, "Influences for Change and the Opportunities These Changes Bring." For the musician, these changes are generally good. Among other things, the changes mean:

- There are more opportunities for more musicians to forge a career in music. In other words, there are more ways to generate income to sustain a living while making music.

- It is easier to reach an audience and easier for an audience to purchase your product.

- The influence of the majors (in other words, the major record companies who are all part of multinational entertainment conglomerates) is reducing.

For the 21st-century musician, the only thing holding back your career is you. Most non-professional musicians can give you a great reason for not starting their career—usually there is something (beyond their control) that has to be achieved first or they just need to tighten up their skills a bit. Alternatively, you will find they have sent demos and are waiting for a response (which will never come).

If you are still at school or college and you're hoping for a career in music, I can see why you might want to polish your skills a bit before you start on your career. However, if you're looking to learn skills, there's nothing better than the school of hard knocks. If you get out and play some gigs, you learn a lot more—much more quickly than you would by learning in isolation. You'll also find that there is a need to learn more, and to learn more quickly, in order to make yourself a better musician for your performances. Added to this, you'll start generating some interest and picking up some fans.

You should remember that you will always be learning and refining your craft throughout your career. As soon as you stop learning, your career will regress.

Music in the 21st Century: This Time It's Personal

One of the things that will make the 21st-century music market different is personal contact. People want to "touch" the act they follow, to feel that they are part of the musician's life, and to engage in a two-way dialogue. People don't just want to hear a CD; they want to go to gigs and participate in the music.

When you're a huge multi-platinum artist, it's hard to communicate directly with all of your fans. However, for a smaller act looking to build a loyal following, this is quite possible. I'm going to talk a lot about business, but in all of the comments that I make, please remember you are dealing with people, and these people (on the whole) want to deal with people rather than some soulless, uncaring, corporate entity. The more you and your organization behave like human beings, the more people will stay with you. If you act like a large corporate entity, then people are likely become disenchanted with you.

An Introduction to the Business Strategy for the Musician

Business strategy? For the musician? This sounds boring, and it sounds like work.

However, you have a choice here (yes, another choice): Do you want a career in music or do you want to find a job and become a wage slave?

If you want a career in music, then you'll have to understand the business aspects. When you're starting out, you will be dealing with the business aspects directly. As you progress and bring in other people to help you with your career, it is important to understand the business side of things so that you can keep control and ensure you don't get ripped off.

Why Adopt a Business Strategy?

Before I talk about business strategy, let me give you some of the logic behind this strategy and some of the reasons why you should consider it.

- First, this strategy will help you become profitable (and stay profitable). Many musicians get into debt very early in their careers due to their lack of income, and they have to take out loans to finance their career. When they then sign a deal, their advance will often help pay off some of those debts. The only problem here is that with the advance, the musicians are getting themselves into a different sort of debt. Often when the deal ends, the musician is still in debt to the record label, and his or her career is at an end (which is why the label deal has ended).

- This strategy will make you more desirable. If you have a solid business that can generate income, then people will want to work with you. This will mean that instead of approaching industry types, such as managers and record companies, saying "we think we're going to be huge," you can approach them with proof about how interested your public is in you. Indeed, for all of your deals, you will be in a better negotiating position.

- Your career will last much longer. Instead of being a packaged commodity that is hot today and cold tomorrow (and dropped by your label), by looking after your fan base you can expect to continue to make money from your music throughout your working life. You will not be on the shelf at 30 (and left with the prospect of having to find a proper job to support the husband/wife and kids).

- You can cut out the middle man. For instance, if you have your own fan base and you know they will all turn up to your gig, then why do you need a promoter for your gig? As you will read later, if your promoter can bring more people to a gig, that's great. However, if you have already reached all of your fans (and potential fans), then do you need someone else taking a cut?

An Outline of the Business Strategy

I'm going to outline a business strategy for a 21st-century music career, starting from the first steps (in other words, assuming that you are just starting out). However, you may already have an established career of which you feel you need to take hold. If this is the case, then apply the strategy when you feel it may be appropriate to you.

One decision you will have to make is where you intend your income to come from. For instance, you could decide that you are purely a live musician, and so your income will be generated solely from live performances. (In other words, you will get your income from the tickets purchased by punters at the gig door.)

Surviving on live gigs alone is likely to be tough, so you might decide you want to sell CDs too, but only CD albums because CD singles smack of a sellout. You may also feel comfortable with some merchandising, T-shirts, and souvenir programs, perhaps. Then again, you may want to go the whole way and generate income from as many (legal) sources as possible, such as all merchandising options (including, perhaps, dolls that look like you), sponsorship deals, and endorsements.

What you decide to do is up to you. For the purpose of this book I will assume that you will consider any income-generating source, but at least initially, the range of sources is likely to be restricted.

(For instance, if the band only started last week, then you're unlikely to be able to secure an endorsement with a major clothing label...but please don't let me discourage you if you've got something great to offer.)

Once you have decided to have a career in music, then you need to dedicate the necessary time and energy (that is, all of your time and all of your energy) to making your career happen. Here's what you need to do:

- The first step is to create a product. When I say "product," I mean something that can be delivered in some form to an audience and that can generate income. This product is most likely to be a song (or a collection of songs) packaged as a live performance or a CD. The whole nature of the product is discussed in Chapter 8, "Creating and Developing the Product," including how and why to expand your product range.

- When you have your product, then you need to start finding your audience. Your audience is the people who will buy your product. Initially, you are likely to find that people are less willing to part with money until they know what they are getting, so you may need to give a few products away in order to generate some interest. For instance, you may do some gigs for free or make a few tracks available for free on a website.

- When you have an audience, then you need to know who those people are. You don't need to know their names or where they live (although both may be interesting); however, you do need to know how to contact these people. The easiest way to contact them will probably be by email, but do not rule out snail mail and the phone (especially cell/mobile phones with which you can send SMS/text messages to a list of people).

- Through contact with your audience, you need to start finding a way to generate income from these people. In other words, you need to persuade your audience to buy, and keep buying, your product. You may use your contact with your audience to tell them about upcoming gigs. Alternatively, you may want to tell them about a new CD or a T-shirt that is available to purchase from your website.

- You then need to expand your product range and your fan base. I will talk further about how to build your audience in Chapter 5, "Building and Keeping the Fan Base," and how to build your product range in Chapter 8. A larger audience implies larger possible income. Without new products, your existing fans cannot be a continuing source of income for you (and their interest will wither).

Figure 2.2 shows a simple way to start thinking about your business strategy.

Figure 2.2
A way to start thinking about your business strategy.

Your Guarantee of Success

In the strategy I have outlined, there is one guarantee of success: your audience.

You don't need talent, you don't need connections, but you do need an audience. Without somebody being there to buy your product, you will not have income. Without an income, you cannot put food on the table or keep a roof over your head.

I will repeat this point: The only guarantee of success is your audience.

When you have an audience, your talent does not matter. You may have a voice that makes dogs howl and only be able to play your instrument with one finger (and then not in time—not that the concept of 4/4 time is understood by your drummer). Your shortcomings do not matter, provided that your audience loves you.

If you have an audience, you will have income, and you will have power. Your income means that people will be interested in you. (If nothing else, they will work out what commission they can generate based on your income.) Your income also means that you will have power to negotiate—you will be able to walk away from deals because you already have your own income.

However, I would caution you against being too talentless. Although your audience may love you today, will they love you tomorrow? In six months' time, will they realize that you are a talentless bunch of no-hopers whose songs all sound the same? If you want a long career, you can't be a novelty act—you need a credible product that will continue selling.

I will discuss the nature of the changes in audiences' tastes in Chapter 5 and how your products should evolve in Chapter 8.

Defining Success

One thing I want to talk about before we go any further is success and what success actually means. There is something of a clichéd view about what success means in the music industry. Many people associate success with multi-platinum albums, huge tours, vast income, many huge properties, substance abuse, and a lot of sexual intercourse. In particular, many people think a career in music equates to riches beyond their wildest dreams. This may happen for one or two people, for instance, with assets of around £800 million (around $1.6 billion). Paul McCartney hasn't done too badly for himself.

However, in any field of human endeavor, some people make a lot of money, but most people do not. Outside of music, those who do not make the huge dollars will still usually earn enough to live a comfortable existence.

I do not wish to discourage you if you have an ambition for a multi-million-dollar income. In fact, I would positively encourage you. If you can follow the principles in this book and become a multimillionaire, then please tell me and please tell everyone else. I am sure the kudos will increase sales of this book. However, I do want you to think a bit about what you want to achieve with a career in the music industry (beyond frequent, guilt-free sexual intercourse) and exactly how much money you need (rather than want).

The nature of success is hard to define and is personal for everyone. I'm sure we've all known of, or have heard about, miserable millionaires and joyful paupers. In thinking about your career, I would encourage you to consider your reasonable expectations from a career in music: Don't just think about how much the top stars earned last year (see Figure 2.3). Once you have your expectations, then you can start planning your career and ensure that those expectations will be included in your plan.

Here are some of the expectations you may want to consider:

- A career in music that spans the rest of your working life (or until you want to end your career in music).

- The freedom to make the type of music you want to make without compromise.

- Sufficient income to provide for your family and loved ones and for you all to be able to live in comfort.

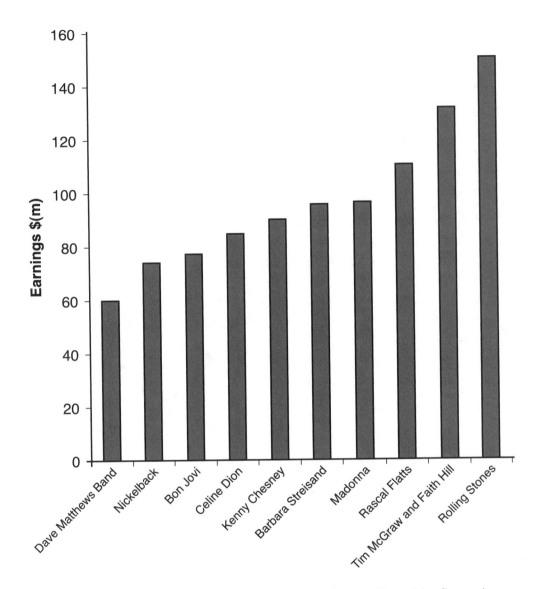

Figure 2.3 Earnings of mega-millions will always hit the headlines. (The figures in this graph come from *Forbes* magazine.) But how much do you really need to earn to consider yourself successful? I will return to this subject in Chapter 11.

- The ability to control your life and make the decisions you want to make (for instance, to be able to spend time with your kids when you want to and when they need you).

- Sufficient income to save for your retirement so you will still be able to buy food when the music stops.

- A flow of income from your music after you have ceased to be active in the industry. That is income from music, not from savings.

As I said, the nature of success is personal. However, for me, a career in which you can earn a living doing what you want to do seems pretty much perfect.

We will look at the amount of money you may need to live on in Chapter 11, "Your Pay Packet."

3 Influences for Change and the Opportunities These Changes Bring

Many changes over the last few years have convulsed the music industry. If you listen to some of the stories, you might think that we're close to the end of the world. In many ways, that could be true for the industry as we currently know it. However, the challenges will probably lead to a stronger, reborn industry with much of the current inefficiency removed, although that's not to say that the corporate behemoths will not add new and different forms of inefficiency.

Some industry commentators suggest that only 5% of artists releasing an album with a major label will recoup their advances. In other words, 95% of artists on major labels do not see any royalties. From a commercial perspective, this lack of success by the majors is a fairly daft situation and one that they seek to rectify over time. Their solution, which has been feeding into their business planning for quite some time, is to sign fewer artists and to be more conservative in their signing policies, making sure that they only sign artists who will have hits.

Ironically, although this reduced-signings policy may seem to work against the musician, it could work to your advantage. The majors are hugely inefficient, especially in their marketing strategies. While they continue with their "tried and tested" marketing strategies (which broadly means advertising), this leaves other options open to you. One of the advantages of cutting out the inefficiencies (and increasing your market by organic growth due to people actually liking your product) is that you can survive on much less money.

The other changes in the industry are not all bad news for the 21st-century music career, either. Many of the changes that have hit the majors, and their reactions to these changes, have also led to many more opportunities for many more musicians. For instance, it has never been easier to get your music to your audience—provided, of course, that you know who your audience is and where they are.

In the new game, once you have reached the audience, there are new rules. One of the most significant new rules is that there is less money and that income will no longer come from one or two main sources. Instead, income is likely to come from many sources. Naturally, as you might expect, each source will create a lesser flow of income than the one or two sources may have historically provided. You will see this theme emerge in the examples that follow.

Ironically, the notion of making less income may actually favor the musician. The musician has far less overhead than the record company —for instance, the musician doesn't have a flashy office to pay for— and so the musician who is being paid directly needs to generate less income to make a good living than the musician who is being paid royalties by a record company that will be keen to keep as much income as it can to fund its overhead (and to pay its staff).

This chapter takes a look at the influences for change (in the music industry and also changes for business in general, which may have implications for how you build and manage your career) and considers the opportunities for your career that these changes bring.

This chapter does not consider all possible sources of income. These sources are discussed in greater detail in Chapter 9, "Economics 101." Nor does this chapter discuss how you can combine all of the disparate possibilities to create a coherent career strategy; this is discussed in Chapter 12, "Putting All the Pieces Together."

MP3s, iTunes, and Music Downloads

One of the most significant changes in the last few years has been the rise of downloads from the internet.

Downloading has taken many forms. One of the most prominent was the (originally illegal) file-sharing services (such as Napster, Kazaa, and Gnutella). The rise of the original Napster and the like, coupled with the availability of cheap and easy-to-use MP3 players, changed the way people got hold of music. In many ways, the unlicensed download sites worked to prove the concept that the public would be happy to acquire music digitally and without owning a physical product.

This is a highly significant change that has resulted in the whole of the music industry's current distribution process being re-evaluated. In particular, the change has major implications for the economics of the music business. With CDs there is a cost to manufacture, a cost associated with distributing the physical product, middlemen who take a cut, and stores who both take a cut and push the product. With electronic distribution, there is no physical product, so the manufacturing and distribution costs are slashed. The "store" still remains, albeit in the guise of a website. When dealing with a conventional store, the record company can provide sales aids (such as posters, free CDs, and so on). However, in the internet-based store the only real sales aid is advertising.

The most significant influence shaping the legal download market has come from outside the music industry: iTunes from Apple. Although originally intended to support the iPod and make it easier for the company to sell its hardware, the iTunes store has changed the way people buy music. At the time of writing this book, there are believed to be more than 350 legal download sites. This is good and bad. It is good because it gives you 350 possible outlets. It is bad because that's 350 possible contracts that you have to enter into and then administer.

Although the download market is still comparatively small—it only accounts for a few percent of total record sales—it is still significant. To give two recent examples of the significance of download sales in the UK market:

- "Crazy" by Gnarls Barkley was the first song to reach number one on the charts without being released on CD. Under the chart rules in operation at that time, this feat only worked because a CD was released the following week.

- Koopa became the first unsigned band to land a UK top 40 hit with their single "Blag, Steal & Borrow." Unlike Gnarls Barkley, Koopa has not released a CD—the rule requiring release of a physical product for inclusion on the charts has been relaxed. In the UK, this now means that the cost of getting to number one has been slashed.

For you, the musician, electronic downloads provide the possibility of going global without pressing any CDs. It also puts you on the same level as established acts in all of the online stores.

Legal downloads and iTunes-style operations are changing the way people buy and listen to music in other less obvious ways. First, there has been a rise in the purchase of single tracks, which contrasts with the decline in the sales of CD singles (and to a lesser extent, CD albums).

People have become bored with the situation where the record industry has been content to pump out expensive CD singles or CD albums with 15 tracks on which only three songs (usually the first three tracks) are any good. Instead, they are now buying one or two tracks from an album—they see albums as little more than a collection of possible downloads.

A second change is that people are now able to buy music that they would be too embarrassed to buy in a record store. This is rather a "music as porn" situation in which people are able to keep up the pretense for family and friends that they are "serious" music lovers when behind closed doors they are happily buying and downloading bubblegum pop.

The entry of Apple into this download market is significant for another reason. For the first time, they brought together in one package:

- The hardware (iPod)

- The compressed file format that plays on the iPod

- The software (iTunes) that includes the facility for people to rip their own CDs and load the content onto their iPod (in other words, take CDs they already own and put them onto their iPod)

- The iTunes store, from which people can buy new music

iTunes (see Figure 3.1) is the only end-to-end music solution on offer to the public. Every other service relies on the consumer putting together various elements.

Figure 3.1 The iTunes store, which is integrated into the iTunes software. The iTunes store is the leading internet download retailer.

At the time of writing, this package is unique. However, the Zune player from Microsoft has just been released (but availability is highly limited). Although Zune doesn't have the history of the iPod, clearly this is a pretty sophisticated piece of hardware backed by some serious software. Given the market in which it has to compete, I am sure it will be developed rapidly.

Although the notion of selling electronic downloads may seem like a panacea, there are still many downsides. First, although your music may be carried by the major music download stores, it will not stand out. There will never be a display to highlight your latest album.

Another downside is the cost of download stores. Although you stand to make a greater percentage selling through download stores, you are by no means going to get a large percentage—there are still significant costs in running an online record store, not the least of which is the cost of credit card processing (where there will be a minimum cost for each transaction).

The Expanding Market for Music in TV/Films/Games

When I was a kid, we had three TV channels: BBC1, BBC2, and ITV (which is the independent, commercial network in the UK). That was it—there were no other options in the UK. In 1982, that choice was expanded to four channels with the addition of Channel 4. Now, with the introduction of satellite and cable services, as well as digital Freeview, there are several hundred channels available in the UK.

Anyone reading this book in the US may sneer at the time when there were only three TV channels in the UK. (Just be grateful that I'm not old enough to remember when there was only one channel.) However, like the UK and the rest of the world, the US has also seen a huge increase in the number of available TV channels, and I'm sure if you go back far enough, there was a time when there were only three channels in the US.

One effect of the increase in the number of channels is the reduction in audience numbers for any particular TV program. Top-rated shows in the UK used to be able to reach viewing figures of around 25 million. Now if a show has 10 million viewers, it is doing exceptionally well. (Even the Queen's Christmas message to the Commonwealth only gets around 6 million UK viewers.) So that's the bad news: Fewer viewers means reduced budgets, and as you might expect, one budget that is easy to cut is the music budget.

However, the good news is that there are a lot more TV shows out there that need music. That means there are a lot more opportunities:

- To get your music heard
- To generate income from your music

These opportunities are not just available for TV. They also extend to film (especially independent films), corporate videos, and a number of other possible outlets. Like the music industry, the film industry has been undergoing many changes. Also like the music industry, it is now easier to get into the film industry. And again like the music industry, it is getting harder to reach the heights in the film industry.

However, that is not such a concern for us—what really matters here is that there are more opportunities to make money from your music in TV and films. The commercial opportunities tend to come in a range of forms. The main options are:

- Specifically commissioned music, for which you are commissioned to provide an original piece of music to accompany a film, TV show, game, corporate video, and so on.

- Tracks licensed for a specific project, in which (for instance) a song is licensed for synchronization with a specific piece of video (such as a TV advertisement).

- Production music or library music, as it is sometimes called. This is music that is pre-cleared for use and where the income is generated from a standardized license. This form of music is increasingly popular because it tends to be cheap, and the license terms are already agreed. Film/TV/video producers like using production music because they have certainty of cost and know that a synchronization license has already been granted.

Another great place for music is video games, which can provide both a source of income and a channel through which to promote your music.

There is much common ground between the popular music industry and the video-game market. Both are aimed at a similar age group (children, teens, and young adults). The nature of video games is such that a track that is included with a game can be played hundreds of times and so can introduce a band and a track to a whole new audience. The possibilities for creating a buzz about a track (with this key audience) through a video game make video games a compelling outlet.

Another interesting facet of the video-game market is how the industry has embraced the internet—for instance, with multi-player games (where each player can be in a separate country playing on a computer linked to the internet) and through leadership boards.

Contrast this adoption of new technology with the music industry that has spent time trying to stop its product from being distributed on the internet. Although we are comparing two highly different industries, the level of innovation in the games industry is still something that the music industry could aspire to if it is to reinvigorate itself for the 21st century.

One last point I want to make about the video-game industry is about product life. Very often video games (which can sell for $50 or $60) will have a lifespan of one year. After a year, the next edition of the game is released, which again sells for $50 or $60. Then every couple of years a whole new gaming console is introduced, necessitating another round of purchasing of new games.

Compare this to the music industry, in which the CD format has been stable for the last 20 or so years. I will talk more about product lifecycle in Chapter 8, "Creating and Developing the Product."

The "Collapse" of the CD Market

Over the last few years the sale of CDs has declined quite markedly. It is difficult to determine the precise reasons behind this decline because you cannot prove empirically why someone didn't do something. That being said, there are a number of reasons that may or may not be related to this decline.

Illegal Downloads

It is impossible to prove the link between illegal downloads and a decline in the CD market; however, many in the industry have cited this as a reason for the decline.

There is a certain logic to the argument: Why buy CDs when you can get music for free? However, it is a slightly far-fetched argument to suggest that if all the people who download illegally were prevented from accessing illegal music, then there would be an increase in CD sales equivalent to the number of illegal downloads. Many people will take what they can get for free, but will never pay for it.

The argument often put forward in favor of free downloads (which may be illegal) is that by having free access to a wide range of music, many people have come across artists who they may not have found in the normal course. This has led to an increase in interest in those artists and indeed an increase in revenue when people have then gone on to purchase these newfound artists' CDs or gone to see their gigs.

I'm sure you have your own views about these practices, so I'll leave you to make up your own mind about the rights and the wrongs of this situation. If you are looking for more arguments about this subject, check out *The Future of Music: Manifesto for the Digital Music Revolution* by David Kusek and Gerd Leonhard. (Details of this book are on my website.)

Pirate CDs

Unquestionably, pirate CDs (that is, CDs manufactured illegally and sold without royalties being paid to any of the copyright owners) have affected the CD market.

It is not an unreasonable assumption that if people are prepared to pay money for a pirate CD, they would be prepared to pay money for a legal CD. What cannot be proven is whether the income that flows to the pirates would flow to the music industry if the pirates could be put out of business. For instance, there may be reasons why people buy pirate CDs. One reason could be price—people may be happy to buy cheaper pirate CDs, but would not pay full price for legal CDs.

As a legitimate music maker who wants to make a career in the industry, there is no upside to the pirate CD market for you.

Bad Music

I've never seen anyone in the music industry put forward this argument, but I will. Bad music—that includes uninteresting artists performing turgid, formulaic songs—leads to a decline in music sales. Second-rate acts and songs lead to second-rate CD sales.

Better Things to Buy

There was a time when the range of goods on which people could spend their disposable income was much narrower than it is today. For instance, 30 years ago there were no video games in the form we understand the product today.

When music had little competition for disposable income, it was easier to generate income from recordings. In today's climate, particularly with many other consumer products being very heavily marketed, the CD is having a hard time. To keep up with the competition, marketing budgets have ballooned.

Reduced Number of CD Outlets

CDs are available in a much wider range of stores—for instance, you can now buy CDs in supermarkets and bookstores. Although this may seem good, it does lead to unintended consequences.

First, these non-music retailers tend to carry a much narrower range of music. Usually they will carry highly commercial chart music and golden oldies. Sometimes these stores will sell CDs below cost price, knowing that cheap CDs are the sort of product that will draw consumers into their stores. The retailers hope that once inside, the consumers will then also purchase some of their products with a higher profit margin.

As a corollary to this, the established record stores are on the decline. Their prices are under attack from the supermarkets and online retailers such as Amazon. The profits they used to make from chart music and golden oldies—which could be used to finance the carrying of less profitable music ranges—are no longer there. As a result, the size of stores is shrinking, and some retailers (such as Tower Records) are going out of business.

Merchandising and Other Non-Music Income Sources

There is one recent development that may not affect you when you first start out, but I'm sure will have increasing influence over time.

Perhaps this trend can be most easily illustrated with an extreme example. In 2002, the UK singer Robbie Williams signed a deal with EMI. Under this deal, EMI not only has an interest in his CD sales, but also all of his other sources of income (such as publishing, touring, merchandising, sponsorship, and so on).

It seems that while the rest of the industry is in no rush to set up deals that go as far as Robbie's does, there is certainly evidence that other artists are making deals where they are selling a wider range of their rights.

In particular, some record companies are interested in having a greater financial stake in touring income (in all its forms). There are several reasons for this; perhaps the most compelling reason is that tours can make a lot of money. If you look at a band such as the Rolling Stones, most of their current income comes from touring. By contrast, their CD sales are comparatively modest. One of the main reasons for tours making so much money is corporate sponsorship, which we will look at in Chapter 9. If you want to check out the Stones' recent earnings, take a look at Figure 2.3 in Chapter 2.

Home Recording

Another significant change over the last few years has been in the area of recording technology. It is now possible to record CD-quality music using a personal computer and free software. If you're more ambitious, there are a number of highly featured software packages that will help you get professional results. These packages include Pro Tools, SONAR, Cubase, Nuendo, and Logic, among others.

Simply owning a computer does not necessarily mean that you can create a release-quality album. At the very least, you need to know how to use the gear, and you probably also need some high-quality hardware, such as analog/digital converters and monitors, not to mention the recording room and some highly specialized software if you are going to get the very best results.

The new technology means it is possible to do a considerable amount of recording without incurring any studio costs. However, in reality, there are not that many CDs at the top of the charts that have been recorded from start to finish in a home-studio environment. (However, at the top of the dance charts, home-based studios may perhaps be closer to the norm.)

The use of new technology gives many new options. For instance, if you want to try a few new songs or create a CD to give out/sell at your gigs, you can record you own tracks and then simply burn a couple of CDs on your computer. This may not be the most elegant solution when it comes to distributing your music; however, it is a simple and straightforward solution that is fairly cheap. Once you have your computer up and running (and have paid for the necessary hardware/software), the main cost (apart from your time) is for the blank CDs onto which you will burn your music. Even if you then only sell the CD for a few dollars, you can make a profit.

Recording and reproducing your own CDs gives you great flexibility. For example, if you want to make only one or two tracks available, you can. If you want to make a CD available for one night only, you can do that, too.

You should also remember that if you record your own material and keep control of the recordings, you have great flexibility if you subsequently think you can do a better job. Obviously you can re-record a track at any time. However, if you own and control the original recordings (which is much easier when you are doing things yourself), then you can just add another part, take the recording to a professional studio to remix the track, or get it professionally mastered.

These options are, of course, open to you if the original material was recorded in a professional studio. However, if a record company is involved, they are likely to own the recordings, so it may not be your choice as to whether anything is re-recorded or remixed.

eServices

It has been possible to sell goods by mail order for a long time. With the rise of the internet, a universal way of buying mail-order goods has come into being, and many people are now happy with the concept of shopping online.

As the level of business conducted over the internet has increased, there has been a need for ways to help people complete business transactions. If you are going to build a career in music, you will need a way to undertake transactions (that is, to sell your products to your fan base).

Receiving Checks

Bank accounts and credit cards have been around for a long time. A bank account is necessary for business, but when you're doing business on the internet, especially when someone wants to purchase an electronic download, it is not particularly desirable to be handling checks or direct credit transfers.

Checks can represent a real nuisance and are not an efficient way of working if you are trying to sell a large number of low-priced products (such as CDs or single downloadable tracks). Let me illustrate this point by talking you through the process.

1. First, the purchaser needs to place the order (which could be done on a website or by printing an order form and filling it in). The purchaser then needs to put the check in the mail.

2. The initial problem is that you need to receive the check. This usually means waiting several days for the mail to arrive, especially if the purchaser is overseas. The possibilities for checks getting lost in the mail are endless.

3. Once you have received the check you need to wait for it to clear or take a gamble that it will clear. If the check is in your own currency, then it should usually clear within a couple of days. (It may be credited to your account sooner than that.) If the check is in another currency, then it can take a while to clear. For instance, with my UK bank account, checks in dollar amounts can take up to a month to clear and be free from any charge-backs. This sort of timing is not uncommon.

    To take the currency issue a step further, if you insist on receiving checks in your home currency, you will lose sales because it may be too much hassle for people to send a check in a foreign currency. However, if you receive foreign currencies and then convert the check, you may be charged a fee. Again, looking at my situation, my bank does not charge any commission on foreign currency transactions; however, it does charge a flat fee for each currency conversion of £5.50 (approximately $11) for amounts under £100 ($200) and £10.50 (approximately $20) for amounts between £100 and £5,000 (approximately $200 to $10,000). Compare that transaction charge to the cost of a CD.

4. Once you have the check and it has cleared (assuming you didn't take a gamble), you then need to complete the order. If you're mailing out the product yourself, then all you need to do is reconcile the order with the check and ensure the product is sent to the correct place. If you're selling an electronic download, then somehow you need to figure a way to ensure that the purchaser can get hold of the download.

None of the problems in handling checks is insurmountable (although if you're trying to sell a CD for $10 and your bank hits you with a currency conversion charge of $11, you may find it difficult to make a profit). However, for the small business, checks can present a real hassle.

Receiving Credit Card Payments

I hope I've made the case against receiving checks, so let's look at other options for receiving money. The most obvious way to receive money is by accepting credit cards. In order to receive credit card payments, you need either:

- A merchant account with a bank or other financial institution and a separate organization to process credit card payments on your behalf.

- An agent who has a merchant account and who will process credit card payments on your behalf. Perhaps the most widely used of these services at the moment is PayPal (www.paypal.com).

The advantage of having a merchant account and using a separate credit card processing service is that you will generally be charged lower fees. However, if you are just starting to receive electronic payments, the all-in-one solution is likely to be much more appealing, especially because you won't have to apply for a merchant account.

You will find that with credit card processing, most of the hassle with foreign exchange goes away. Or rather, you can set prices in your home currency, and your customer will be charged in their local currency. With these sorts of transaction, you will often find that there is a commission paid for the currency conversion. The commission payments may be levied on both you and your customer.

At the time of writing, Google Checkout (checkout.google.com/sell) was comparatively new. This service is similar to the offering from PayPal. The one distinct disadvantage (at the moment) is that payments can only be made to a US bank account, so this service will be of little use to you if you are not based in the US.

Order Fulfillment

When you have received payment, then you need to deliver the product. How you fulfill the order (that is, how you choose to get the product to your customer) will depend on the nature of the product. If you are selling a CD, then this will need to be physically sent to the purchaser. However, if you are selling an electronic download (such as an MP3 file), then the download needs to be made available to the purchaser in a form he or she can readily access.

If you are selling a download, then the easiest solution is to use a download service, such as PayLoadz (www.payloadz.com). With this sort of organization, you can link the payment and the download so purchasers can get hold of their products immediately. (As you might have guessed, PayLoadz has designed its service to be highly integrated with PayPal.) However, if you're selling music downloads, then you're more likely to want to sell at the online record stores, such as iTunes.

You don't need to use a download service; you could use your own website, in which case you have several options:

- Send the product by email to the customer. This works, but not everyone will be happy about receiving an email with a large attachment. You may also find that some anti-spam software will delay these files (or lose them or break them).

- Give the purchaser a download link on your website. You can do this manually by sending out an email link. Alternatively, you could have your own download service on your own website. To get your own download services up and running, you will probably need some custom web programming, which may be expensive.

The difficulty with any delivery process that involves human intervention (such as sending out an email) is that there can be a delay before the customer receives his or her product. These delays may be quite legitimate at your end (for instance, you may be asleep or you may be playing a gig). However, the slower the product is delivered to the customer, the less likely he or she is to make a subsequent purchase from you.

If you are dealing with physical products, you don't have to do all the work yourself. You could use a service provider to undertake this work on your behalf. Some of the options you could consider are discussed in the next two sections, "On-Demand Delivery" and "Fulfillment Services."

On-Demand Delivery

One recent development that is not solely related to the music industry has been "on-demand" services. This is a very useful step forward if you are looking at ways of getting your product to your fans.

Conventionally, if you want to sell a CD, you (or your record company) will make a recording and then go to a CD pressing plant and ask them to press several thousand CDs for you. You could then sell these CDs. The downside to this arrangement is that you need to make an investment to get your CDs pressed, and if you don't sell them, then you could face a loss.

With an on-demand service, instead of pressing several thousand CDs, you wait for someone to buy your CD. The service provider then takes the money from the purchaser, presses a CD (and, of course, prints the artwork and so on), and then delivers the CD to the customer. The on-demand service provider takes its fee (which is usually fixed) and pays you the balance.

There are many other on-demand services, such as print on-demand services. Like CD on-demand services, these will provide printed materials at the point that the customer places an order. These services allow you to sell your own T-shirts, mugs, buttons (badges), posters, programs, and so on without incurring the up-front costs of printing/production and holding stock.

You may also find these services particularly useful for several reasons:

- You can get up and running very quickly and easily.

- When you are up and running, it is (comparatively) easy to change things. For instance, you won't have several thousand CDs sitting around if you decide you don't like your album anymore. Equally, you will usually find that if the service provider isn't up to scratch, it is comparatively painless to change the provider.

- With an on-demand service, you can compete with the major players (in other words, the established acts that are already trying to sell CDs, DVDs, and merchandise). Although you may not be able to compete in terms of revenue raised from CDs, DVDs, and merchandise (because these services are inherently inefficient, as mentioned below), you will be able to have a comparable product range that should give you a certain amount of credibility.

- Another advantage of the on-demand services is that through their delivery services, they provide a way to get your CD/merchandise to a fan base over a wide geographical location.

Two examples of providers of these services are Lulu (www.lulu.com), which provides on-demand print and CD/DVD services, and Café Press (www.cafepress.com), which provides on-demand merchandise, print, and CD services.

The downside to the on-demand services is that they are not cheap. To give an example, a CD from an on-demand service may cost in the region of $5 to $9 (plus postage). If you're a new act looking to sell your CD at a highly competitive (in other words, low) price, with these costs you may sell a lot of CDs but not generate much profit.

If you do choose to use an on-demand service, you still have the option to sell your products directly. However, you then need to source your products. So, for instance, if you want to sell your own CDs at gigs, you would either have to get a batch of CDs pressed at a pressing plant or order a number from your on-demand service. In either case, you will need to make an investment, and you will then have to carry stock. If you are ordering from your on-demand service, then you will have very thin margins.

Fulfillment Services

As an alternative to using on-demand services, you may want to use a fulfillment service. These are organizations that will deliver your product to your customers. This may not be an obvious service to use—to many, it feels like paying money to have someone put your CD in the mail—however, there can be a great value to these services.

In deciding whether these services have value to you, let me ask you a question. What do you want to do: make music or spend all day processing orders and sending out CDs and so on? If you want to make music, these services are worth considering for the benefit of the extra time that they will bring you. Seriously, think about the process a mail-order firm goes through—credit card transactions, printing invoices, packing CDs, labeling envelopes, and mailing the packages—then decide how much it is worth for someone to do that for you.

There are also more specialized services, such as those offered by CD Baby (cdbaby.com; see Figure 3.2) that will create a webpage for you, promote you within their community, and get your music distributed through the electronic download services (such as iTunes).

Another example of a fulfillment service is Fulfillment by Amazon (www.amazonservices.com/fulfillment). At the time of writing, this service was in a beta phase. However, the potential advantages are clear: You can sell your product(s) through Amazon and have Amazon deal with the whole process, from taking the order to shipping the product and then paying you.

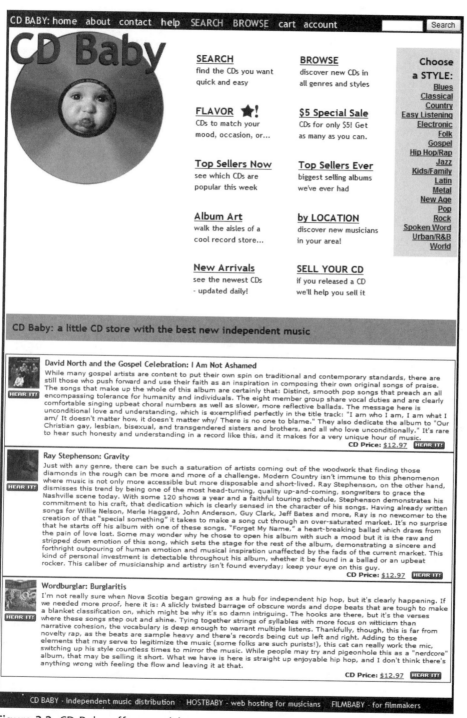

Figure 3.2 CD Baby offers musicians a way to get their music promoted and distributed to a wider audience.

The disadvantage of these services is that you still need to get your own CDs/merchandise produced, which will require an investment. You will then need to hold the stock and supply it to your delivery service. The advantage of these services is that you can make more income compared to what you can make using the on-demand services.

If you do choose to use a fulfillment service, you still have the option to sell your products directly. So, for instance, you could still sell CDs at gigs.

American Idol/X Factor

The phenomenon of *American Idol* and *X Factor* may be leading to the (false) impression that all you need to do is impress Simon Cowell (or another player in the industry), and your career is set.

For those of you who may be unfamiliar with *American Idol* and *X Factor*, these are televised talent shows where the prize is a recording contract. Both shows share a judge, Simon Cowell, who is one of the big cheeses at Sony BMG. In both shows, Simon plays the role of Mr. Nasty in a pantomime-dame sort of way. There are many similar shows around the world.

The difficulty with these shows is that some people can develop the false belief that fame is easy and that talent is unnecessary. The early stages are intended to exploit those laboring under this false illusion by giving viewers the opportunity to sneer at talentless no-hopers. These shows seem to have become very dominant, with no other pop music shows able to compete on television. That being said, for some highly talented people, these shows do provide a way to get significant exposure.

My biggest concern with these shows is that the contestants are not developing their own loyal fan base. It seems the shows attract their own viewers who will watch and vote each year. Some of the shows' viewers will even buy the CDs of that year's successful artists.

However, the viewers do not appear to continue following the artists when the next year's show begins; instead, they remain loyal to the show. This means few artists develop a successful solo career from their participation in the show. Just looking at *American Idol*, perhaps the only contestant so far who has developed and sustained a career of any note is Kelly Clarkson, who won the first American Idol in 2002.

The musician looking to build his or her own career who does not want to go down this route finds an advantage to *American Idol* and the like: It clears away much of the clutter. Many wannabes will flock to *American Idol*, which leaves you clear to pursue the other less obvious courses that may prove more lucrative.

For the musician who does not want to participate in these talent shows, the shows also demonstrate routes that may not be worth following. For instance, I would suggest that (at least initially) you spend little time trying to publicize yourself on mainstream TV because so much music programming is dedicated to *Idol*-type shows.

MySpace, YouTube, and Other Forms of Internet Relationships

Over the last year, MySpace (www.myspace.com) and YouTube (www.youtube.com, which is now owned by Google) have become hugely popular and have become useful marketing tools for musicians. The services achieve different aims and should not be confused:

- MySpace (see Figure 3.3) is a community network. In essence, you join and set up your own MySpace webpage (which can include your biography and music clips, as well as a link back to your regular website). You then ask people to become your friend. You link to your friends' MySpace pages, and your friends link to your MySpace page. The idea is that if someone is interested in one of your friends, then that person may find you by following the link to your page, which is on your friend's page. Again, the theory is that you can create and tap into a community of like-minded individuals.

Figure 3.3
MySpace: a community networking site on the internet.

- By contrast, the concept behind YouTube (see Figure 3.4) is much simpler. It is a place where you can share video clips. This gives you a great opportunity to get your message out and for YouTube viewers to see your video. The difficulty is that because YouTube is so popular, you may get lost in the deluge that is available to viewers.

Figure 3.4
YouTube: a great place to share video clips.

Although these two services are undoubtedly great ways of generating interest, and there are tales of people being signed on the strength of their MySpace following (Lily Allen in the UK being one example), I would caution you about getting too lost in the concept. It can be easy to become a MySpace/YouTube star, but this may count for nothing. In particular, becoming a MySpace/YouTube star does not address how to convert this highly localized "stardom" into:

- Income

- A lasting career

I will return to this subject of converting highly localized, unremunerated fame into something sustainable and more financially rewarding in Chapter 5, "Building and Keeping the Fan Base."

Associates' Arrangements

In a bid to create publicity and increase sales, many online retailers offer an associates' program. An example of one retailer offering this sort of arrangement is Amazon.

The way these arrangements often work is that you create a link on your website to a certain product on the retailer's website. If someone then follows that link and purchases the product, you receive a commission, which will typically be in the range of 4% to 10% (see Table 3.1).

So how does this help you?

First, if you have a product that is widely available (such as a CD or DVD) but that you are not selling directly, you can create links on your website to purchase the product(s) from the online retailer. This means that you will get paid twice: First, you get the royalty, and second, you get the commission from the retailer.

Second, this gives you another source of income. Say, for instance, you are a band performing Celtic music. This sort of music typically has a much narrower audience than a mainstream pop group could expect.

Table 3.1 The Current Referral Rates for Amazon.com Associates

Total Items Shipped	Commission Rate
1–20	4%
21–90	6%
91–330	6.5%
331–940	7%
941–1,880	7.5%
1,881–4,700	8%
4,701–9,400	8.25%
9,401+	8.5%

However, many members of the Celtic music audience also have an interest in all things Celtic. This is where you have an opportunity to increase your income and to help your fan base connect with and learn more about the background to your music.

To give you some examples, a Celtic band could consider including links to these sorts of products:

- CDs from other bands who perform music in a similar style. Perhaps you could include links to some of your heroes or your major influences.

- Books about:
  - The origins and history of Celtic music
  - Celtic instruments
  - Celtic myths that may have influenced the subject matter of some of your songs

If you want to see an associates' arrangement working in practice, you can check out my website. My book *Cakewalk Synthesizers: From Presets to Power User* is available from Amazon (as well as being available from other online retailers and good book stores). I have included links to this book on Amazon.com, Amazon.ca (Canada), and Amazon.co.uk (UK). To see how these links can look, go to www.noisesculpture.com/cakewalk and you will find the links toward the bottom of the page.

For the purchaser of my books, there is no disadvantage to using these purchase links on my website. The purchaser is not charged a different price, nor is any personal information about the individual passed on to me. There is an advantage for the reader in that he or she can read about the book on my website and then go and purchase it immediately from Amazon. For me, the advantage is that I can increase my income first by encouraging people to buy my book and second through then getting commission from Amazon.

You will also see that on my website I have added links to the books that I recommend you check out in this book. I think readers appreciate you telling them where they can find further information about a subject that may be of interest to them. That I can make a few extra cents from the arrangement is just a bonus to me.

Personally, I will only recommend a book that I have read and that I think is good. However, this is my approach. You do not need to like a product to be able to receive commission from an associates' program.

Ringtones

This is a development that baffles me. Let me illustrate with an example of a song that is on the UK charts at the time of writing this book.

If I want to get hold of "I Don't Feel Like Dancin'" by the Scissor Sisters, I can go to iTunes and get a download for £0.79 (roughly $1.60). However, if I want a ringtone for my cell (mobile) phone, it will cost me £4.50 (roughly $9). This ringtone:

- Is not the full track

- Does not feature the Scissor Sisters, but instead uses a soundalike

- Is not endorsed by the Scissor Sisters

Added to this, if I play the track on my iPod, the quality of reproduction will be pretty good, but the sound of a mobile phone ring is quite tinny and fairly distorted.

I can't see any reason why anyone would want to buy a ringtone in this manner. But maybe I'm just getting old and reactionary because ringtones are hugely popular. What is more surprising is that people will spend far more on a ringtone than they would on a download for their iPod or MP3 player. Indeed, I have come across people who will not consider buying music for their MP3 player, but who are happy to purchase ringtones.

If you can get into this market, do! There's obviously a lot of money to be made somewhere (mostly by the credit card companies, I would suspect).

Unique Ideas

In addition to these developments, many songwriters and performers are looking at unique ways to generate income. One example of someone who has used her creativity both with her music and the marketing of it is Katherine Schell (www.katherineschell.com), a Chicago-based musician. In July 2006, she held an eBay auction for the rights to her song "The Gravity Situation." Under the terms of the auction, the purchaser was offered the exclusive commercial rights to the song for one year.

Katherine is not alone in adopting this sort of new idea. A songwriter was recently reported in the UK when he was trying to sell the rights to his song one line at a time.

Will these ideas work for you? I don't know, but I would suggest they probably won't because someone else has already done them. However, I am sure that you could find an equally novel way of generating income (and, let us not forget, publicity) that would work for you.

The Fan Base

4 Exploiting with Integrity

In the 21st century, the key route to success is through marshalling a large fan base and using the spending power of the fan base. Any artist with a large fan base can:

- Generate income by selling products to the fan base

- Negotiate with third parties (such as major record companies) from a position of strength (due to the spending power of its fan base)

There will never be a situation in which you as an artist do not need a fan base (of some sort).

The fan base is also the best sales force and ambassador for any artist, as well as being a harsh critic when an act fouls up. If an artist abuses the trust of its fan base, then the relationship with its fan base is over. This could even mean the end of the artist's career.

This chapter considers how you can generate income from your fan base while retaining mutual trust. In the next chapter, I will look at how to build and keep the fan base.

Exploitation

Before I proceed, I want to talk quickly about the use of the word "exploit" (and its variants).

You may well be quite uncomfortable with the use of the word—I am sure you do not want to do anything as ruthless as exploiting your fellow human beings. It's good to be uncomfortable with this concept; it shows you are a caring human being who hasn't lost your integrity.

As you will know, the word "exploit" has two main interpretations:

- To benefit unjustly or unfairly from a situation
- To make full use of and derive benefit from

I am using the term in the second interpretation, so this chapter is about how you can make full use of your fan base and derive a benefit from that use. The benefit you will derive will be more than just financial.

I could use a different term. However, I have chosen to use the word "exploit" to remind you that there is the possibility for you to overstep a line. To my mind, the key in exploiting the fan base is to remember that you are in a relationship, each party to the relationship needs to benefit, and the benefit needs to be roughly equal for each side. As Figure 4.1 shows, each party expects something from the relationship. That is why I have called this chapter "Exploiting with Integrity."

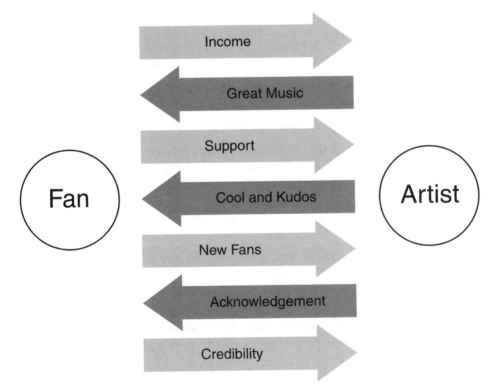

Figure 4.1
Both fans and artists expect something from their relationship with each other.

Why Do You Need a Fan Base?

For an artist, the fan base is everything. Among other things, a fan base will bring you:

- Income
- Power and influence
- Credibility
- Support at gigs
- New fans
- Radio/TV coverage/chart position

In short, nothing else really matters apart from the fan base.

Let's look at these benefits in turn.

Income

The central chunk of your income to support your career will come from your fan base. They will do the things that bring you money, such as buy CDs and other merchandise and come to your gigs.

There are other potential sources of income out there (for instance, from television or sponsorship). These other sources are particularly significant if you don't have a fan base or if you don't have a significant fan base. However, without a fan base, you are beholden to other people (such as music supervisors) to decide to use your work (and so generate income).

Even if you already do make your income from other sources (for instance, you may already compose music for video games), there is no reason not to start to develop your own fan base. It will give you two advantages:

- You will be able to sell your services more easily, provided you can demonstrate to potential employers that they will sell more of their product by using your services. (You need to use a "hire me and I bring a following" type of argument.)

- You will be able to piggyback off reputation for creating music when you start selling your product. So, for instance, if you release a CD, you will be able to market it with the line "from the creator of the music for [whatever your game was]."

In short, the fan base is the source of income for a musician. Although there are other sources of income, as a general rule of thumb, no fan base equates to no money. An unhappy fan base or one that feels exploited (in the bad sense of the word) will lead to a severe reduction in income.

I will discuss the many sources of income in more detail in Chapter 9, "Economics 101."

Credibility

If you're in the music business (whether as a manager, a record company, a gig promoter, a journalist, or whoever), who are you going to take more seriously—an artist who performs a gig in a bar every month or so, or an artist who has sold 1,000,000 CDs? Having a fan base converts potential into fact. In other words, you can be a credible person (or group of people) to deal with.

Record companies only want to sign you for what can be sold. If no one is going to buy your recordings, then you won't get signed. If you already have an audience, then you are a proven quantity.

Power and Influence

A step forward from having credibility is having power and influence. Credibility will get you through the door and bring you to the negotiating table. Power and influence mean that you can cut the deals that you want to cut on your terms.

When you speak on behalf of your fans (or, more to the point, when you speak on behalf of their wallets), you can start to shape your business.

Support at Gigs

Imagine a gig at which no one turned up. Imagine a gig at which people turned up but stayed in their seats and clapped very politely after each song (or didn't even clap).

Now imagine a gig at which the audience turns up, sings along with the songs, shouts out for their favorites, goes wild at the end of each song, demands an encore, and then crowds around the stage door after the show is over.

Which would you prefer?

New Fans

One of the best ways to grow your fan base is through word of mouth. Your fan base will work as something between a sales force and your ambassador.

Your fans will reach more potential fans than you ever can. More to the point, potential new fans are more likely to listen to the opinion of a trusted friend than they are to listen to the words of an advertisement that appears to be trying to hawk a dodgy product.

Radio/TV Coverage/Chart Position

One way to get radio and TV coverage is for people to call and ask for your CD/video to be played. A good fan base will do this for you, creating a lot of buzz about your newest releases without incurring any costs for you.

Another way to get publicity is to get in the charts. If nothing else, this will get you heard on the chart shows.

The band Marillion took a novel approach to getting their single "You're Gone" onto the charts in 2004. They asked their fans to buy the single during a specific week (and encouraged fans to buy more than one copy). The fans did, and the single entered the charts at number 7, Marillion's highest chart placing for nearly 20 years.

This created quite a buzz about the single. First, Marillion was back on the charts for the first time in many years. Second, there was the story of how the band marshaled their fans to get their chart placing. You can read more about Marillion in Chapter 14, "Tales from the Sharp End."

The Fans' Expectations

We've looked at what a fan base can do for you. Let's now look at the other side of the coin: What can you do for your fans?

Remember that we're trying to create a relationship with the fan base. We want a loyal fan base who will purchase our product (and not just once) and who will act as our ambassadors to increase the size of our product-buying fan base.

We want to exploit (in a good way) the resource that is the fan base. To do this, you need to have a deep understanding of what your fans expect in return for what they give you. Think of a marriage in which each partner brings something different to the relationship. The same principle can be applied to the relationship (or hopefully marriage) between artist and fan.

One thing that might help to focus your mind on the fan base is to think of these individuals as your clients who purchase your services. Most service providers will have a contract with their clients, setting out the rights and responsibilities, as well as the legitimate expectations of both parties and the measures of success. Although you will never have such a formal relationship with your clients (your fan base), take a moment or two to think about the terms that could be included in a contract with your fans.

What legitimate/reasonable expectations could your fan base have? These are many and varied and will depend on the nature of your act. However, there are likely to be some common themes, which probably include:

- Great music, whether live or recorded. There is never any excuse for giving a poor performance or releasing a bad track.

- New products to buy. Fans want new things to buy. One CD every 10 years isn't going to be good enough. They want regular CDs (without compromising the quality of your output). They want live DVDs. They want T-shirts so they can show the rest of the world that they love your music and share your values.

- A relationship. Fans want to have a relationship with the artists they follow. They want to feel that they can "touch" (in a metaphorical sense) the acts they follow. In short, they want contact with real human beings. This can be achieved in many ways:

  - Often, just reading or seeing an interview will give a fan a sense of the human being(s) who makes the music that moves them. We will look at ways to ensure that your fan base sees interviews (and other publicity material) in Chapter 6, "Publicity in the 21st Century."

  - Technology affords many opportunities to interact. For instance, you can send your fan base an occasional email. Although someone else may write the text, if the communication is said to come from the artist and is written in a style that could be right for the artist, it will form a bond. However, if the text is written in a style that is not consistent with the artist and therefore suggests that someone else wrote it, it will create a divide.

  - Another technical option is an internet forum. This gives many fans an opportunity to share their views about an artist. If the artist drops in to the forum from time to time, this will be very well received. However, forums also give people the opportunity to vent their anger if things have gone wrong, so this can be a double-edged sword.

- Acknowledgement and respect. Fans expect to be thanked for their efforts. Fans expect to be thanked in CD notes, when they hear you interviewed, and at gigs for turning up and for their warm reception. In fact, any time they hear you communicate, fans expect to be acknowledged. If ever you mention that your fans are less than intelligent or have poor taste in music and so on, it is probably the end of your career.

  As a subset of this, fans do not want to feel neglected or forgotten. If a loyal, long-established fan base feels that you have gone to pursue other more lucrative markets, they may turn against you.

Often when a British band goes to the US, there is a negative reaction. Usually the band will only spend a month in the US, but if there is a gap of nine months between two releases, then the UK fans believe that the band has been in the US for the duration and has forgotten their original fans.

- Cool and kudos. Fans do not want to be associated with artists who have (in their view) dangerous beliefs (and I'm not just talking about "edgy" views). More than that, they want you to take a lead on certain issues. What constitutes dangerous issues and the issues for which you should take a lead is very subjective in both cases and will very much depend on the audience you are targeting.

  For instance, if you are targeting a teenage male audience, they are unlikely to want to hear about politics, but they may want to hear about girls, and indeed, they may be impressed by tales of your "conquests." By contrast, if you are targeting the housewife market (housewife being used as a generic description, not in a pejorative sense), then your audience may expect you to align yourself with worthy causes, such as breast cancer, in addition to creating great music.

  In short, your individual fans want to feel better about themselves, and they want other people to feel good about them and respect them, due to the fan's relationship with you. You don't necessarily need to make people look cool by their association with you, but it certainly doesn't do any harm.

That being said, there are limits to what a fan can expect, and I think the vast majority of fans will respect these limits. (Remember, you will only rarely come across a stalker.) For instance, I don't think that your fan base needs to know where you live (beyond your city of residence), and your family's privacy (especially that of any children) should always be of the highest priority.

Communicating with Your Fan Base

I've already mentioned communicating with the fan base in the context of fans' expectations. I now want to talk a bit more about communicating with your fan base. In particular, I want to talk about how you communicate and how frequently you communicate.

Communication is a two-way process: It is not something that you "do" to your grateful fan base. It is really hard to make a communication sound and feel like a two-way dialogue, especially when you have a marketing message that you are keen to get out. The other point to remember is that communication is not what you say; it is what the other person (that is, your fans) understands.

How Do You Make Communication a Two-Way Dialogue?

First, you need to understand that you cannot make communication a two-way dialogue unless you sit down individually with each fan for a one-on-one chat. Instead, you need to make your communications *feel* like a two-way dialogue. There are several things you can do to help this.

Respond to Questions

Assuming you have a way for people to ask questions (or at least for you to be able to pick up a general feeling about what people are thinking), you need to make sure that the more frequently asked questions—especially the more important questions (from the perspective of those asking the question—are dealt with in a timely manner.

You can, of course, anticipate certain questions. If the lead singer quits your band, then people are going to want to know why, what he/she is doing next, whether the band is going to split, whether there will be a replacement, whether the replacement will be as good as the previous incumbent, and so on. You should be ready to answer these sorts of questions before the news becomes public. Better still, you should anticipate these questions and answer them as part of making the announcement.

You can also encourage questions. As mentioned earlier, you could set up an internet forum at which the artist (or members of the band, if there is a band) drops in from time to time to add a few words.

However, if you are going to go down the forum route (even if the forum is not intended for answering questions), remember that the forums will need to be monitored (especially if you have a younger fan base). If the comments on the forum get abusive and start running out of control, then you could have problems with adverse publicity as well as legal problems.

If you're looking for other ways to respond to questions, you could also encourage questions by phone, SMS/text, email, snail mail, and so on, and then answer them on your website or in a newsletter or similar medium.

The Human Touch (Again...)

An obvious way to create a two-way dialogue is to have two (or more) people speaking to each other. We call this an interview.

It is comparatively cheap to produce a DVD these days. Letting your fan base see a DVD of you being interviewed is a way to communicate directly with the fan base. If you want to involve your fans to a greater extent, a number of your fans could be involved in the interview process.

I'm not convinced that many fans would see it as great value to pay for a DVD of you being interviewed. Most fans understand that interviews are undertaken for publicity purposes. You could send out a DVD to fans for free or perhaps make the interviews available for free on your website, maybe as a video podcast.

Alternatively, you could interweave some other footage into the interviews to make a more valuable package (value being perceived from the fans' perspective). For instance, if you were making an album, you could commission a documentary of the making of the album and include clips of you recording the album. The documentary could then be sold alongside the album, and it could also be licensed to TV stations.

The other really obvious way to communicate with fans in a human fashion is to talk to them. It's not always possible to talk after a gig, so why not invite some people to meet you before a gig? You just need one or two people to have met you and to put out a good word for you (perhaps on an internet forum), and your reputation will be cemented (albeit temporarily, until people think that you've forgotten them).

How Frequently Should You Communicate?

It may be a glib answer, but you should communicate as frequently as you need to. There is a fine balance to be struck: You need to communicate frequently enough that your fan base knows you still love and care for them. However, you mustn't communicate so frequently that you become a pain and they think of your messages as junk mail or spam.

In practice, the frequency of your communication is likely to be determined by the stage of your career and what you are communicating. However, you should never communicate for the sake of communicating —you should always ensure you have something to say (which in practice means you have something to publicize, such as a tour or an album).

As a general rule of thumb, I would suggest:

- When you are starting out you may want to communicate around once a month (provided you have something to say).

- When you are still quite fresh, but you are established (perhaps you are releasing CDs), then you might want to communicate once a quarter.

- At the point that you have been established for quite a while and may be releasing a CD every two or three years, then you might want to communicate once every six to nine months.

- When you are at the stage that you are winding down your career (perhaps 10 to 15 years before you retire), then you might want to communicate every one to two years.

You may want to communicate more frequently. For instance, you may send out special messages if you have some tickets left for that night's gig or you're looking for some fans to get involved as extras in your next video. Equally, you may communicate less frequently if you've just got nothing worth saying.

How Should You Communicate?

Technology offers many new ways to communicate. However, some of the older methods are still good choices. Very often how you choose to communicate will depend on the message you need to impart and the nature of how your fan base likes to receive messages.

To cut to the conclusion of this discussion, I recommend you communicate in different forms. Each member of your audience will like to receive communications in a different manner. There is the potential to alienate sections of the audience by communicating solely in one manner. This strategy reduces the chances of permanent alienation.

The following sections discuss some of the main choices.

SMS/Text Message to Cell/Mobile Phones

SMS (text) messages are great if you have a message that is short and urgent, and where the information only has value for a very limited time. For instance, if you have spare tickets for a gig, then you might want to send an SMS message to let fans know about the opportunity.

By contrast, if you want to send out a long newsletter with photos, then an SMS message is unlikely to be appropriate, irrespective of the nature of your audience.

From a practical perspective, SMS messaging is often easier to manage when you have a smaller list of recipients.

Although this is a sweeping generalization and the trend is changing, SMS messages on mobile phones tend to be used more intensively by teenagers and young adults. So if your fan base is mainly made up of preteens, then sending out an SMS message may not generate the necessary response because many of your fans may not have a cell phone (yet!), although, as the age of owning a cell phone falls, this will become a more viable option.

As telephony services develop, you will be able to do more with the phone, and the services will become more uniform. For instance, in the UK it is a simple matter to send an SMS message to a land-line phone. Some phones can receive SMS messages (although this is very dependent on the model of phone and the services provided by the phone companies), and for others the SMS message is spoken by a robotic voice. I am sure that by the time the next edition of this book is published, there will be more options.

If your contacts list is sufficiently short, you may even call everyone on the list personally to impart your news. Hopefully, assuming you are building a successful career, this won't be a practical option for too long.

Email

Email is a great way of communicating:

- It's simple.

- It's fast.

- You can send one message to many people.

- You can send a short message or a long message.

- You can send attachments (such as photos or a form to fill in to apply for tickets).

- You can include links to internet sites (for instance, "Click here to see pictures of our gig last night").

However, email is not a panacea and does present many challenges.

One of the first challenges is keeping email addresses up to date. People frequently change their email addresses—they change schools or colleges, they get new jobs, they change internet service providers, or they close an email address because it has been receiving too much spam. To ensure that your message gets through, you need to find a way to ensure your list of email addresses is kept up to date.

Spam (that is, unsolicited commercial email) is a huge problem for all of us. It clogs our email boxes, and for legitimate mass email senders (such as a musician trying to keep in touch with his or her fan base), it presents the problem of how to send multiple emails without them looking like spam. One thing you can do to prevent your emails from looking like spam is to simplify the message. Many spam messages include graphics (which may be a cover for viruses). If you send a message in plain text (perhaps you could link to graphics on your website), you will find you are less likely to have your message stopped.

People who have a particular problem with spam often adopt some sort of filtering solution. Often the solution involves the person maintaining a list of people from whom he or she can receive any message without the message being stopped. This practice is called *white listing*. You should encourage your fan base to ensure that the address from which you send your email messages is white listed. You should then maintain a consistent email sending address to ensure that your messages pass through the spam filters unhindered.

There is another reason not to include graphics: People don't like them, especially if they have a dial-up internet connection (in other words, not a broadband/ADSL/DSL connection). If you send an unsolicited email that takes 10 minutes to download, you will not be popular.

I've already mentioned graphics in the context of spam. Let me now add a few thoughts about the presentation of your email in general. As an electronic medium, you have great flexibility over how you present your email. You can use colors, graphics, different-size fonts, pop-ups, and any number of devices to grab the reader's attention.

Don't.

If your message isn't strong enough to stand on its own, then rewrite the message (or wait until you have something important to say). The beauty of email is that you have the reader's undivided attention; you don't need to stand out from the crowd. Adding lots of flashing lights is just going to distract the reader and annoy him or her.

You can do a few things to help the reader:

- Put in a sensible subject line so the reader can identify that the email is from you and what it's about.

- Write in short paragraphs. Long paragraphs are always difficult to read—it is even harder to read long paragraphs when the text is displayed on a computer screen.

- Add headings to break up the text and to show where one subject ends and another one starts. The only formatting I would ever suggest you use in an email is to show headings in bold. Anything else is superfluous and tends to make emails look like ransom notes.

  Some people like to summarize the content of the email at the start and put links to each piece within the email. I don't like this for two reasons. First, the links don't always work, and second, if you need to do this, then your email is too long.

- Make it short. Get to the point quickly and then go away. People are busy and don't want to listen to your self-indulgent drivel. If you've got more to say, then refer the reader to your website (or anywhere else where further information might be available). On the whole, people like short emails but are happy to spend hours browsing websites and "finding" information for themselves.

Mail

I've talked a lot about technological options, but please don't forget the more traditional mail services. Although they are not "free" like email or cheap like SMS messages, they are in many ways more personal and more effective. Many people still like receiving letters (that aren't bills) and enjoy receiving tangible goods through the mail.

The real advantage of the mail is that you can send things. For instance, you can send a newsletter, posters, or a DVD interview (as mentioned earlier). There are several downsides to this, though. First, the goods that you are sending cost money. Second, postage costs—it isn't free. Third, it takes time to address and stuff envelopes (which again may incur costs if you have to hire someone to complete this task).

What Should You Communicate?

When considering what to communicate, there are two aspects. First, the topics you should communicate, and second the details of those topics to include. I will consider both of those points.

Before I look at what you should communicate, can I just mention what you should *not* communicate? The purpose of communication is several-fold, but primarily you are trying to:

- Promote something that you are selling
- Foster the relationship between you and your fan base

Just communicating for the heck of it means you are generating noise. If you are dropping an email just to say hi, then you are wasting your fans' time. Communicate when you've got something to say. You've got something to say when there is something happening in the future that will interest your fan base. So, if the band members have all just been on holiday and are feeling really chilled, that is not something to communicate. However, if you have just spent six months in the studio, and your new single will be out next month, then that is something to say.

Equally, when you communicate, you should communicate the significance of your news. For instance, if you say, "We signed a record deal," who cares? However, if you say, "We signed a deal, so the new album will be in shops next week," then that puts the news in a context that really means something to fans.

When you come to look at the details you need to communicate, there are two approaches. You can give all of the details or you can give none of the details and just communicate the headline news. Let me explain the difference with a practical example. Suppose you are announcing a gig. The pertinent details here are:

- The date of the gig and the time it starts
- The location of the gig
- The cost of tickets and where they are available
- Any special restrictions (for instance, if you're playing in a club at which you have to be 18 or 21 to be admitted)

This is the bare minimum information that must be communicated. There's much more you could say, such as whether you're playing any special songs and whether there will be an opening act, and so on.

Now let's say you decided to communicate this gig by email. You could either send out an email with all of the details (which would be quite long by the time you explained all the purchase options), or you could send out an email that says, "We're playing a gig in London on November 25th," and include a link to your website for further details.

The advantage of referring people back to your website is that you can give much more information than you could easily give in an email. For instance, you can include a link to a map of the gig's location. Also, you could include links to purchase tickets, thereby encouraging people to buy them.

Another advantage of this approach is if you make any changes (for instance, if there is a mistake in the published date of the gig), then you can change the webpage very easily. Obviously if you make a change like that, I would expect you to drop a brief email to say, "Whoops...we made a mistake on our website, and the correct date is now shown."

By contrast, if you included the wrong date in an email, even if you send a correcting email, there is always the chance that someone will look at the wrong email and end up being disappointed (or embarrassed/angry if he or she turns up at the venue on the wrong night).

Mind Your Language

Even if the whole basis of your act is that you swear like troopers, when communicating directly with fans (in other words, when sending SMS messages, emails, letters, and so on), I recommend that you remove any profanity as much as possible.

I recommend this for several practical reasons:

- First, many people, particularly corporations, use profanity filters to block emails that may contain bad language. You may craft the most literate and amusing email, but it will be to no avail if it gets caught in a nasty spam filter.

- The other reason for caution in your language is that you don't know where your communication is going to end up. Emails can get sent to the wrong people, letters and emails can be opened by other members of a family, and so on.

You should also use the fans' language when writing as far as possible. That is to say, you should use terms that they use in a manner that they would understand. To give an old example, when Michael Jackson says "bad," he means good, not bad. You should refine your language in a similar manner, although I would caution against using the vernacular if it is going to sound false. We've all heard middle-aged people trying to get "hip with the kids." It never works, and it isn't pretty, so don't do it!

As a final point (and the irony of this comment is not lost on this author), remember that not everyone speaks English as a first language. We're dealing with music here, so it's not necessary to use your most flowery prose. (Save that for your lyrics, if you really must.) The simpler and more straightforward you can keep your communications, the better.

The Mechanics of Bulk Communication

The practicalities of how you communicate need some thought, so I'll address that in the next few sections.

Mechanics of Bulk SMS/Text Communication

There are several ways you can send one SMS message to many people:

- Most mobile phones will allow you to send one message to several people. However, this can be a real pain. All phones differ, but generally you need everyone's number stored on your phone (and there may be a limit to the quantity of numbers that can be stored), and then you need to create a list of people to send the message to. This can prove to be a real fiddle.

  Once you have your list created, then you need to write the message. Even with predictive text, this is a painfully slow process, and there are no spell-checkers to help you. Once you have written the message, you then need to send it to the mailing list. Provided you don't slip up, this is usually a fairly straightforward process.

  Of course, if you then lose the phone, you've effectively lost contact with your fan base, and you've lost contact with your income. Not a good situation.

- To make life easier, many mobile phones allow you to connect your computer so you can type your message and manage your mailing list. If your phone has this feature, it will make sending SMS messages much easier.

- There are also many internet services that allow you to send SMS messages. You type a message (you can use Word or your favorite word processor to check the typing), then you load the message and a list of the phone numbers to which you want to send the message. You hit a button, and the messages are all sent for you.

These services are not particularly cheap. (They tend to cost in the region of 5 to 10 cents per person per message.) However, they are much more convenient than using your cell phone to do all this. Doubtless with increased competition, these prices will fall.

Mechanics of Bulk Email Communication

A regular email program (such as Microsoft Outlook or Outlook Express) will allow you to send emails to more than one recipient.

If you want to take a step up from that, you can find several specialized programs for bulk email. One example is MailList King from Xequte (www.xequte.com/maillistking); see Figure 4.2. These programs all do a broadly similar thing, but you will need to check individual features and play with the demos to ensure that your requirements are met.

The main functions you can expect this type of program to perform are:

- Maintaining a database of all your contacts. You can assign individuals to groups. For instance, you might want to differentiate those people who have purchased a product from you from those people who have never purchased from you.

- Sending an email to multiple contacts. You can send emails to every contact, only specific contacts, or a group of contacts (for instance, those who have purchased a product).

- Automatically manage the joining and leaving process. You can usually use form mail scripts on your website to facilitate this automation process.

Form mail scripts (which are pieces of programming that you can add to your site) may help you build up a mailing list. With these sorts of scripts, people can access a page on your website where they can type in their email address. They then hit a button, and you will receive a message that the person wants to be added to the mailing list. The advantage of this course is that your email address is hidden from spammers. If you publish your email address on your website, it will be picked up, and you will receive spam.

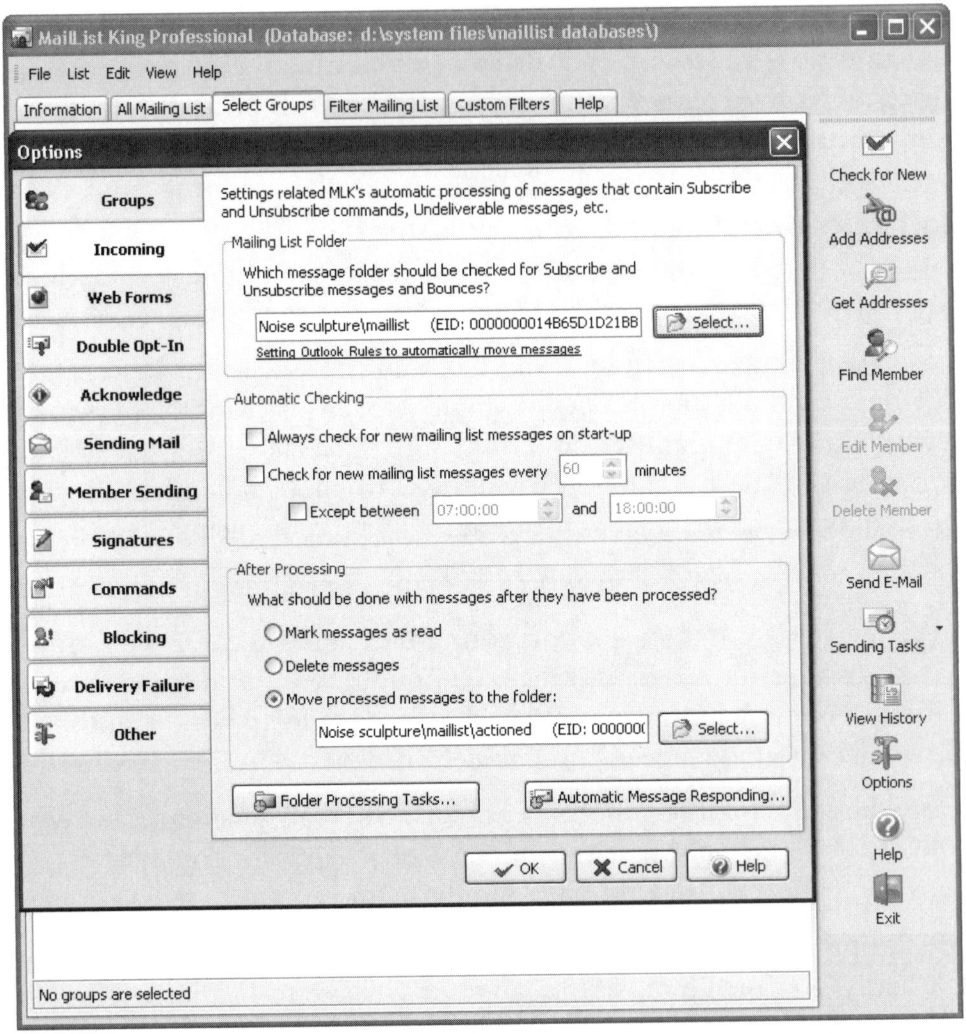

Figure 4.2 MailList King, a specialized bulk email and database program. Check out the company's website for more shots of the program in action.

One last thing: If you send one email to multiple recipients, please remember to put the multiple recipients' email addresses in the BCC (blind copy) field, not in the To field. This has two advantages:

- First, you do not disclose the email addresses of your whole mailing list.

- Second, it prevents a whole heap of hassle and lots of emails flying about if someone hits Reply to All to respond to your message.

Mechanics of Sending Out Letters in Bulk

Do I really need to spell this out for you? You send the same package to everyone on the list. It is a very tedious, manual process, so you may want to outsource the work.

So Will You Exploit with Integrity?

In closing this chapter, I want to reiterate my point about exploiting with integrity.

Think about when you go into a restaurant. You eat a meal, and you are then charged for that meal. The charge is greater than the cost of the ingredients. The charge is greater than the cost of the ingredients plus a share of the cost of running the restaurant (including property and staff costs, as well as taxes). Provided it was a good meal, you are happy to pay the bill and will probably even add a tip (through generosity, because you feel it is deserved, or just because you feel bad about not leaving a tip).

So does the restaurant exploit you?

Good exploit? Yes, probably. They give you something you can't get at home—a meal without hassle (perhaps better than you could cook yourself), ambience, choice of food, wine perhaps. The reasons are many and varied.

Bad exploit? Probably not.

If you like the meal, you will probably return to the restaurant and will probably recommend it to your friends. And here we are reaching the heart of the point I am trying to make. The factor that is going to grow your fan base the fastest is word of mouth—trusted friends telling each other about your music and recommending it because they like what you do. Remember, if word of mouth is going to work, then you need to give people something to talk about.

You don't need a huge marketing campaign. Such a campaign may have some impact, but you will never get great bang for your buck; the approach is too scattered to have real, lasting impact. By contrast, word of mouth is free and has much better results, although they may take longer.

And if you're thinking about exploiting people in a bad way, please don't. You might get away with ripping people off initially. However, you won't get away with it for long, and certainly not for long enough to have a proper career. You can rip people off if you're happy to keep starting up under a new guise, but at the end of the day, why bother? You will do much better to treat people ethically and think about a long-term career.

5 Building and Keeping the Fan Base

I've said this before, but I'll say it again because it's important: Any career in music will succeed only if there is someone to buy the product. The people who will buy the product are the fans. You need to cherish and nurture your fans (as people) if you are to survive and have a career in music.

This chapter looks at how to build, nurture, and maintain a fan base. Going further, it looks at how to develop someone with an interest into a regular flow of income. Although it's great to be able to brag about how many hits you get on your website, that number is irrelevant. All measures of interest in you as an artist are irrelevant: People may be looking at your website because someone has suggested that it is an example of the worst possible features in website design. All that matters is whether you can convert interest into income.

As you increase the portfolio of products you have for sale (for instance, when you have a number of CDs, a few DVDs, and a range of merchandising), each new fan will become more financially valuable to you because he or she is able to spend more money on you.

The Conversion Process

Before we go any further, let's look at the process by which you develop interest into income. There are several stages:

1. Generate some sort of interest so that people come to you.

2. Develop the interest into someone you could call a fan.

3. Persuade the fan to spend money on you.

4. Ensure the fan is happy about spending money and keeps spending money on a regular basis.

83

Figure 5.1 shows that conversion process and illustrates how a new fan can then bring in more fans by word of mouth.

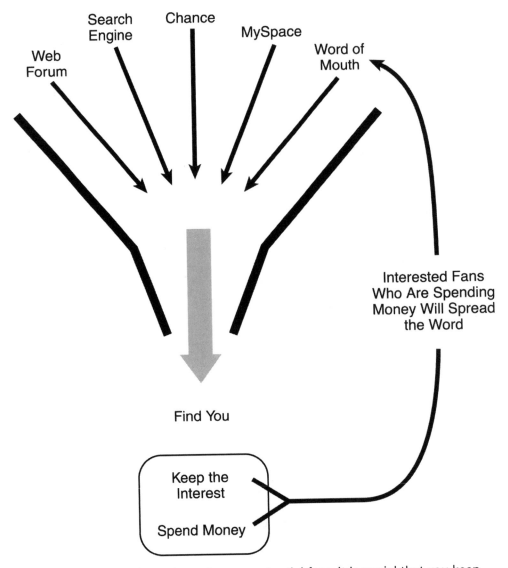

Figure 5.1 Once you have drawn in your potential fans, it is crucial that you keep their interest and create a situation where they want to spend money (on you).

As soon as you start making some noise (figuratively), you will get interest. Your key challenge is to convert that interest into a fan base and to convert that fan base into an income stream. It would be a rather foolish act to try to raise your public profile without being able to capitalize on the interest.

In this chapter, I want to look at how you can proactively manage that conversion process.

Generating Interest So That People Come to You

People are likely to come to you through one of two routes:

- Personal recommendation. This is direct word of mouth from someone who could already be regarded as a fan.

- Chance. People may come across you by chance if they hear a track on the radio, see an interview with you in a magazine, or come across you while browsing the internet. (Perhaps someone mentioned you on an internet forum, or maybe the person found you as one of the results of an internet search or found you on MySpace.)

If you are really lucky—really, really lucky—then people will hear some of your music, will love it, and will want to buy it. That's great: It provides you with income, as long as the new potential fan can find out where to buy the product. Your challenge then is to make sure that person becomes a true fan and keeps spending money on you.

However, you may not always be that lucky. Many people won't hear your music or will want to hear more before they decide whether they like you. Whenever somebody wants to know more about an artist, the most logical place to look for information is a website. This could be your own website or a page on a service such as MySpace or SoundClick (www.soundclick.com). Realistically, if you don't have a website, it is very difficult for you to ensure your potential fans get the information they need to decide that they like you.

I will discuss websites further in Chapter 6, "Publicity in the 21st Century."

Developing Interest into a Fan

It may feel great when you look at your website statistics to see that thousands of people have been hitting your site. As I mentioned earlier, however good this may feel, it means nothing. It means nothing because you don't know who these people are, and they are not spending money with you.

To take a significant step forward, you will need to get these people to tell you how you can contact them. In practice, this usually means you need to find a way to persuade people who are interested in you to give you their email addresses.

Giving out an email address is a very significant step forward. Most people will want some sort of reassurance in the form of a privacy policy before they give out their email address, and even then many people will remain skeptical. Your privacy policy may be explicit (in the form of "Click here to see our privacy policy") or implicit, with a note to the effect that "we hate spam as much as you do and will *never* share your email address with anyone."

So what will persuade someone to give you his or her email address (or other contact details)?

If you ask nicely, then I'm sure some people will be happy to give you their email address. However, I would be a bit suspicious about anyone who asked for my email address and didn't give me a reason why. If you ask nicely and explain what you're going to do with the email address, then I think you might get much better results.

For instance, if you say something to the effect of, "Please let us have your email address so we can keep in touch with you and let you know about our gigs and releases," then you may get more favorable results.

Many people aren't going to want to give you an email address unless they feel they are really getting something in return. For instance, some people may be happy to give you their email address in return for access to download some tracks and videos. Others may give up the information for a free DVD. For these people, you need to be more subtle in your approach.

Instead of simply asking for an email address, you can give access to a password-protected area of your website, perhaps by encouraging people to sign up for a virtual "backstage pass" or something else suitably musical (but perhaps slightly less corny). You can then email the password to the email address and make sure that the potential fan signs in to the area using his or her email address and the password you have sent.

Taking this approach achieves several things. First, you know that the email address is genuine because the person has to be able to receive the email you send out to use the virtual backstage pass. You can be fairly sure that the email address in your records will be kept up to date if someone uses it to sign in. (You can normally expect people to sign up again if they change email addresses.) Clearly this approach will need some programming on your website.

Once you've created your virtual backstage area, then you can make any amount of material available, such as music, video, or screensavers. You could take a step further in the information you are gathering by giving people tangible goods, such as a DVD. Many holiday destinations operate on a similar basis—you give them your (postal) address, and they send you a video/DVD of their destination. You could do something similar, perhaps offering a DVD with a few tracks and an interview or two.

The benefit of offering tangible goods is that you get a postal address. This is interesting (because you will find where fans live, which can be useful if you want to gauge whether it is worth gigging in certain locations), but may not always be useful because you will often not want to send a letter. (Usually you will want to send an email or SMS message.) The downside to getting the postal address is that you will have to send the tangible goods, which will cost money to produce and send.

You will also find that there are some people who simply will not give you their email address or any other personal details. On the whole, these people are less likely to become fans with whom you can develop a relationship. However, you can still reach these people through conventional retail outlets, and they may come to your gigs (if they feel they can get tickets without having to disclose too many personal details).

You can, of course, find other ways to get other contact details. For instance, if you give away (or sell) cell phone ring tones, this gives you a great way to collect cell phone numbers.

Persuading Fans to Spend Money

So now you've got the potential fans interested. They may even think of themselves as being fans. So how do you get them to spend money?

You don't.

It just happens. Your role is to provide the right product for your fans to buy. Let then know what they are buying and—provided they want to—they will buy. Remember, we're exploiting fans in a good way, not a bad way. You're a musician, not a secondhand car dealer.

Sometimes the buying happens quickly, and sometimes it happens slowly. Sometimes you don't realize it has happened. If your songs are available from iTunes, then you won't know the identity of the purchaser. Even if the only place where any of your products can be purchased is your website, you may not know that you have converted someone into a purchaser—a friend could have bought their ticket for a gig or given them a CD as a present.

Even if some people don't buy (or take a long time to buy), there is still a benefit for you. You will have their contact details, so you can keep in touch. For their part, although they may not be spending money on you, they may be acting as your ambassador and telling all their friends about this really cool act they came across.

However, please do not think that having someone's email address means that you have made a sale. People need to be reminded of your product (hence you need to communicate regularly), and they need a reason why they should buy your product. If you just *tell* them about your product without giving them a taste (such as a short audio clip), then you will not make any sales.

Keeping Fans Happy

Let's assume everything has gone according to plan, you are building your fan base, and your fans are happy to spend money with you.

Great! Congratulations.

You now know how hard it can be to start building a fan base. That hard work should never cease; you will always want new fans. However, there is one thing easier than trying to find a new fan and converting that person into someone who will spend money—keeping your existing fans.

Existing fans know and like you. Existing fans will have spent money with you and will be happy to spend more money with you. Whenever you release a new product, you can be sure that many of your existing fans will buy it at the earliest opportunity. For these reasons, existing fans should be your highest priority.

In many ways you don't need to do anything out of the ordinary for these existing fans to keep them happy. However, you should keep them happy. There are two simple things that you can do to make existing fans happy:

- Come up with new products: new CDs, new DVDs, new posters, new merchandise, and so on. You get the idea. Fans want to know that you are thinking of them and working to create new stuff for them.

  When you create new products, they need to be excellent and not simply good. To use something of a cliché, they need a "wow" factor. If a product is only good, then your existing fans will think twice before they buy anymore products from you. Products are discussed in more detail in Chapter 8, "Creating and Developing the Product."

- Interact with your fans. When you interact with your fans, they feel that you care and, in addition to buying your product, they will continue to work as your sales force and ambassadors.

The other thing you need to do is not upset your fans. This issue is discussed later in this chapter, in the "Losing Fans" section.

Finding Potential Fans and Building the Fan Base

In Chapter 6, I will look at more of the options for publicity. For the moment, I want to look at the main places where you can get directly in touch with potential fans.

I've talked a bit about growing the fan base. Because it is such an important factor in your career, I want to look at some specific ways you can find your fans and grow the fan base. This really is one area where you have to be very proactive—if you're not prepared to be proactive here, then you are unlikely to have a career.

There are two things to remember when looking at the number of your fans:

- The numbers will not grow in a linear manner. Some weeks you will pick up many new fans, and others you will only pick up a few fans. You will probably find that you pick up more new fans when you make a noise (or shortly thereafter) and fewer new fans during your quiet periods.

- When you are relying on word of mouth, the increase in numbers can be startling. At some times you may even see exponential growth in the number of your fans (where one person tells two people, those two people each tell two people, making four new people, then those four people each tell two people, making eight people, and those eight people each tell two people, and so on; see Figures 5.2 and 5.3). However, exponential growth is (ultimately) unsustainable (you will eventually run out of people to tell) and doesn't reflect human nature, where you will usually find one person telling lots of people and many people not passing on the word.

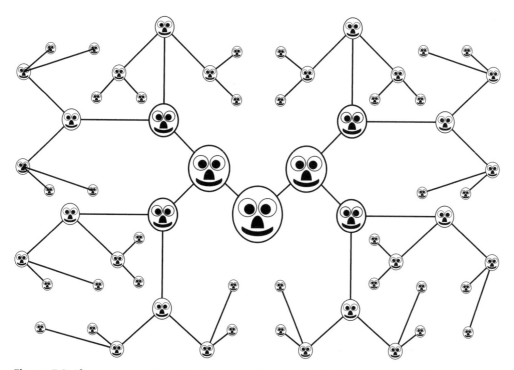

Figure 5.2 If you can reach out to two people, who each talk to two people, who each tell two people about you (and so on), then your number of contacts will grow rapidly.

To connect with a potential audience, you need to find the place where people who could make up your audience go (whether physically or metaphorically). You then need to go there. This destination could include:

- Websites
- Magazines/fanzines
- Radio shows, TV shows, internet sites
- Gig venues

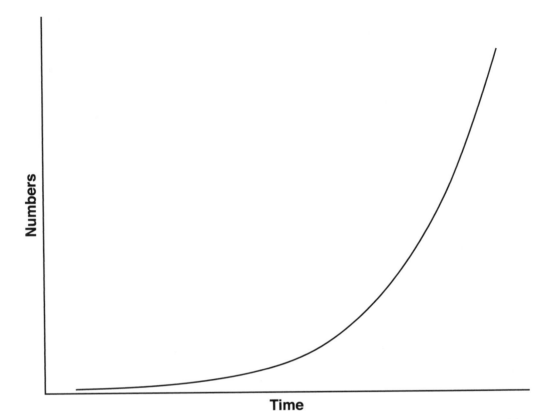

Figure 5.3 As Figure 5.2 shows, your total number of contacts will grow more swiftly as you have more people finding new contacts for you.

To a certain extent, finding fans is a numbers game—the more people you approach, the more people you are likely to find. However, you should perhaps be a bit discriminating. For instance, if you're a thrash metal band, maybe your grandmother's friends would not be the best source of new fans. Then again, your grandmother's friends may have their own grandchildren who would like your music. You never know....

Anyway, the following sections discuss a few of the places to start looking for fans. Remember, these people are of no use to you until you know how to contact them, so get ready to start collecting email addresses.

Family and Friends

The obvious place to start your quest for new fans is with your family and friends. Your friends may be happy to come and support you at gigs, but they are unlikely to want to buy every piece of merchandise you have. In fact, many will expect you to give them stuff for free in exchange for their support. However, your friends will have friends (and those friends will have friends). Use word of mouth, and you will start to grow your numbers.

Tell a Friend

You can also encourage people to tell their friends (and other acquaintances). For instance, you could offer an incentive to people to disclose their friends' email address. You could set up an arrangement where if someone gives you the email addresses of five of his friends, you give him a track to download onto his iPod.

Website

I've mentioned your website several times and will discuss it in greater detail in Chapter 6. However, for now, remember that you need to have a way to capture emails (or other contact details) through your website.

Gigs

Gigs are an excellent place to find new people, but gig venues (which may be dark, sweaty rooms) are often not great places to get email addresses. However, since gigs present such a great opportunity to reach new people, you should try.

There are two main ways you can use gigs to collect email addresses (or other contact information). First, you can ask people: Send someone around with a pen and paper and ask for email addresses, or put someone in a prominent place (the line for the restroom, perhaps) and ask for email addresses. Alternatively, direct people to your website. Maybe the easiest way to do this is to give out a flyer with your web address and tell people to check out the website for details of other gigs.

A great way to grow a fan base with gigs is to swap gigs with another act: You play a hometown gig and they act as support, and they play a hometown gig with you acting as support. Of course, it helps if you are from different geographic locations (even different sides of the same city). If the other act is as well organized as you, it will also have its own mailing list, so each act can then email its own fan base and direct its fans to the other act's website. Of course, you can also pick up more email addresses by sending someone to collect them at the gig.

Music and Merchandise

Another really obvious way to solicit contact details is through the goods you sell. If your only sales outlet is your website (and you sell directly, fulfilling the orders yourself), then you will already have contact details for everyone who has bought something from you. However, if you do not sell everything directly, then you should think about encouraging people to join your mailing list.

You can do this in several ways:

- You could include a card with a CD or DVD so that people can send you their contact details. Equally, this card could include a reference to your website, and you could encourage people to stop by and sign up.

- If you are using an on-demand service (refer to Chapter 3), usually these services will not disclose the identities of purchasers. However, they will give you the opportunity to send a brief email to the purchaser. With this email you could thank the purchaser for buying your goods and encourage him or her to drop by your website.

Press and Broadcasting

I will look more at the press and broadcasting in Chapter 6. But before we get there, let me add a few comments here.

Press and broadcasting cover a very wide range of media, including radio (terrestrial, satellite, and internet), television (in all its forms and variants, such as video podcasting), and newspapers and magazines (real and online).

You would be mad to ignore these outlets. However, as a means to increase your fan base (and increase numbers on your mailing list), press and broadcasting are fairly blunt instruments. Think about radio, for instance. Very often you do not know whose song is being played. Even if someone hears you and likes what they hear, you have to hope that your name is given out clearly and that the listener then writes the name down and searches you out on the internet. This may happen (especially if your record is played several times on radio); however, you are more likely to find that this is a tough way to create a fan base.

Before I move on from the media, I want to mention fanzines briefly. It is easy to look disparagingly at fanzines because they are often "amateur" productions. However, fanzines are often very closely aligned to their target audience, so if you find one that covers your niche, you will find a very quick way to access a large potential audience. This audience is likely to be very engaged with and very passionate about their music.

Added to this, fanzines are usually run by people with a genuine passion for music, who are more interested in finding something cool and including it in their magazine than they are in chasing the commercial imperative.

When you tour (if you tour), it is well worth taking the time to meet as many fanzine editors as possible because they will introduce you to many fans.

Losing Fans

There are bad things in this world. One bad thing is losing fans, as Figure 5.4 shows.

You will usually lose fans for one of two reasons:

- Boredom. It could be that your act has grown stale, or it could be that the tastes of the fan have changed.

- Active dislike. If you do something really stupid, it is quite possible to change devoted fans into a well-motivated group of upset individuals who could do serious damage to your career.

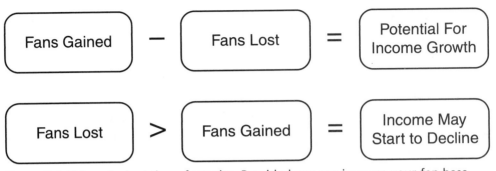

Figure 5.4 Take a look at these formulas. Provided you can increase your fan base faster than you lose your fans, you can increase your earnings from your fans. However, if you lose fans at a higher rate than you gain fans, then you are likely to see your income start to fall.

All lost fans are usually lost forever. The former group (that is, the bored fans) may come back to you at a later stage, but this is unlikely. However, those who have chosen to actively dislike you are almost always lost forever, as well as being vocal in their criticism of you. Clearly this vocal criticism will not help in your efforts to expand your remaining fan base.

We'll look at the boredom factor in the context of Chapter 8. For the moment, I want to talk about some of the things that will alienate your fan base and cause the people who have provided your income to actively dislike you.

Bad Things You Can Do with Email

There are several bad things you can do with email (and SMS messages). I would suggest that the first time you use your mailing list to do one of the following things is when you will instantly lose fans (and find out how quickly they tell their friends about your appalling behavior):

- Selling your mailing list, especially if you sell it to an organization that supports, for instance, the clubbing to death of baby seals. In this case, you would lose fans for two reasons: first for selling the list, and second for being associated with something that most of your fans are likely to regard as very uncool.

- Spamming your mailing list, which in this context means bombarding your mailing list with unsolicited emails. You should also be careful if you have several email addresses for one person (assuming you can notice this) because people tend to get annoyed if you send one email more than once (even if it's their fault that you have multiple email addresses on file for them).

- Using the mailing list to advertise products that are not your own. For instance, if you start sending advertisements for power tools, then your fan base is likely to become disgruntled.

Remember, we live in a high-tech world, and most people are pretty tech savvy. They instinctively realize when they're being ripped off or used. Many people have disposable email addresses to check where spam and the like originates, so if you start abusing the trust people have put in you by giving you their email address, then you are likely to be found out and exposed very quickly.

I would also suspect that if any of your fans suspect you have undertaken any of these activities (even if you have not), the results will be equally disastrous.

Bad Things You Can Do with Your Website

I will talk about website design in Chapter 6, but before we get there I want to mention a few things that will alienate your fans (and your possible fans).

Associate links (for instance, to Amazon) on your website are fine within reason. If you have a link so that someone can purchase one of your products at Amazon, it will not be a problem. If you are linking to a related product (for instance, borrowing an example I used in Chapter 3, if you are a Celtic band placing links to books about the origins and history of Celtic music), I'm sure no one will object. However, if your site is linking to all sorts of (apparently) unrelated products, and it just looks like a bad imitation of Amazon, then people are likely to distrust your motives and feel alienated.

Some sites carry advertisements. You may be able to get away with these, but to my mind this is a truly naff thing to do and is likely to turn people off. You really must have a good reason to convince your fan base that advertisements are justified. This, along with other forms of rampant commercialism, is likely to alienate many people.

Other Bad Things You Might Do

You can also alienate your fan base through your actions (and sometimes inactions). For instance:

- If you are accused (or convicted) of a crime, your image will be tarnished. Whether the tarnishing will turn off fans depends on the crime, the level of reporting, and the nature of your fan base. For instance, most crimes of violence are likely to be unpopular with your fan base (unless you're a gangsta' rapper, in which case your fans may be somewhat more likely to accept criminal behavior on your part). On the other hand, drugs may not be a problem unless you have a squeaky-clean image or a young fan base.

- Selling out, as in giving up on your principles in return for money, will cast you in a bad light with your fans. Try not to do it or allow the perception that you have sold out to arise.

- Fans want to interact on a human level. If you are from the "treat 'em mean to keep 'em keen" school, then you may have difficulty with long-term relationships (with your fans and your partners).

There are many other ways you can upset your fans. Before you take any actions, take a moment to consider your fans' possible reactions and whether there will be any adverse consequences for your career. I'm not suggesting you shouldn't do anything edgy or dangerous—just that you should consider the implications before you throw your career away.

Going Global

In this wired-up world in which we live, going global is very easy. Indeed, if word of mouth about your act is strong, then your fan base will probably have spread the word about you internationally before you can think about the implications. Being successful on a global basis is much harder.

If you are communicating with your fan base by email, and your website is supporting a great relationship with your fans, then it doesn't matter where you are, and it doesn't matter where your fans are.

However, there are some occasions when the global spread can make life difficult. Here are a few examples:

- Some countries have a poor reputation for financial fraud or do not have sufficient financial infrastructure. You may find it difficult (if not impossible) to receive credit card payments from residents of these countries.

- Fulfillment of orders overseas may lead to postage costs that you did not expect. This can be easily remedied by a bit of research and some caution when setting postal rates. Also, in some countries, the mail service can be truly awful.

- You may not be able to get out to every country and play live. Then again, you may not always be able to get money out of these countries, so some places are best avoided.

If you are looking to expand your fan base proactively, then playing overseas is a good way to do so. However, you may have difficulty in the logistics of getting there and difficulty in gaining critical mass to support your activities.

This is one place where you can bring in a combination of fan base–building and gig-swapping to help you get started. I don't offer this as a simple solution, but it may help you take that step from your local markets to a global market.

What Do You Do if You Don't Have a Fan Base?

So far this book has assumed that you are a musician who will have (or will be able to have) a direct relationship with your fan base (provided you can just get motivated). However, there are many musicians for whom this relationship is not practical, so they reach their audience through an intermediary.

There are many musicians in this situation, for instance:

- Composers and songwriters
- DJs, MCs, and beat creators

For these people, there are two options: Carry on working through an intermediary or find another way to get your music directly to the public. This section looks at some of the direct options.

Current Options for the Musician without a Fan Base

Many musicians who do not have their own fan base are (for a variety of reasons) non-performing musicians. Let me give a few examples.

If a songwriter writes a song, then before the song can reach an audience, the songwriter (or the songwriter's publisher) has to find an artist to record the song. This effectively puts the songwriter's income at the mercy of the artist (and the artist's fan base). If the artist makes a poor recording of the song and/or has a small fan base, then the songwriter will not see very high royalties. Now, of course, the counterarguments are that the songwriter can still place the song with another artist, and the artist can always make a great recording. Both of these options can be lucrative for the songwriter.

On the other hand, a music composer is often dependent on receiving a commission. Subject to fulfilling the terms of that commission and getting paid, there is little the composer can do to influence the fee. If the commissioning body doesn't have any more money to pay the composers, then that is that.

Both of these situations illustrate the fundamental problem for musicians who do not have their own fan base. DJs have a similar situation in that they are hired for specific gigs, and (with a few exceptions) they don't have the opportunity to develop their own fan base. That being said, there are examples of DJs and MCs who have their own releases. (Norman Cooke, a.k.a. Fatboy Slim, comes readily to mind.)

However, DJs, MCs, and beat creators are all often called to a role much like session musicians or special guests. In their role as a session musician, these individuals are dependent on their relationship with the producer (or whoever hires them).

Some New Possibilities for the Musician without a Fan Base

For all musicians without a fan base, there is, of course, the opportunity to keep on doing what you're already doing. However, as I've mentioned, this runs the risk of your income being subject to the vagaries of the decisions of those who will (or will not) hire you. Only you can decide whether this will provide you with the income and the career that you seek.

There is another option: Create a product that can be marketed and create a community to which you can sell that product. In short, put yourself in the same situation as performing musicians and start community building.

So how can this be achieved?

Options for the Non-Performing Musician: Create an Act

The most obvious route for the non-performing musician (and here, let's take the example of a songwriter) would be to form a band, create a show, and go in search of an audience. From a practical perspective, the songwriter would need to be both songwriter and manager (at least initially). With this dual role, the first tasks the songwriter would need to complete are:

- Writing the songs for the band

- Finding the musicians

- Teaching the musicians the songs and getting the act into shape

- Developing the products that can be sold (primarily CDs and limited merchandising in the first instance)

- Finding ways to reach out to the audience—finding the fan base and arranging gigs

Clearly, this is not going to be a solution for a quick buck. Remember that what we're looking at here is how to develop a long-term career in the music industry, not how to make some money and retire to the sun.

If the notion of years of gigging is one that does not appeal to you, remember that just because you formed the band, that does not mean you have to join it. However, if you're not going to be a member of the band, then there are some very practical issues you need to consider.

For instance, if you are not present (either in your role as manager or as a member of the band) at a gig, then you need to have someone you can trust to collect the money and look after the arrangements (such as liaising with the promoter, keeping the band in line so they don't get drunk before the show, and so on). You could easily reach a situation where you have the same logistical concerns that a major band has for a tour (albeit on a smaller scale), and all you're doing is playing a few bars and clubs. You could then find that the band doesn't want to play your material and walks.

As I say, this is could be quite a difficult situation. It could also take a considerable financial investment. However, do you like the alternatives: no career or a career that is at the mercy of other people?

You may want to think about the type of band that is appropriate to play your music. For instance, if you create a band of hard and heavy rockers, they may feel it necessary to live up to the Spinal Tap excesses they believe are required of them. If you feel a boy band is more appropriate, then you may get away with much lower costs (in terms of mayhem and not needing such a quantity of equipment) and greatly lessened emotional agony on your part.

In many ways this option is not new—there have been production companies around for years. For some production companies, the line between production and management is sometimes a fine one. Often the production company will start as the de facto manager and will get a more experienced manager involved later.

The twist here is that instead of creating an act and licensing them through a record label, here you would take responsibility for building and managing the fan base. In essence, the fan base would be your property to exploit. So, for instance, once you have a first act up and running, you could then establish a second act and use the same fan base to market that second act.

This option can also apply equally well for a composer. (In this context, I am thinking of a classical composer.) There is no reason why a composer should not put together a group of musicians to regularly perform his or her work. You could achieve this in several ways:

- The first option is to hire an orchestra, hire a venue, and put on your own show. Clearly, this is the expensive and risky route. Until you have established a fan base who you can reasonably expect to buy sufficient tickets to give a performance critical mass, then you might want to think about some of the other options. Realistically, you would probably not hire the orchestra and venue; instead, you may only hire the orchestra and look for a promoter to deal with the venue and selling the tickets.

- Establish a small ensemble that is available for functions. There are many functions where, for instance, a string quartet can play. Often these will be weddings, civic functions, corporate functions, or even funerals. Can you imagine what a selling point it would be to offer a string quartet that could provide a new piece of music written specially for the function?

  There is no reason why a number of different musical sections should not be available for hire. It is likely that the smaller ensembles would get the most work (because they would be cheapest). The advantage of starting small is that it gives you, the composer, the option to start building a fan base, and each function is another opportunity to market.

Of course, composers can still pursue the route followed by countless composers and look for a patron, whether that be in the guise of an individual or a corporate, government, or charitable body.

One advantage that composers (and non-performing songwriters) have is that they can create more than one act to perform their material. This can significantly improve the income and the exposure for the composer. The only way a conventional act can create another act to exploit the spending power of their fan base is to create their own tribute band. This could be an interesting concept, but it is probably a flawed idea. Imagine what would happen if the tribute act became more popular that the act it was imitating.

Options for the Non-Performing Musician: Record Your Own CD

Another option for the non-performing musician is to create an act that doesn't have a live performance element. In essence, your course would be to record your own CD and then to promote it through a community that you would build.

Although this option may be cheaper, it is a far more risky strategy because you are cutting off one of the key means by which you can interact with your fan base on a human level (and in doing so, you are cutting off the income—including merchandising income—that can be generated from live performance). However, if you can create a product that is sufficiently appealing and then find an audience who likes the product, then you may have a chance.

You might find this idea appealing, especially because it seems to be a comparatively "easy" way—you probably already record your own material, and it's not so difficult to get a CD pressed (and distributed using a fulfillment service), and you can always get your music onto iTunes and the other download stores. Perhaps you might be thinking that you'll create a community, have a hit, and *then* form the band to do the live stuff (maybe once you've generated some income from your hit). If you are, then give up now. It will never happen for you.

You simply won't be able to differentiate yourself from everyone else in the market who is hoping that strategy will work. Take a look at a service such as CD Baby (cdbaby.com) and give some consideration to how you are going to stand out from the crowd. There are literally thousands of people trying to do this. Unless you can start building a fan base, you will not stand a chance of making a commercial success.

However, it's not all doom and gloom; there are other things you can try. Let me give you one example.

People don't go to gigs to listen to music. If they want to listen to music, they can stay at home and play CDs. At home, the sound quality is much better, you don't get beer spilled on you (well, not usually), and there's never a line for the restrooms.

People go to gigs for the experience and for the pleasure that the experience brings. If you are not going to gig in the conventional sense, then you could at least give people some sort of experience that they could attend. For instance, say you create new-age, spacey-type music and you have recorded an album. Why not arrange an event at a planetarium, where your music is played to accompany a show of some sort? Most countries have more than one planetarium, so approach several venues—you could even set up a mini tour for yourself.

As well as giving your fan base an opportunity to experience your music in a different way, this could give you the opportunity to get out and meet the people in your fan base. And, it provides a venue for you to market some of your own merchandise.

Perhaps you could even take this further. Say you find two other people who create similar music to you and are in a similar situation to yours. These may even be people in different countries. If you could each organize a similar event in your own locality, you could potentially share some of the costs and increase your fan base. Think of this as being equivalent to gig sharing for a conventional band.

Not everyone creates new-age space music. If you want to pursue this route, then you will have to find a way to create an experience that will be sufficiently engaging that your fan base (and your prospective fan base) will want to be involved.

If you're after a very high-risk strategy—high risk not necessarily because of cost (although it probably will be expensive), but because it could take a lot of your time, and you could end up looking foolish—then pursue a hit single. With downloads counting toward sales figures, it is logistically possible for an independently released track to reach number one on the charts.

If this strategy succeeds for you, then you will gain a lot of publicity, and you will have more credibility. (Many doors open if you can attach the words "hit single" to your name.) If you fail, then you will have learned how tough it can be to have a hit single. If it was that easy, then all of the major labels would have hit singles all of the time with all of their acts.

Options for the Non-Performing Musician: Film, TV, and Games

In Chapter 3, I looked at the expansion of the film, TV, and games market for music. This market provides a great opportunity for non-performing musicians and musicians without a fan base to generate some income.

These opportunities are open to everyone, and you should consider pursuing them whatever course you take with your career (so you should consider pursuing them even if you are a gigging musician). However, these opportunities do not give you the chance to increase your income by increasing your fan base. The only way to generate more money through these opportunities is to create more product (in other words, more tunes that can be used) and be lucky with your placements.

Options for Solo Musicians

The last group of people I want to look at are solo musicians. In this context, I am including instrumentalists (singers, trumpet players, bassists, and so on), DJs, MCs, and beat creators. In fact, anyone who may not be part of an act is included in this group.

For these people, like the non-performing musician, the key is to create a product that can be sold and to pursue a fan base. You can create the product in the same way that a non-performing musician can. Alternatively, you can create a product with you as the lead performer. Let me elaborate.

In the conventional music industry, there is a high cost to doing business. This means that artists have to reach a certain level of commercial success to be financially viable. However, if you are prepared to forgo the relationship with a record company and carve out your own career, then you can work with much lower costs. Lower costs mean you can sell far fewer CDs and still have a financially viable career.

To pursue this opportunity, you still have to create a cohesive product/act. If you're a highly talented bass player and you only play bass, then you might get lots of session gigs, but you wouldn't expect to turn up at a record company and demand a recording deal unless you had some sort of act and could make a convincing case that your act would be commercially viable. If you're happy to understand this logic, then you will understand why you won't have a self-managed career without creating some sort of act with products that can be sold.

6 Publicity in the 21st Century

In the 21st century, the notion of the press pack being the cornerstone of the marketing effort is a long-forgotten memory. Today, perhaps the most significant piece of marketing for a musician cannot be directly controlled: the act's Google ranking.

The purpose of publicity is to generate interest, not sales. In Chapter 5, I discussed the process for converting interest into fans, fans into sales, and sales into a stream of income. Publicity means nothing if it is wasted on interesting people who will not convert—you need to get money-spending punters.

Publicity takes a lot of time and can cost a lot of money. If your publicity isn't going to reach people who you can (ultimately) convert into a stream of income, then don't bother with the publicity—you will be much better served by growing your fan base organically, as discussed in Chapter 5.

As well as looking at some of the new publicity options, this chapter will look at conventional means of publicity because these can still be effective. However, I will also suggest some of the reasons why the conventional route is not your most efficient way of proceeding. Remember what we're trying to do here—we want to grow the loyal fan base that will spend money. We're not interested in reaching people who will never spend any money with us.

You will see that I have split this topic into two sections:

- Active publicity. This includes reaching out to people to try to get them interested.

- Passive publicity. This covers what those people can learn about you when you have drawn them in.

See Figure 6.1 for an illustration of the routes for active and passive publicity.

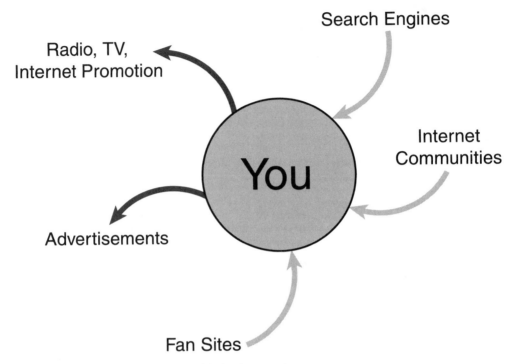

Figure 6.1 Active and passive publicity in practice.

Active Publicity

Active publicity can take many forms, but in essence it requires you to take action in order to persuade someone to expose you (and your music) to their public. This could be action that you take to get yourself into a newspaper, get your track played on the radio, or see your video played on TV.

In essence, we're looking at three things here:

- Advertising—paying someone to mention your product.

- Getting your music played or reviewed in any of the main media channels.

■ Publicity—creating stories that can be featured in the media. These stories can range from publicity stunts to human interest stories.

Many people have a mistaken notion that if they sign with a record company, then that label will "make" them a star. This is untrue. The label will expect and will push the artist to do his or her own publicity (and the label will help focus the publicity activities by bringing in public relations people). In short, the label will push an artist to do what the artist needs to do and what the artist should be doing if he or she doesn't have a record label.

However, the record company will encourage artists to connect with their fan base in a very disconnected way. They will look at marketing as a one-way flow—from the artist to the fan. They will not see it as a two-way communication, nor will they make serious efforts to ensure the relationship is converted into a marriage.

You should be aiming to foster natural, organic growth, so in many ways this form of active publicity is an anathema and a waste of resources. Although I would never suggest that you ignore any broad-based form of publicity, I think you will find that trying to connect directly with people will be more effective in the long term.

There are three main areas of active publicity that you are likely to pursue: radio, TV, and press. I am including the internet equivalents of those three under those main headings. However, publicity through traditional radio, TV, and press is also becoming less effective for several reasons:

■ The markets are stagnant.
    ■ Consumer spending on TV is increasing only slowly, and the 16-to-24 age group watches less television, both in terms of the amount of television that this age group has historically watched and in relation to the amount of TV watched by other age groups.
    ■ Consumer spending on radio services is fairly static.

- The markets are fragmenting—with many more services available, the audience is being spread more thinly.

- People are increasingly getting their information from other sources (which primarily means the internet, where broadband is growing well and prices are falling).

The difficulty with any form of advertising is that you can't be sure you will reach your target demographic, especially if you are aiming for the 16-to-24 age group, which comprises the largest proportion of the CD-buying public.

The current growth areas in the communications services field are mobile phones and social networking sites on the internet. If you are lucky enough to have a publicity budget (if you do, it is likely to be very small), then I suggest you focus it in the areas of mobile phones and social networking sites (or whatever the current hot areas are).

If you want to read more about the trends in the communications services market, Ofcom (the Office of the Communications Regulator—the UK regulator of communications, including telecoms, radio, and television) regularly publishes research. For details, go to www.ofcom.org.uk/research/cm. This material is specific to the UK market; however, the principles and the trends are very similar for many other countries' markets.

Advertising

There are many places that you can advertise, including radio, TV, newspapers, magazines, billboards, and the internet.

If you want to start placing advertisements, then you are going to have to deal with advertising people. These people are the enemy: They will imply that they can bring you the world. They will not, but they will charge you a lot of money.

The statistics that advertising people can produce will suggest how effective each of the media outlets is at reaching your target audience. So for instance, they will be able to say that Show A on Radio Station B has an audience of C million people, and D% of those people are in the 18-to-45 age group.

Now, consider a conversation with your bank manager if you want to borrow money. What is going to impress him or her more—several million people hearing your advertisement on the radio or a known number of fans who have purchased your product and who have therefore generated a known amount of income?

In short, advertising people will not be able to deliver any measurable results. You will not be able to *prove* that their actions have increased your sales. However, they are likely to have a positive effect.

One area where a lot of money is spent is TV advertising. Many record companies will heavily advertise products where they know there is an audience and past experience has suggested that they will recoup their advertising expenditures. However, as television becomes less significant for the younger age groups, it remains to be seen whether TV advertising will be the way that ensures CDs are sold in the future.

Promotion

The line between advertising and promotion is a fine one. To make the distinction, what I mean by promotion is publicity work generally for a specific project. For instance, if you have a single to promote, then you might perform that single on as many television programs as possible, or if you have an album to promote, you may perform some live gigs (or undertake a tour).

Promotion is expensive; however, it is not necessarily as expensive as advertising. It may also be more effective than advertising.

One thing that promotion may do is give you an opportunity to connect with your fan base (as well as the chance to find new fans). Clearly you should always remember what it is that you are promoting. However, why not use the opportunity to do something a bit special?

For instance, if you are promoting your new single and you are doing a radio interview, then why not take an acoustic guitar and perform the song live (with just a voice and a guitar)? You may not always be able to do this, but it will give you the opportunity to connect with people and to prove you are a real performer who loves what you are doing.

Capitalizing on Active Publicity

It is very difficult to make sure all publicity counts. For instance, if after weeks of hard work you manage to get your record played on the radio, then people must know either the name of the song or your name.

One thing you can do is make sure that the title of your song is obvious from listening. If you're not sure whether it's obvious, play your song once (and only once) to someone who hasn't heard it before and then ask that person what the title is. If he or she doesn't get it right, then that song probably shouldn't be played on radio.

If you're skeptical about this, check out some top 40 songs. How easy is it to pick out the title? Now, listen to some songs that haven't made the top 40 and see whether you can pick out the title. Of course, there will always be exceptions—for instance, you cannot figure out the title of "Bohemian Rhapsody" from the song. Although there will be these exceptions, please don't delude yourself that you have written the next "Bohemian Rhapsody!" Or rather, please do delude yourself, but then learn to live with failure when no one buys your single.

There are other things you can do to capitalize on any publicity. For instance, if you are going on TV, then make sure that the name of the act is obvious (for instance, have the band name on a banner at the back of the stage or put it on the kick drum).

Whatever publicity you are doing, please don't mistake it for actually converting fans into a source of income. Unless you can attract people and they can find you, they will not become a source of income, and all your hard work will be worth nothing.

When Did the Press Pack Die?

Many years ago, marketing types would talk about the "press pack." The notion behind the press pack was that this was a bundle of information that could be sent out for publicity (usually attached to a press release). Typically, a pack could include a short biography, some photos, and maybe a track or two.

As technology evolved these got more impressive, and some people started to send out multimedia CDs with the information and the tracks on the CD. The CDs could even include video clips (perhaps with an interview or similar).

But then everything changed. Press packs and electronic press packs do still exist; however, with every artist having a website (and the ability to communicate with his or her fan base), the need for a press pack is reduced.

You may be pressured to produce a press pack, and there may be times when these are useful. (For instance, if you are approaching someone about a gig, that person may want to see a photo and read about your background.) However, as a general rule, I would suggest that you don't bother.

I would particularly suggest that you don't bother sending a press pack to journalists. If the media outlet is small enough to be interested in you (for instance, it may be a local paper), then no one will care much about the media outlet. (Do *you* care about your local paper? Do *you* read your local paper?) However, if you are generating sufficient interest, then the media will come to you. In particular, the more useful media outlets will come to you.

I would also suggest that you apply the six degrees of separation theory to getting publicity. There is bound to be someone in your fan base who knows a journalist (or knows someone who knows a journalist) who will be useful to you. Journalists will think you are so much cooler if they find you, rather than if you are just another act begging them for publicity.

That being said, as we go through this book, you will see that there are some limited occasions (typically when you have reached a certain level of success and you want to step up your game) when you need to think about a strategy that includes involving the media.

The Role of PR

As you will have gathered, I'm fairly skeptical about the benefits of advertising. My skepticism is not because I think you will not get results, but because I do not believe you get the results you pay for, unless those results are to raise your profile with people who will never buy your product.

I do not want to damn the whole of the marketing industry. There is one piece of marketing that I think can be very useful and that I want to single out. If you have an experienced PR person at your disposal (who may work for a record company or for an agency), that person can be very helpful. The kind of PR person you should be looking for must have lots of contacts who they can call.

With this route you will be getting lots of well-placed publicity and you will be controlling the message to a much greater extent. Just taking any publicity you can get leaves you prey to whims of journalists trying to make a name for themselves.

Singles

For many years singles have been the mainstay of music promotion, and although their influence is not as strong as it once was, they are still a highly important marketing tool. In some markets, the notion of a single is obsolete, and instead an album track will be heavily promoted. For the purpose of this section, similar principles apply.

The advantage of a single (or promoted track) is that it creates an event about which you can shout and get publicity in many different forms of media. For instance, you can promote a single on TV or radio, in the press, on billboards, on the internet, and in live performances. This promotion can be as paid-for advertising or by personal appearances, interviews, and so on and can be in one country or many countries.

The disadvantage of a single is that the promotion costs are very high, and (in the territories where a physical product is released) the margins on the product are typically very low, although the economics have changed considerably with the introduction of digital downloads. Unless you can find a unique marketing angle, then you will probably have to promote a single in a conventional way.

Whether you are promoting a single in the conventional manner or through a unique (and perhaps untried) angle, you will have to work very hard to stand out from the crowd. And if you are thinking about releasing a single without a fanfare and a huge amount of publicity, don't. You won't make any money or find any new fans, and you will find that the release has been a waste of your time, money, and effort that was doomed to failure from the outset.

Passive Publicity

We've looked at some of the strategies you can employ to actively publicize your music. I now want to talk about some of the passive strategies you can consider.

The purpose of a passive strategy is to help people who are:

- Looking to find you
- Trying to find information about you

As you might expect, much of this strategy is implemented on the internet. I will discuss what your website should look like in more detail later in this chapter, under the section "Building the Perfect Website."

Helping People Who Are Looking for You

People will find your website in one of three ways:

- By typing in your URL (you web address). In order to do this, they must have seen your web address written down (for instance, on a flyer given out at a gig), or they must have been told it (in which case, well done on having such a memorable URL).
- From a search engine such as Google.
- From a link on another website.

There are many things you can do to help people find you, which I will look at in the following sections.

Getting Picked Up by Search Engines

Search-engine ranking is a black art. Many people will sell you services to help improve your ranking. I'm not convinced that many of these services do much good. If you want to read more about the latest thinking about search engine optimization, one site I recommend you check out is Search Engine Watch (searchenginewatch.com).

Ignoring all of the science, there are some sensible things you can do to give search engines a chance of finding you, such as:

- Ensure you use text and not graphics. It is very tempting to use attractive graphics for key headings, such as the artists' names. If you do this, then ensure that each artist's name (in full) is included in regular text. Remember, search engines will search text—they cannot search (and read) graphics.

- Ensure all of your key information is included on your site. For instance, if you have a well-recognized song, make sure its title appears somewhere. People may search for your songs instead of just searching for you.

- Ensure any unique words associated with you are included. If there is anything that can help narrow down a search and differentiate you from other websites, then use it. Better still, invent a whole new word, and when people search for that, they will find you. Okay, that last one's a bit cheap, but it is quite fun. Added to that, it will confuse etymologists for years to come.

- Have links from other sites. Some search engines rank the importance of a site according to the number of links to the site. One way you can increase the number of links is by forum postings. Just make sure you include your site's URL in your signature, and the link will be set up for the search engine to find.

Helping People Who Want to Find Out More about You

I'm guessing that when I suggested you set up your own website, you understood my reasons completely. Indeed, I'm also guessing that you didn't need to read this book to decide that having your own website would help your career. However, you may start to wonder what I am doing when I suggest that you highlight other websites that mention you—surely by pointing people in different directions, this could get confusing and could draw income away.

And you are right to be concerned. However, remember that your success is based on a community around you, and here we're talking about publicity.

Okay, enough self-justification. What am I actually suggesting you *do*, here? Two things:

- Find other communities that mention you. Participate in those communities and support them.

- Link to other websites/communities that have information about you.

Let me explain further.

Participate in Other Communities

You will be able to find whether you are mentioned in, and linked to from, other communities (whether that be MySpace, a web forum, or similar) by looking at your website statistics. These should be able to show you where you have been linked from. Follow those links back, and you will find a whole array of other communities.

Take a look around these communities and then participate—drop in for a chat or just to say "hi." Be open and honest about who you are, include your URL in your signature, and perhaps use your logo as an avatar (the small image that identifies individual users on internet forums). There's no need to spend too long, and you definitely don't want to hang around if there are any arguments. All you are trying to do is show that you are a friendly sort of person.

This sounds too simple, doesn't it? And in many ways it is. However, you have done a few things here:

- First, you have reached out to people on a human level. This gives you a certain degree of humanity.

- Second, you have added some more links back to your website. The more links there are back to your website, the more people are likely to flow toward your site. Also, the more links there are out there referring people to your website, the faster people will find you (the more links, the more your site becomes a magnet).

- Last, you have tapped into another community—in other words, a whole group of people (not just one person). Each member of that community may then bring a new group of people with him or her. Many communities link to other communities, and community people often bring whole communities with them, not just one or two friends. As you reach out to communities, you have the potential for the number of your fans to grow very quickly.

Another way to find who is linking to you is to search for yourself (using Google or your favorite search engine). Search on the name of your act, the names of the individual musicians, and your URL. You may be particularly surprised by the results when you search for your URL.

Other Websites/Communities That Have Information about You

As you gain popularity, people will want to write about you. One place that people may write about you is in the forums, and we have already covered this.

You may find that unofficial fan sites crop up. (Your site should be the "official" fan site.) If unofficial sites spring up, I would suggest that you be very grateful and do everything you can to help these people. Just make sure their site doesn't look too much like yours, if for no other reason than you don't want people to think it's a fake.

One of the main reasons to support the unofficial sites (and to ensure they don't look fake) is that they give you credibility. Anyone who alights upon these fan sites will be impressed by the fan's devotion and will often want to know more about the act. Hence, these other sites will help to pass more traffic to you.

When you reach a certain level (don't do it before you've played your first gig), then think about a Wikipedia (www.wikipedia.org) entry.

Wikipedia is an online encyclopedia that is updated by anyone who wants to (which could mean you). If you do start an entry, make sure you keep it up to date. If you don't start an entry, then check Wikipedia periodically just in case anyone else has written about you (in particular, to check that they haven't accidentally got any of their facts wrong). You should, of course, check your listings in any other online encyclopedias or similar reference sources.

Building the Perfect Website

There will be many discussions about what constitutes the perfect website. Here are a few of my thoughts about the features of a good website.

Let's start with a few general principles. Your website should be:

- Fast

- Easy to navigate

- About you

Notice that I didn't mention the visual impact? Don't worry, I will come to that.

The Need for Speed

Your website should load quickly. Once loaded, page changes should be fast (if possible, immediate). Finally, anyone navigating through your website should be able to get to the intended destination page quickly. If you're not fast, then people will get bored or frustrated and will go elsewhere (and you will lose the potential income that could have flowed from that person).

You can design a website to be fast. However, if you start using a professional web designer or allow "marketing" people to give their input, you will be pressured to do things that can dramatically slow down your website.

There are two things that significantly slow down a website (that is, cause it to take a long time to load and to change pages)—graphics (especially video) and audio. As you know, in your line of work, audio and visual features on a website are very important.

There is a trend to use short video clips that load automatically when you go to a website. Some of these can look quite good. Other sites have a large number of images. These too can be quite impressive. Some sites start to play the artist's latest tracks automatically. However, all of these approaches will dramatically slow down the loading time of the webpage. Some will cause the webpage to be so slow you will wonder whether your computer has crashed.

There are many reasons for including impressive graphics and tracks that play automatically:

- When it finally loads, it looks good.

- People don't realize just how long the features will take to load. Often the web designer will demonstrate the features in a meeting, where he or she can run the video or other media feature directly from his or her computer, thereby avoiding showing the download time.

- Peer pressure—everybody else is doing something similar. This is coupled with a perceived need to appear "fresh," "new," or "cutting edge."

- The belief that because it is a musician's website, music has to be stuffed down the throats of anyone who alights on the site.

Let me make a plea: Please don't do this. Please don't even think about this. Instead, please create a simple home page that loads virtually instantaneously and contains links so that people can easily find video/audio clips and so on and download them if they want to.

Obviously, the home page should be visually appealing. However, this can be achieved in a quite simple and straightforward manner through some carefully chosen visual images. These images can then be optimized for web viewing so that their loading time is reduced to the absolute minimum.

It is not necessary to have animated graphics to impress people. Indeed, with animated graphics there is a much greater chance that your site will look naff or cheesy, whereas with something simple there is less to get wrong in terms of design decisions.

Easy to Navigate

Too often the navigation for a website is engineered by the website designer (who will usually be a computer programmer of some sort). This is a bad, bad thing to do.

Website navigation should be designed from the perspective of the user (in other words, the fan or potential fan). It should be designed around how the fans think about you and how the fans expect to find information about you. Navigation should not be constructed on the basis of how the underlying data files are organized.

Navigation from the Home Page

The first step in helping people to find their way around your site will be the home page (the page you see when you first load your site). The home page should clearly have visual impact and should be welcoming. (In other words, it should be interesting and not crammed with lots of confusing text.)

If there is something you are particularly promoting or you have some recent breaking news, then that should be featured prominently on your home page. For instance, if you have just sent an email to your fan base about some gigs and you have referred people to your site for the details of the dates and where the fans can get tickets, then your gigs should be prominent on the home page.

In practice, this means words to the effect of "Gigs announced" should be immediately visible when you load the home page, and somewhere under that there should be text to the effect of "Click here for details of the dates and where you can get tickets." (Obviously, that should be a clickable link that takes you to the page of details.)

Navigation Bars

One way that people often find their way around a site is with navigation bars. These are usually groups of buttons on the left side or across the top of the screen that help viewers find their way around a site. For an example of a navigation bar, see Figure 6.2, which shows a screen grab of my website. The navigation bar is on the left side. You will see there are four buttons, labeled "Home," "Books," "Mail list," and "Contact." As you click on each of these buttons, the main part of the screen displays a different page (though the buttons and the top graphic remain unchanged).

My website has a simple aim: to promote my books. Accordingly, my site is very simple, so I only need four buttons. Each button has a text label that is fairly self-explanatory. I recommend you use the minimum number of buttons you can get away with, although you should never use fewer buttons if this will make your site counterintuitive in its operation. As a general rule of thumb, anything around six or seven buttons is fine. You might want to go up to nine buttons, but I would never suggest exceeding that number.

Figure 6.2 The author's website. Note the navigation bar on the left side, which helps viewers find their way around the site.

The text on the buttons should be immediately legible and should unambiguously suggest where the viewer is being led. If the text on the button is insufficiently descriptive, you may also want to consider a rollover message (some text that displays when you roll your mouse cursor over the button).

This may all seem obvious, but I am sure we have all seen sites that are hard to understand immediately. Remember, your fans are sensible individuals (hey—they wouldn't follow you if they weren't), and you're not making it easy because they are stupid. You are making it easy because you respect them and you want them to get to the information they want without wasting their time. If they have to waste their time or they get frustrated, they are very unlikely to spend money on you.

Structuring the Navigation

You need to give some careful consideration to how broad and deep your navigation system is. Let me elaborate. You have got some "stuff" that you want to disseminate to your fans and potential fans. The "stuff" is a mixture of different things—for instance, information about you, the artist, contact details, music or video clips, pictures, and so on. You need to fit this information into a framework so that viewers can find their way around your website in a manner that immediately makes sense to them.

As a first step, that information can be split under some main headings. These main headings will become the navigation buttons. However, under these general headings, you may have a lot of different pieces of information. Those different pieces of information can be separated to make navigation clear. Under those new subheadings you may have another grouping of information that could be separated under sub-subheadings.

As you can see, this is getting confusing! Just think how your viewers may feel. Let me give an example to try to illustrate this point. Suppose you have a button labeled "About." This is where you have all of the information about the artist, including, for instance, biographies and news. You may have two different types of news: current news (news that is still relevant) and archived news (old news that you retain for completeness). Under the archived news, you may then store the news by year. With this arrangement, you could have four layers:

About > News > Archive > Year

This has a certain logic to it, and many people would be able to follow this structure. However, suppose you are looking for a press release in the 2006 archives but you can't find it, so you want to check out the 2005 archives. You could start from the top and follow the same path down the tree and instead of selecting 2006, select 2005. However, it would be preferable if there was some way in the navigation system to step up (from 2006) and then step down again (to 2005).

The ease with which people will be able to find their way around your site will be governed by two factors: the number of layers (in this example there are four layers) and how you can navigate up and down between the layers. The more layers you add, the more complicated your website will be and the harder it will be for people to find what they are looking for.

The solution to ensuring that the number of layers is minimized is to have a sufficient number of main headings (in other words, a sufficient number of navigation buttons or whatever you are using to assist navigation). However, as I mentioned earlier, there is a limit to the number of navigation buttons you can have before browsing around your website becomes confusing. As you will understand, you need to strike a balance here and create a website that works for you.

As a general rule of thumb, if you can restrict yourself to two layers, you will be able to create a website that is fast to use and is simple to navigate. With some hard work, you could create a site with three layers that is reasonably fast and reasonably easy to navigate. When you get to the fourth layer, then you are likely to reach the point of confusion. You should also remember that each branch on the navigation tree does not need to be the same length.

You may be wondering about the example I gave earlier, in which the news archive was stored at the fourth level. As suggested in the preceding paragraph, if you go to the fourth level you may reach confusion (as I illustrated). As well as going too deep, I think my example displayed another error: It put the news under a counterintuitive location. You may disagree, but I would suggest that most people looking for news about an act would not look for this under the heading "About." If you regularly have news, then it is probably best to have a "News" navigation button and put all of the news there.

Figure 6.3 gives an example of how you could structure the navigation system on a band's website.

Alternatives to Navigation Bars

I've mentioned navigation bars at some length. Don't feel you have to have these. With your music career, you are working in a creative industry, so you can be creative with your website too. However, don't get too creative—if people don't understand your navigation system, you will lose customers (even if you've employed some of the most intelligent and innovative tricks in the book). I have suggested navigation buttons because they are simple and, more importantly, they work.

Instead of using navigation buttons, you could have a page with a number of links. Often you will find this system is adopted for the second layer of navigation. Let me give you an example of how this could work. Assume you have decided (having read my ramblings) to have a "News" navigation button. When you click on this, it could open a News page. On the News page, you could have links to your most recent news articles and links to "Archive 2006" and "Archive 2005" (for instance). This would combine the two navigation systems.

You can use any form of navigation you want. For instance, you could have a graphic that has different clickable regions, each of which takes you to a different area. This may work, but it could come across as a gimmick. Also, it may not work so well if you want to go from a second level to a third level. However, just because I can't find reasons to follow one course, that doesn't mean you shouldn't look for new and innovative ways to help people navigate your site.

If your website is too hard to navigate (in other words, its operation is counterintuitive or people cannot find what they're looking for *immediately*) even with your best effort, then you've got too much stuff.

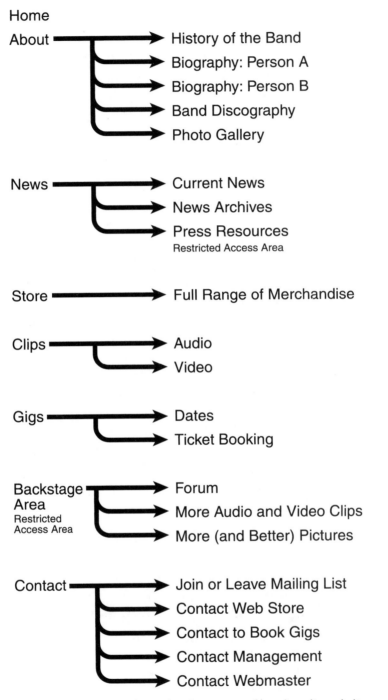

Home
About → History of the Band
→ Biography: Person A
→ Biography: Person B
→ Band Discography
→ Photo Gallery

News → Current News
→ News Archives
→ Press Resources
Restricted Access Area

Store → Full Range of Merchandise

Clips → Audio
→ Video

Gigs → Dates
→ Ticket Booking

Backstage Area
Restricted Access Area
→ Forum
→ More Audio and Video Clips
→ More (and Better) Pictures

Contact → Join or Leave Mailing List
→ Contact Web Store
→ Contact to Book Gigs
→ Contact Management
→ Contact Webmaster

Figure 6.3 An example navigation system for a band's website.

If you've got too much stuff, then cut the content, A website should be promoting you; it is not a detailed reference of your whole performing career. (Leave those highs and lows to your biography and the documentaries that will follow after its publication.)

Equally, if you think your site needs a search engine, then start worrying —your life is clearly getting far too complicated. Search engines are great with research-driven sites. Your site should be about promoting your music and increasing your fan base, not about research.

Amount of Information on a Page

The amount of information that any one page carries will have a dramatic effect on the comprehensibility of the page. Equally, the size of each paragraph will have a marked effect on the comprehensibility and the ease with which someone can physically read the information.

In an ideal world, you would not have a page of information take up more than one screen. (in other words, if you open any particular page on your website, all of the information should be displayed without the need to scroll down or across.)

However, there is a difficulty here. There are many different screen sizes, so the amount of information that can fit on a single screen will vary. As a minimum, most laptop screens are around 15" in size. (There are smaller and there are bigger, but on the whole that is the current minimum specification.) By default, most laptop screens are then set to 800×600 or 1,024×768 resolution. These are good sizes to consider when thinking about how much information you can get on a screen.

However, there will obviously be times when this aspiration is wholly impractical. At these times you should take a pragmatic approach, but still do everything possible to aid navigation.

For instance, if you are including a history of a band, you may have a lot of information. You could split this information over several pages, but you may not like how this looks. Alternatively, you could just have one long page. Although inelegant, this could work. If you are going to have a long page, then I would suggest you have lots of (bold) subheadings so that the text is broken into clearly delineated chunks for the reader. You could also make it easier to navigate through the page with links to jump to certain parts.

As another example, if you're including gig information, it may not be practical to split this over several pages. In this case, I would suggest you group chunks of information together. For instance, you could group the dates by country, by state, or by the month in which the gig occurs. Whatever you do, choose something that is easy for the person wanting to buy tickets to follow.

Does It Promote You?

It may sound like the most obvious thing, but your website should be about promoting you and your music. I make this point because often it gets forgotten.

People use their site to try to show off or to settle old scores. Anything that is not directly about your music is a distraction that will distance your fan base from you. As distance increases, your income will decrease.

Visual Impact

It is crucial that your website has a clear, crisp, engaging visual image. There is nothing worse than a website that looks old and tired. However, the way to ensure you don't look old and tired is not to invest in the latest whiz-bang technology (which is likely to be advocated by old and tired web designers who are keen to try out their new toys). Instead, the answer is to design the site (visually) so that it looks as appealing as possible. The best way to do this is to find a designer who can create web-optimized graphics, but make sure that they don't try to do anything that uses excess bandwidth.

If you are concerned about what the designer is suggesting, ask him or her to put up a demo website. Then go and find someone with a slow internet connection (if possible, a dial-up connection) and try it out. If it's even vaguely slow, then get the visuals changed.

You may be tempted to do the visuals for your own website. I would caution against this unless you have experience in this area. So often homemade visuals just look, well, homemade. From the start you will be giving the image of an act that is cheap—in other words, not very successful and perhaps not worth following.

One last word of caution: Although your website should look great, try to ensure that it doesn't look too "corporate." By this I mean if someone could look at your site for the first time and think, "That's a website for a pharmaceutical company" or "That's a website for an aerospace contractor," then you may not be appealing to music fans.

Things That Frustrate Your Viewers

There are lots of things you can do with your website that will really, *really* frustrate your viewers. Here is a list of just a few of those things:

- Websites that require specific software to view. Some web features (particularly the horrible animated graphics I have already railed against) need specific plug-ins to be installed on the viewing computer. Some people may take the time to install the plug-ins just to view your site, but many will not bother and will look elsewhere for their music.

- Really slow websites. Even when the necessary plug-ins are installed, you shouldn't use them automatically. Using animated graphics and automatically playing music will cause a website to slow down while the necessary files are downloading. While the files are downloading, it can appear that the website is not working. Again, this may encourage a potential new fan to go elsewhere.

  Please do have music on your website. Please have videos, too. You are a musician after all. However, please make these optional (in other words, the viewer has to click a play button).

- Websites that are incompatible with certain web browsers. There is a wide range of web browsers, each of which will view HTML (and other web-based code) in a different way. You should ensure that your website has been checked with as many different browsers as possible before you go live. In particular, you should ensure that your website works as intended when it is viewed with Microsoft Internet Explorer, Firefox, Opera, and Safari (which is part of OS X for Macs).

- Script blockers and other disabling features. Many people have script blockers activated to help reduce the risk of hackers and viruses. These blockers will stop certain features on your website from working as you intend. If your website makes use of any scripts (such as a piece of JavaScript to make your navigation menu function properly), then there should either be a non-script alternative or a warning that notifies the viewer that the website will not function as intended without scripts being enabled.

- Websites designed for a particular screen size. As I have already mentioned, there are many different screen sizes available, and different users select different resolutions. The combination of these factors may mean your website has to fit into a very small space or a very big space. While you can't account for all sizes, please do check that your website looks good at a range of sizes and resolutions.

Make It Sticky...

Please don't.

There is a really horrible buzzword among web people: "sticky." What they mean by this term is that people go to your website and keep going back. Often people suggest you should update your content regularly (for instance, weekly) to make a site sticky.

Stickiness can be useful if the website generates its income from advertising revenue or has a massive amount of stock for sale (for instance, Amazon).

However, for you, this is not a good thing. A sticky website suggests that you are not communicating with your fan base. If they need to come back and keep looking at your website, then they obviously don't trust you to tell them when things are going on. If they don't trust you in this little way, are they going to trust you with other things (such as their money)?

The only time it may be good for your site to have any sticky features is if you have a forum where your fans can communicate with one another and with you.

Choosing a URL

A URL is a universal resource locator. In English, that means your website address.

You are likely to be constrained in your choice of URL if your act's name is not readily available. Although your choices may be limited, do try to choose a URL that is unique, memorable, and easy to communicate verbally.

I would suggest you register several URLs—for instance, a .com and .net version of your URL. You may want to register a local version (for instance, .co.uk), and although that may be a sensible idea to ensure that no one else uses it, I wouldn't suggest you use it in public because localized URLs have a habit of looking very parochial.

If you do register several URLs, then only use one (the obvious choice being .com). Only use the others to automatically transfer the viewer to your main URL.

Do Something of the Moment

As I am writing this book, one feature that is becoming very prevalent (but may not quite have reached critical mass) on websites is podcasting. This is not simply a nice idea; it is something that many people are doing, including some very serious websites, such as the BBC.

In case you haven't come across podcasts (where have you been?!?), these are audio or visual files distributed over the internet. A user subscribes to a podcast feed—this subscription may be paid or unpaid—and the user's podcast software will automatically download a file whenever a new podcast is made available at the feeds to which they have subscribed. The downloaded podcast can then be transferred to a mobile media player (such as an iPod or other MP3 player) or listened to on the user's computer.

Users can subscribe to podcasts using the Apple iTunes software. Other popular podcast software includes Juice (juicereceiver.sourceforge.net), which is free to download and use and which is available for Windows, Apple OS X, and Linux formats.

For musicians, podcasting is a great opportunity to get your message out there. Added to this, you should already be very familiar with the technology to record an audio podcast because it's the same technology with which you would record your songs. Once you've made a podcast file in MP3 format, the only vaguely difficult bit is creating your podcast news feed.

One of the great things about podcasting is that it allows you to get a lot of content in front of your audience that they can then listen to when they want, but it doesn't slow down their use of your site.

At the time of writing this section (November 2006), podcasting is very much of the moment. If podcasting has been and gone by the time you read this, then another technology may have come along and gained widespread acceptance. If this is the case, then embrace the new technology and use it to further your aims (but as I have said before, don't use any technologies that slow down your website).

Make It Personal for Your Fans

If there is anything you can do to make your website more personal for your fans to foster and reinforce your connection with them, then do it.

As an example of a simple thing you can do, take photos of your fans at your gigs and then get them up on the website as soon as possible (ideally before the next morning). Anything you can do to foster a sense of belonging should be considered.

The Product

 # What Do You Actually Do?!?

I want to start looking at your product. But before I do that, I think it is important for you to have an idea about who you are and what it is you do. If these are difficult questions for you, then it will be even harder to create a cohesive product that you can sell to your fan base.

Let's look at this issue from a different perspective: What does your act offer to your potential fan base and why would the fan base spend money for those offerings? Take some time to think about it. It's very important.

If you're offering junk that is of no worth to a fan base, then you're going to lose your fan base and your income. No income equates to no career.

Who Are You? What Do You Do?

Have you seen or read interviews with artists who say something to the effect of, "Our album defies categorization," or "We're creative people —we don't like to be pigeonholed?"

Now, I don't want to constrain your creativity, but one thing you need to do is establish your genre. You can define the genre as broadly (or as narrowly) as you like, using whatever terms you feel appropriate (however contradictory). Equally, you can change your genre how and when you want.

You need a genre for two reasons. First, you need a genre so you have an idea of your identity—an idea about what it is you actually do. Once you have defined a genre for yourself, then you will have a clearer understanding about when you are changing and developing your genre.

You also need a genre so that new people know what you do. In broad terms, people know what they like: They know that they like death metal but not freeform jazz (or vice versa). Without an identifiable genre, you may be passed by.

I love the notion of an artist who feels comfortable working in many different musical styles. However, let's look at the commercial realities for a moment. If you're a death metal band and you suddenly start playing freeform jazz, then you're probably going to lose a large chunk of your fan base.

Very few acts can change and keep their fan base. However, many acts can develop as their fan base develops. Evolution, not revolution, is the key here. Also, very few acts can claim to be truly diverse in the way that say, Led Zeppelin, was.

Zeppelin played rock (at times, heavy, thunderous rock), blues, and folk, as well as throwing in some country-tinged material and showing some reggae influences. Zeppelin disbanded in 1980, and I'm not sure that there has been a band since then that has achieved their level of success with so many diverse styles. My hunch (and it is a hunch) is that Zeppelin's fan base accepted the wide range of styles because the band always had a cohesive, identifiable sound of their own that was very much due to the individuals in the band.

Who Is Your Market?

Once you know who you are and what you do, your next quest is to figure out who your market is.

Don't fool yourself into thinking that you will appeal to everybody. Try to really narrow down who your market is. For instance:

- If you're producing really lightweight but highly melodic pop music, then you may well appeal to the pre-teen market.

- If you're producing pop/R&B and you're a male singer, then you may appeal to the female teenage market.

- If you're producing very aggressive metal/rock, then you may appeal to males age 15 to 24.

- If you're a middle-aged crooner singing sentimental love songs, then you may appeal to the 45+ female market.

As you have no doubt realized, these are really crude generalizations and will never be totally accurate. Also, there will always be people who are interested in a style of music you don't expect (the grand-mother at the death metal gig, and so on).

However, these broad generalizations can be useful as a starting point for thinking about your strategy for finding an audience. If you don't know who your potential fan base is, then how will you go looking for these people?

Is There an Audience?

I'm going to ask you to be really dispassionate for a moment. Try, if you can, to emotionally disconnect yourself from your music. Imagine you are hearing your music for the first time. Now answer one question: Is there an audience for this kind of music?

If there is an audience, who are these people and how big is the market?

Let me give you two examples, one musical and one not: classical guitarists and poets. No one would suggest that either of these art forms is anything other than completely worthy. However, the number of people who can actually make a living by playing classical guitar (as opposed to teaching) and writing poetry (as opposed to teaching creative writing) is tiny.

That being said, there are people who will buy classical guitar music and poetry. If you are a classical guitarist, and you are reading this book, and you can bring me a sublime recording (of yours) of the music of Antonio Lauro, I will buy it. As a side note, if you haven't heard any of Lauro's music, you should. Check out "Natalia" and "Andreina" from his *Valses Venezolanos*.

Before you stride purposefully into the world, ask yourself how big your potential market is. Is it a Justin Timberlake–sized market or is it a classical guitarist–sized market?

If the market is on the smaller side, that should not necessarily be a problem. One of the benefits of the strategies outlined in this book is that you can be very efficient from a financial perspective. This means you may be able to generate income (to sustain a career) at a much lower level than would be necessary if you signed with a record label.

Also, if you are doing something that is more obscure, then you may be able to charge higher prices. To take me as an example again—and I am not alone; this is a well known economic phenomenon—I am happy to spend more money on acquiring the music of Antonio Lauro than I am on acquiring a normal CD, due to my liking of his music and the scarcity of good recordings. (It's basic supply and demand economics, along with my love of perfectly crafted tunes.)

Another benefit of operating in a less popular niche is that you are likely to be working in a less crowded market, so you should be able to capture a larger share of the market.

When assessing whether there is an audience out there, be careful to ensure that there will be a suitably large audience for you. For instance, you may be in a band made up of a bunch of fat, balding guys in their fifties (no offense intended to fat guys in their fifties—it's just a nice stereotype for illustration) who play Rolling Stones–type music (not covers, just music in a similar style). You may surmise that given the size of the audience for the Stones, then there is an audience for you. And you would be wrong.

The Stones have their audience and will always have their audience. They have created and maintained that audience by virtue of their hard work over at least the last 45 years. People want to see the Stones; they don't want to see a bunch of fat losers (their opinion, not mine) performing second-rate "dad" music.

So I will ask you again, because this is really important: Is there an audience out there for you?

Before you answer that question, let me just add another thought. Do the people you are aiming for have the time, the money, and the inclination to buy your product and to come out and support you?

For instance, if you are aiming your music at what could be lazily categorized as the "housewife" market, will that demographic support you?

Almost without exception, all of the housewives that I know are run ragged by their kids. They spend the whole day chasing and cleaning up after their kids. The priority in their life is their kids, not music.

Although I am sure you could create music that an average housewife would like and would be happy to listen to (on the radio) while she completes her daily chores, the notion that a housewife would have time to find out about your act and support your act is, I believe, misguided. Kids, teenagers, and younger adults will have more time (and, ironically, will often have more disposable income) to invest in music, so the music market is aimed at this younger age group.

What Does Your Audience Want?

So you've decided what you do, you've identified your audience (and you're sure they'll support you), so what are you going to sell them?

This may sound like a daft question, so let me elaborate. You need to identify what the audience wants and ensure that what your act does (and produces) dovetails with what the audience wants in an act. In other words, your products need to be designed in light of your audience's needs. When you look to understand your audience's needs, this is the time when you need to understand the composition of the audience. (Don't just rely on your expectations of the makeup of the audience.)

Ask yourself a few questions: Does the fan base really want a poster? Probably not if the fans are not kids/teens. Does the fan base want a CD, or would they prefer to buy downloads? Alternatively, are they the sort of people who would value (that is, pay for) a special-edition CD that costs more than a regular CD?

You will never get the answers to these questions perfectly correct; however, the more you know about your audience, the more informed your decision-making (and therefore your product design) will be. This is another reason why you should spend time getting to know, and communicating directly with, your fan base.

Tuning Your Act to Fit Your Audience

Over time you will get to know your audience. If you don't, your career will be short (see Figure 7.1). As you get to know these people (individually and collectively), you are likely to be able to fine-tune your output to match their needs.

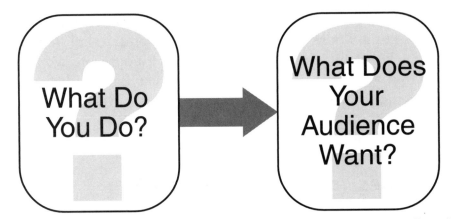

Figure 7.1 What do you do and what does your audience want? Is there a direct link between the two? If not, then you may have difficulties building your career.

This is a good thing. It means that you can be more efficient in your product offerings, and you will generate more income. It may also mean that you increase your fan base because you have hit a winning formula.

However, do be wary of change. With each change you could alienate your existing fans, leaving them feeling as if you have sold out. If you are making a change that you are happy with (and that may also be part of the maturing process), then I don't think you need to apologize for your changes. If this means you lose fans, then unfortunately there is little you can do to stop that. In this situation, it is important that you ensure the parting is as amicable as possible.

On the other hand, if the changes are ruthlessly commercial ones, you may find it hard to defend your position, and you may find that former fans tend to say unpleasant things in the anonymity of cyberspace.

And just to be clear, I am not suggesting that you change everything about your act in an attempt to chase dollars. Instead, I am suggesting that you focus on the aspects of what you do that are more popular with your audience.

Evolution

You may know your market very well. Indeed, you may know many of your fans personally. However, your audience may change over time. To oversimplify, you are likely to be in one of two situations.

Renewing Audience

If your act is focused on a particular demographic—for instance, the pre-teen market—then the individuals who make up your audience may grow out of your act. This is nothing to be too concerned about, provided you can keep renewing your audience.

In many ways, if you are renewing your audience you can keep the same act—you don't need to do anything new because your material will be new to the audience (but you must obviously ensure that you remain current). Although this is a bit cynical, it does illustrate an important point: With an audience that does notage (because the audience keeps renewing and you are therefore always focused on a specific age group), you cannot change or mature as an act. It is often a big mistake to think that you can mature and carry an audience with you. Unfortunately, as the audience matures, they will just see you as either cheesy or kids' stuff (or both).

For an illustration of this, look at the boy bands that have tried to take time out and return as new, mature versions of themselves. It rarely works. Equally, look at the former boy band members who have tried to have a lasting solo career with a more adult sound: Justin Timberlake may be one of the few examples of someone who has been able to make the change.

Maturing Audience

By contrast, you may have an audience that will let you grow with them. This is likely to be the situation if you are creating more adult-oriented music.

This audience will remain interested while you continue to provide a soundtrack that reflects their life. However, they may get diverted away from music. For instance, upon having children, many parents focus on their kids and not music.

However, assuming you can keep the fan base over the long term, you need to ensure you do not develop ahead of your audience or in ways that your audience does not appreciate. For instance, if you started life as a Hell for leather death metal band, then your audience may be happy for you to mature into a more classic rock band over time.

Getting Stale

As your audience changes, you will have to make sure you do not change too fast to ensure that you do not lose your audience.

However, you must make sure that you don't change so slowly that you become overly familiar. If you get to the point where your fan base can't be bothered to go see you because they think they will see the show they saw last year, then you're in trouble and will probably lose your fan base.

8 Creating and Developing the Product

The notion of "product" sounds sordid, doesn't it? It probably feels uncomfortable in the same way that talking about exploitation in Chapter 4 was uncomfortable.

However, you're going to have to get used to the idea. At the end of the day, product is what you sell. If you don't sell any product, then you won't have any income and hence no career. So make a choice: Get over your squeamishness or go and get a proper job. We are now going to deal with the business aspects of your career.

What Is a Product?

Before we go any further, let me explain what I am calling a product (see Figure 8.1).

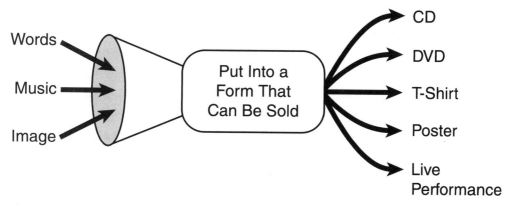

Figure 8.1 The process of product creation takes something intangible (a word, music, and so on) and converts it into a tangible form that can be sold (such as a CD or DVD).

In simplistic terms, a product is something you can sell, so a few chords and a line or two from a chorus don't make a product (although they may be part of the product development process). However, more than simply being something that has the potential to be sold, a product is a freestanding item, tangible or intangible, that is packaged and can be sold. Ideally, it is something that you can sell again and again and again.

So for instance, the following are examples of products:

- A CD
- A DVD
- A T-shirt
- A poster
- A live performance

There is a strong argument that you could call a live performance a service rather than a product because you are selling entertainment (which could be deemed to be a service) to people. However, I don't want there to be any confusion in terms between products and services, so I am calling *everything* a product. If it is something that you give to your fan base in exchange for money, then it is a product.

Product Process—From Creation, through Development, to Market

When you start thinking about products, you need to think about the process, from creating a product, to selling it, to providing after-sales service. Most products will follow a process that has the following steps (see Figure 8.2). For now I want to briefly introduce these main steps—I will then go on and discuss them in greater detail.

Product Development

The first stage of creating a product is the development stage. It is at this point that the product is conceived and researched. Only once you are sure that the idea is viable should the product be taken forward.

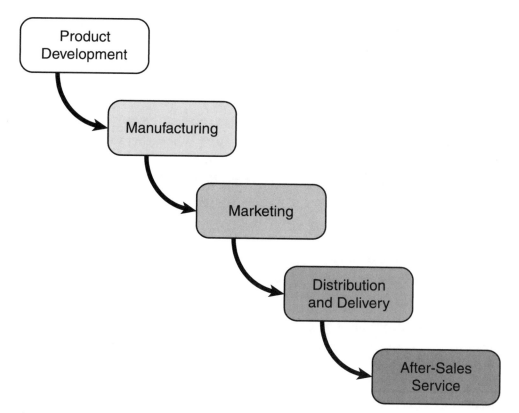

Figure 8.2 The product from creation, through development, to market.

Part of the product development is obvious and natural—for instance, writing songs. However, other parts may be unnatural (or at least not something that you will have experienced before). For instance, you may not have familiarity with the process involved in creating a T-shirt.

Manufacturing

The manufacturing stage is when the product is created. It is at this point that you actually get something tangible, whether that is a recording of a song or a test of a T-shirt. This is the first chance to see, hear, and touch something real.

You will often also find that there are problems at the manufacturing stage. The band may not be performing as well as you had hoped in the studio, or the T-shirt may be of a substandard quality. This may be the only opportunity you get to ensure the quality is everything you hoped for, so take the time to ensure the quality is perfect.

Marketing

In the marketing phase you will raise awareness of your product with your fan base. Traditionally, this is the time when the act goes on the road, playing live shows and making as many TV/radio appearances as they can. For many musicians, the two hours on stage each night are the reason they got into the business—the remaining 22 hours of each day are mindless tedium.

Distribution and Delivery

There is no point is selling products unless you can get to your fan base.

There is no art or craft in efficient delivery; it is pure administration. That being said, when it goes wrong, it is a nightmare for you and the fans, so it is well worth finding someone who can organize this aspect of your business.

After-Sales Service

Selling your product and getting it to the fan is not the end of the story. You're going to need to respond to complaints. For instance, merchandise may not arrive, CDs may not play, or the booklet may be badly printed. Whatever the complaint and whether it's your fault or not, you'll be expected to ensure that these things are fixed.

Developing the Product

Now that you know what I am calling a product, what product are you going to sell to your fan base? This is where product development comes in.

You've probably looked at the products I've listed in the previous section and thought that you want to do all of them. (This is not unreasonable; most musicians do want to produce CDs, DVDs, T-shirts, posters, and live performances.) You've probably also got lots of other ideas for products you would like to create.

Let's look at some of the factors that should influence your choice of which products to develop.

Size of the Product Range

Although it may seem like an odd consideration, the number of products you offer is an important issue.

You should aim to have a reasonably wide range of products so that you can offer something for most of your fan base. If you limit your product range, then you are limiting your potential income. (If there is nothing more for people to buy—perhaps because they've already bought everything you have to offer—then they won't give you their money.)

Equally, if your product range is too broad, that will create other problems—for instance, you will have large amounts of stock to store, insure, and keep track of. Also, with a wide product range you may end up spending more time on your products and less time on your music.

When you first start out it will be quite easy to limit your product range because you will be starting from zero. Perhaps your bigger problem will be charging for products.

Although new products do give more sales opportunities, they don't guarantee income (especially if you flood your market). Take a look at "The Cost of Developing Products" section later in this chapter, which, among other things, looks at the cash flow implications of creating new products and buying stock.

Only you can decide what is right for you in light of your fan base. To the extent that you are uncertain about the scope of your product range and the number of each product that you will stock (and you should be uncertain about developing any product for which you do not have an order that has been paid for), then don't be too ambitious: Start small and grow.

Which Products Do You Need? Setting Your Priorities

Now that you've got an idea about some of the products you can develop, it's probably a good idea to prioritize the development of these products. This will ensure that you have a steady flow of new products rather than everything arriving in one lump, and that you don't spend all of your time thinking about products and none of your time making music.

Planning will also help you to think about future products. You may have just released your CD, so it would seem a sensible approach to plan when the next CD will be released, given that it may take a year from conception to release. With a bit of planning you can ensure that you get everything you want sorted out. For instance, with some planning you could find a time when the producer you've always wanted to work with is available.

As a first step in the planning process, split your ideas into two piles: those things you should do and those things you should think twice about.

The things that you might think about developing include:

- Products you need because they define who and what you are. Two examples of products that define you are CDs and gigs. I can't see many people existing as musicians without developing one or both of these (although, as an example, TV composers may define themselves by single tracks rather than by a whole CD).

- Products that generate a healthy income and a profit. I will talk more about this issue under the section "The Cost of Developing Products," later in this chapter.

- Products that advertise you or raise your profile. A great example of this is T-shirts. Think about it: People will pay you money to advertise your brand on their body!

Then there are some things that you should think twice about (and then think again). As a start, this category will include products for which you need to carry a large stock, which have low margins, or which you just don't understand.

So what products should you create? That depends on your fan base and what it is you actually do. If you are creating a product that your fan base wants to buy, then you won't have to work hard to make sales, but you may have to work hard to ensure your fan base knows about the availability of the product—especially if you don't have direct line of communication with your fan base.

By contrast, if you create product that your audience doesn't want, then you're likely to have a lot of stock on your hands. Think about the notion of "want" in human terms, not just in relation to a general demographic. Ultimately, you should develop products about which you are passionate. Develop things that really matter to you and things that you care about. These are the items your fan base is far more likely to be interested in and will want to buy.

In this book I don't offer you money, but I am trying to help you find a way to do what you love and to generate sufficient income to live. It is your career, and you need to feel good about yourself. If you develop products that you are truly passionate about and that you truly believe are good, then it doesn't matter whether you sell 1,000 or 10 million (or just a few to your family and friends)—you will still believe you have a good product and will feel proud. And you will know that you haven't ripped off your fan base with second-rate tat.

Market Testing

One of the biggest difficulties in developing a new product is knowing what your fan base wants and what they will buy. It's pointless to develop a new product if no one is ever going to buy it.

One way to find out what products would interest your fan base is to carry out some research—in other words, ask people directly. This can be useful to a certain extent; however, one of the downsides of market research is that people aren't always straightforward. If you ask people whether they would buy a certain product, they may say they would. However, this doesn't mean that they will buy the product.

For instance, the person you surveyed may have been willing to buy when surveyed, but may have run out of money by the time the product is available. Alternatively, people may change their minds, or the product may not be what they expected from the description given when they were surveyed.

Whatever the reason, they won't buy.

A better way to know what the fan base might want is to know the fan base. If you get to know your fan base over a sustained period of time and you have conversations with individuals (two-way conversations, asking questions and listening), you may get a better feel for what they want than you would get if you followed the survey approach. However, you will still not get a perfect idea.

You will only truly know what sells once it has sold.

Research can be helpful, and I would always suggest that you get as close as possible to your fan base; however, if you want to know whether something sells, then the best course is to try selling it. If you start small so that you don't take too much of a loss (perhaps only releasing a product through an on-demand service), you will be able to gauge interest. Then, on the basis of actual sales figures, you can grow your product.

So for instance, you may know that your fans will buy T-shirts, but you don't know whether they will buy baseball caps. You could set up a baseball cap with an on-demand service and order, say, 50 caps to try to sell at gigs. If they don't sell, then you won't have lost too much. However, if they do sell, then you could look into having them produced at a lower cost (in other words, at a cost that may allow you to generate some profits).

Making Your Product the Best You Can
There are several keys in the strategy I am setting out in this book. For the moment, I want to look at two elements: the direct relationship with your fan base and making excellent music. By bringing these two elements together, you are getting close to developing a product that will sell itself. This is a good thing because, as you will have noticed, the strategy in this book does not rely on extensive advertising and hard selling. Instead, it relies on people wanting to buy.

Before I look at other products, let me look at your music products and take the example of producing a CD.

There are many elements that affect the overall quality of a CD, including:

- The songs. You need well-written, properly structured songs with instantly memorable tunes and lyrics to immediately draw you in. Songwriting is an art and a craft, and you should continually seek to improve your writing ability, whether through courses, a song-writing consultant, reading about other songwriters, continuing to practice your skill, or working with other writers.

  One book that gives an insight into how a hit songwriter works is *Tunesmith: Inside the Art of Songwriting* by Jimmy Webb (writer of "Up, Up and Away," "MacArthur Park," "The Highwayman," "Galveston," and "Wichita Lineman," among others). I highly recommend this book. You may not like Jimmy Webb or his songs, but you can still learn huge amount about the craft by reading his book.

- The songs should be well performed. There is no excuse for an average or lackluster performance. Remember, your recording could be available in 10, 20, 30, 40, or more years' time, and you could still be receiving income over this period. Surely, for a work that will have that longevity, the extra take just to nail the track is worthwhile.

  When it comes to performance, are all the musicians as good as they could be? Are you recording with a singer who has never had a singing lesson is his or her life? Does the bassist have trouble with the notion of 4/4 time? Does the guitarist keep old dull strings on his guitar? You need to do anything and everything you can to improve the quality of your product before you sign off on a recording.

- The songs need to be well recorded. This doesn't mean that you need an expensive recording studio; it just means that you need to ensure the absolute highest audio fidelity—and don't kid yourself that your ropey old computer will do. Equally, don't kid yourself that a shiny new computer will make you sound great when there are more fundamental problems (such as lack of talent, a poor recording room, or similar factors).

I've also got to question your commitment to creating a product of the very highest quality if you're not going into a studio with the best producer you can find (and, of course, afford). You may be good, but ask yourself how many hit records there have been over the last few years that haven't had a top-flight producer? Some, but maybe not that many who have gone on to have a lasting career. You really need to find a producer who will ensure that you sound like a bunch of slick professionals and not like a group of highly talented amateurs who don't quite make the grade.

- Once the tracks have been recorded, they need to be mixed and mastered. You may be able to record yourself. You may have even bluffed the production bit. However, before you go any further, ask yourself whether you have the talent to mix and master your material. I am sure there must be some artists somewhere who record, produce, mix, and master their own work, but I think these people are few and far between and may not sell huge numbers of records.

    If you want the best product that you can have, then find the best mixer you can afford and find the best mastering engineer.

- The final step once the recording, mixing, and mastering have been completed is to get the CD pressed. All your hard work will be in vain if the reproduction, printing, and packing are not completed to the highest standard.

Although you may get each element right on its own, it is also fundamentally important that the elements work together. For instance, if you have the best producer, the best mixing engineer, and the best mastering engineer working on your project, then they all need to know what you want and expect. If each individual has his or her own separate vision of where your product is heading, then these individuals may work against each other. The producer may add lots of bass parts, the mixing engineer may feel that the bass end is too muddy, and the mastering engineer may feel the track lacks body and so he or she boosts the middle of the audio frequency.

Someone needs to take hold of a project and ensure that all of the parties understand what you want. (When I say "you," I mean you the client—the person who is paying everyone's salaries.) If they then don't do what they're told, don't pay them.

To succeed, your product must be of the very highest quality. You won't sell just because you've sent an email to your fan base. You have to create something that your fan base wants to buy—this is very much the strategy of build a better mousetrap, and the world will beat a path to your door. Remember, you are not stuffing your product down people's throats with advertisements, so you need something that is really good in order to convert interest into sales (and quickly). If you create a stinker of a product, the word will spread very quickly.

I have discussed one particular musical product here (the production of a CD). The principle of producing the best product you can applies to any product, whether it be a gig or a mug. If you're not selling top-of-the-line products, then life is going to be tough for you.

Releasing the Product

One of the biggest problems will be deciding when a product is ready to be released to the public.

For an artist signed to a major record label, the decision to release an album is usually fairly simple. If the producer says it's ready, and the label thinks it's ready, then it is ready, and the CD will be released.

If you're trying to release a product (any product, not just a CD) without having someone with that level of financial involvement, then you need to be really certain that you aren't releasing your product too soon. When you think that you may be close to release, make sure you distance yourself from the product (as far as you can) in order to stay as objective as possible.

Also, again to the extent possible, consider the opinion of other people. In particular, if you have paid someone to be involved with a product (for instance, a producer), and his or her reputation is on the line too, then make sure that person believes you are ready to release.

Life of the Product

I want to discuss two issues here—first, the lifespan of a product, and second, product renewal.

Lifespan of a Product

Conventionally, after a CD is released it will be re-pressed while it is selling. When it stops selling, no further copies will be pressed, and it will no be longer available. That is the end of the income from that CD.

The situation is markedly different now, and there is no reason for music ever to be unavailable. This means an album can keep making money for years after it is first released. There is a number of ways that an album can continue to be available (and generating income):

■ With on-demand pressing, you can make a CD available until the end of time.

■ If you are in control of the masters and arrange for the CD to be pressed, then you can keep ordering CDs (as long as you can keep the stock and keep selling the CDs).

■ Lastly, you can keep your music (whether individual tracks or the whole album) available via download services (which are all trying to acquire and make as much material available online as is possible).

Given that an album may now be available forever (or at least as close to forever as we're likely to get), this increases the necessity to make the product of the very highest quality in the first place.

Generally, keeping a product available is a good thing (unless it costs you money). Perhaps the main reason why you might wish to prematurely cut short a product's life is in order to replace it with something new that you will be able to sell to people who bought the older product.

Product Renewal

Product renewal comes in two forms:

■ Giving additional features to an existing product in order to make it more attractive

- Launching a whole new product to replace an existing product that is withdrawn from the market

This sort of product renewal can be difficult in the music industry, so let's look at the example of how the video-game industry renews its products:

- To encourage new purchases of an existing games console, further titles can be released. This creates "more" reason to buy the console. In addition, giving away free games when a console is purchased lengthens the lifespan of the console by increasing demand.

- To encourage renewal, a whole new console can be released that is incompatible with existing games. Of course, the stated reason for the incompatibility is to give new features. As noted earlier in this book, game manufacturers are not beyond making their product obsolete by releasing a new game every year with additional features.

The key difference between these two approaches is that with the first option you are getting more sales from the original product, so you are widening your user base. With the second approach, the existing user base is being asked to replace a product that has become obsolete (and all of the games for the obsolete product can be regarded as obsolete too).

These sorts of practices do happen in the music industry. Here are a few examples:

- Greatest hits albums bring in new fans (and can sometimes sell to existing fans who want to own all of an artist's catalogue).

- Greatest hits albums with new tracks bring in new fans and sell to existing fans who are keen to get the new tracks.

- Remixed and remastered versions of old (usually classic) albums are intended to be sold to existing fans as an "upgrade" to their existing album.

- Live albums sell the same songs to existing fans.

- Limited-edition merchandise, such as a tour T-shirt, becomes available. Because availability of the T-shirt is limited to a certain timeframe, a new T-shirt can be sold once this one has become obsolete. Any piece of merchandise can easily be made into a limited-edition product that can then be replaced by new limited-edition products. Perhaps the most obvious limited-edition product (that will generate income every year) is a calendar.

The complete wholesale renewal of the product (like the new video-game console) is a harder task to achieve. The music industry last did this very effectively when it made vinyl obsolete with the introduction of CDs. However, since then it has not managed to renew its products so well. That is not to say it hasn't renewed—for instance, MP3s, remastered albums, and attempts at higher-quality CDs (whether SACDs or similar, or 5.1 mixes) have had some effect.

For your early products, just focus on getting a successful product launched and ensuring that you make a profit. Remember the possibilities of renewal, and don't make any decisions that would make it harder for you to renew your products.

When you have a portfolio of products, then you can consider whether it is feasible to produce a version two or a version three of any products. Before you do renew your products, consider two issues:

- Will renewing the product make it easier to sell the renewed product? In other words, will the existing product already be recognized/established in the market? Alternatively, will renewable make it easier to reach a wider fan base?

- Will renewing the product make it harder to sell in the market? Will the renewed product just be seen as a re-tread of a tired old product that should simply be dropped? Equally, will renewal tarnish your reputation?

Only you know how your fan base will react and only you can decide upon the right course for your business.

Development Time

I now want to focus on some of the logistics of product development. As I have discussed earlier in this chapter, as a crude rule of thumb, the more products you can produce, the higher your income will be (within reason). However, in order to develop a high-quality product that will enhance your reputation and will sell, you need to invest a lot of time.

You need to balance these two competing interests to ensure you have time to do what you love (make music) and generate sufficient income.

Planning

You need to take development time into account in order to organize your life. Most artists follow a structure in which they record an album, release the album, and then tour to promote the album. The tour is usually booked before the album is finished, so a few month's gap is left for overruns. If you don't plan well enough, you could be touring before you have finished and released the album you are meant to be promoting.

Without wanting to belabor the point too much, remember that planning also takes time, so you should include an allowance for planning when you are planning. (I know it sounds like planning how to plan, but it's better to remember it than to get it all badly wrong.)

Critical Path

When you are planning a project, there are some activities that can only happen once something else has happened. For instance, you cannot mix a track until it has been recorded, and you can't press a CD until the songs have been written.

Equally, there are plenty of activities that are not dependent on other activities. For instance, you don't need to have completed the mix of an album in order to commission the artwork.

The key to successful planning is ensuring you have a timescale for each part of the project and then recognizing which parts are dependent on a previous task having been completed and which tasks can be completed independently. Clearly, the tasks that are dependent on a previous task are the hardest to plan, particularly when you a trying to schedule several people together (such as a producer, a mixing engineer, and a mastering engineer).

Logistics of Product Development

Turning to focus on the logistics of product development, as a musician you will know that there are no shortcuts when you create music. You cannot half-write a song and hope that you are inspired to write the remaining part when you get up on stage and start playing the song. If you've only half-written a song, you will find it is impossible to teach the rest of the band the song.

If you are a songwriter, you will know that songs get written in many different ways. Sometimes inspiration comes to you, and the song writes itself in as long as it takes you to play it. Other times you need to keep returning to a song over a long period of time, perhaps agonizing over one word or one note for several weeks. Maybe you write with a partner or you and the whole band all get in the room and play. Everyone throws in lines and melodies, and together you create perfection that could not be created by any of you individually.

You will also know there is no right or wrong way to write a song, although it will often feel like you are only using the wrong ways. This is the nature of the creative process, and how you create is up to you.

However, although I would not wish to put any constraints on your creativity, I would like to make a few suggestions:

- First, understand your creative process. If you are a songwriter and you can write 10 hit songs in an afternoon, that's great. However, if, like normal people, it takes you a lot longer to write songs—perhaps a couple of days, or maybe each song is written over several weeks—that's fine. Just make sure you have factored the writing into the product development process.

  Equally, if you ask someone else to get creative on your behalf—for instance, you might ask someone to create some artwork for a poster—then try to understand the person's creative process and the timescales to which he or she works.

- In the 1950s and 1960s, whole albums could be recorded in a matter of hours. I think the Beatles' first album was recorded in three hours. Those days are gone—I don't think you could get a kick drum set up in less than three hours these days.

  You should always ensure that there is sufficient time to record, but you may want to constrain this time if you are working to a tight budget. It is very easy to sit around and say, "We should be able to record this whole album in a few days, as long as we have rehearsed enough." However, it will always take longer than you expect, especially if you are aiming to create the highest quality product. Unfortunately, the only way you will learn exactly how much time you need is to spend the time.

- As well as understanding the creative process, develop a thorough understanding of the whole process. Make sure you (or whoever is running the project) understand which function each person involved in the project fulfills and how much time his or her process will add to the project.

Intervals between Products

The interval between products will depend on the nature of the product, the expectations of your fan base, and the current stage in your career. Let me take a CD as an example.

If you are a new band, then you could probably release a CD with a few tracks (say three of four) ever few months when you are first starting. You would probably be growing fairly rapidly, so each new release should be a big step forward, and you would probably have a small fan base who will be keen to buy your CD (as long as it is reasonably priced). Although you could release according to this schedule, as you will read later in this book, I think there are good reasons not to release CDs too early in your career.

When you are a more established act, you will probably spend a lot of your time playing gigs. To ensure you sell sufficient CDs to make a reasonable profit on the project, you will need to ensure that you don't release CDs too close together. You may also find that with all the gigs you are playing, you have less time to write and record new songs.

Accordingly, you are likely to have to leave an interval of around 12 to 18 months between CDs.

You could perhaps even stretch to a gap of two years. However, at two years or longer, your fan base may start to feel deserted and may forget you as they look elsewhere for their music.

However, if you are a long-established act (think in terms of the Eagles or the Rolling Stones), then you can leave at least three years between recordings. As long as you can contact your fan base (which means you need to ensure you keep your databases up to date during long gaps between CDs), then you will find a ready audience when you return.

Product Pricing

Product pricing is crucial. Charge too much and no one will buy the product. Charge too little and you won't make a profit.

In the next section ("The Cost of Developing Products"), I will discuss the cost of developing products and the economics that determine when a product starts to make a profit (or, more importantly, the point at which a product ceases to make a loss).

Development costs will have a significant influence on pricing. However, there are many other influences—some are scientific, but most are less so. Perhaps the two most significant questions when it comes to pricing are:

- What price will people pay? In other words, how much can you charge before people will refuse to buy your product? The secondary issue here is at what level your fans will think you are abusing their good nature and taking money straight out of their pockets. If you reach this price point, you will lose fans quickly.

- What price will make the product sell? In other words, how low do you have to go to encourage sales? You should also remember that there is a point at which your product will look "bargain bin"—if you reach this, then you will lose credibility. You should also remember that rubbish never sells.

You may be thinking that you'll set the price of each product according to the manufacturing costs and then add a bit for profit. This is admirable, but probably rather naïve. As the next section about the cost of product development will demonstrate, it is difficult to know when a product will break even. Also, even if you price a product on the most reasonable basis, people will still feel ripped off.

People feel ripped off because they will ascribe a value to your product based on their own beliefs and values. In other words, they will value your product based on what they feel it is worth for them. It is for this reason that manufacturers apply differential pricing. Let me give you two examples of this from the car industry.

Take the example of two models from the BMW 3 Series; some of the features of these cars are set out in Table 8.1.

Table 8.1 Differing Features and Prices of Two Cars in the BMW 3 Series Range

Model	Engine Size	Power (at 5,750 RPM)	UK List Price
Saloon 318i four door	1,995cc	127 bhp	£19,995
Saloon 320i four door	1,995cc	148 bhp	£21,625

The prices quoted here are understood to be the manufacturer's current list price in £ sterling. I am not quoting a dollar price because I am only using these figures to illustrate the difference.

These two cars look exactly the same (apart from the model badge at the back), yet one is £1,630 more than the other. Both have the same engine and the same equipment (as far as I can tell—I haven't taken these cars apart to check). So why the price difference?

One has a more powerful engine and a "better" badge than the other. In other words, you are paying £1,630 for someone to tweak the engine in the more expensive car. There is no other apparent difference between the cars—for instance, there do not seem to be any more parts in the more expensive car to justify any higher manufacturing cost.

In reality, the cheaper car probably has exactly the same engine as the more expensive car, but with its power artificially reduced so that it doesn't compete with the more expensive car. In other words (and this is just a guess on my part), the cheaper car probably costs more to produce than the expensive car.

This is one example of a situation in which manufacturing costs have no relation to sale price. The price differential is because people want to pay more for something they value more. What they really value more is the badge on the back of the car telling the entire world that they have a better car.

As another example of differential pricing, look at the price differences between VWs and Skodas. For many years Skodas had a reputation for being exceptionally bad cars made in the Eastern Bloc and were the butt of comics' jokes. (You know the sort: How do you double the value of a Skoda? Fill it up with gasoline.)

Skoda is now owned by VW, and some people claim the quality of the Skoda exceeds that of the VW. In essence, all of the models in the VW and Skoda ranges share the some workings; all that differentiates the cars (apart from the price) are the body shells and the location of the factories. (Skoda factories have historically been in lower-wage locations, such as Eastern Europe.) However, people will happily pay considerably more for a VW than they will for a Skoda.

This may seem like madness, but in reality people are choosing what they want to pay. People who have the extra spending power are buying the VW or the more expensive BMW. People who don't have such a spending power choose the cheaper BMW or the Skoda.

Think about the brilliance of this for a moment. If you're the person who works for BMW or VW and you're in charge of pricing the products—a decision that will affect the whole of the business—then you don't have to get your prices right. Instead, your customers will tell you what they want to pay for your product.

Now think how this principle could be applied to your products. Let's take the example of a CD. Pressing a CD may cost you $1 per unit for a short run. This price would include a jewel case and a printed booklet. You could produce this at a lower cost by dropping the leaflet and using a cardboard sleeve. Perhaps this would come out at $0.80 per unit. Alternatively, you could create a special edition of the CD using a DVD-sized case and having a special booklet inside. (You could maybe market this as a collector's edition.) This might cost $1.50 per unit to produce.

When it comes to selling these products, you might be able to sell the regular CD for $10, the cheap version for $7, and the collector's edition for $20. If you could achieve these prices, then the income from the collector's edition CD would be three times the income from the cardboard-sleeved CD (see Table 8.2).

Table 8.2 An Example of Differential CD Pricing

	Manufacturing Cost	Retail Price	Profit ($)	Profit (as a Percentage of Manufacturing Cost)
CD with cardboard sleeve	$0.80	$7.00	$6.20	775%
Regular CD	$1.00	$10.00	$9.00	900%
Collector's edition CD	$1.50	$20.00	$18.50	1,235%

Before you get too carried away looking at the big numbers, remember that I will talk more about profit margins in the next section. However, you will see that you have options to create different products so that you are selling essentially the same product (the CD) for three different prices depending on what people want to pay.

CDs aren't the only products for which you can apply differential pricing. For instance, you could charge more for a long-sleeved T-shirt than you would for a short-sleeved T-shirt. Perhaps you could charge $5 more, or perhaps $10 since you are likely to find that your T-shirt supplier will charge you more for the raw materials. There is no real logic for this—if suppliers felt the need to charge more for materials, then they would charge more depending on whether you buy small, medium, large, or extra-large T-shirts—however, you will pay more, so they will charge you more.

Are you getting to see how it all works now? Okay, now go away and think about how you can create a range of products that will be valued differently by different fans with different spending power.

The Cost of Developing Products

In the next chapter ("Economics 101"), I will discuss the economics of a career in the music industry. For the moment, I want to talk about the economics of products.

Time Is Money

How many times have you heard that phrase and wanted to scream? Unfortunately, it is true.

There are things you can do as an artist that will generate money (for instance, writing a hit song), and there are things that do not generate money (sleeping, for example).

Every minute that you are alive has a certain cost. You have to buy food, you have to put a roof over your head, you have to put gas in your car if you want to drive anywhere, and so on. Although you may not be spending money at any one particular moment, over the course of time you do have to spend money.

Therefore, your time as an artist is valuable. If you spend an hour on one product and a year on another project, you will have incurred different costs. Hopefully, the longer project will generate more income. If it doesn't, then I suggest you complete more of the single-hour projects —they are far more lucrative for you.

When I talk about the cost of time, this is the principle that I am discussing.

The Profit Margin on Products

When you sell a product, you will receive income—in other words, money. This is great; money is really useful for buying stuff like food. However, you can't spend all the money you receive because you will have incurred costs in getting your product to your fan. The difference between the selling price for the product and the cost of producing the product is the profit.

The profit is money that you can spend (or money that you can invest to develop more products). If the cost of producing the product exceeds the price you get for selling a product, then you have incurred a loss (which is a bad thing—if you do it too often you become bankrupt). I make no excuses for spelling out in detail many of the costs you may encounter. If you don't recognize and factor in these costs, you will run the risk of incurring a loss.

There are many costs in developing a product; these fall into the broad categories of development, manufacturing, distribution, marketing, and after-sales service (which I discussed at the start of this chapter). Let's look at how these may apply to you in a real-life situation. Please bear in mind that many of these areas overlap and may be difficult to separate if you are working on a project, so some of the distinctions I have made may seem slightly artificial.

The Cost of Developing Your New Product

The development stage of any product is the real creative stage. The most obvious example of product development for a musician is writing songs. New material is the quintessential core of a musician's new product. For the non-writing musician, finding the right material can be as time-consuming as writing music for other musicians.

Writing new songs can take considerable time. Many artists who sit down to write an album's worth of material will spend many months honing their material before they are ready to go anywhere near a studio, and even then the songs may need a lot of polishing.

In music, the costs of development are usually the cost of the artist's time (which usually equates to his or her living expenses for the development period). However, there may be other costs—for instance, if a band is writing an album, they may hire a studio in which to write. They may need roadies to look after their gear, and the studio may provide an engineer. All of these costs need to be factored into the development of the product.

However, not all products have a development cost. For instance, if you write an album's worth of songs and then use those same songs for live shows, there is no new development cost for the second use of the same piece of development. In other words, you don't have to write the songs again in order to perform them in a live setting.

As you use your raw material (in this example, your songs) in more ways (album, live shows, DVD, film soundtrack, and so on), your development costs as an absolute figure will not reduce; however, the costs, set against the total income from the development work, will look far more efficient.

I have only given one example of a development cost. There are clearly others. You can also think about research costs under this banner—for instance, if you are researching the market for producing merchandise.

One of the key factors to note about development costs is that they are usually fixed. In other words, once you have spent the money, it is gone and cannot be recouped. Therefore, you need to think about a development budget before you spend the money, not after.

Manufacturing Costs

Manufacturing is the process of taking the raw material (often the song) and turning it into a form that can be sold (such as a CD). There can be several stages to the process (and there are different cost implications associated with each stage). Take the example of producing a new CD for which the songwriting stage has been completed. There are then two manufacturing stages:

- Recording
- Pressing

Recording may be part of the writing process, and there may be little cost if the artist self-records. If this is the case, the main costs are likely to be the artist's time, electricity, and the investment in recording technology. However, for larger projects it is common for an artist to record in a studio, in which case the costs will include the studio hire, roadies, engineers, and so on.

Within the recording costs, there is also the expense of mixing, mastering, and getting the music into a format that can be sent to the CD pressing plant (or uploaded to a download store, such as iTunes).

As with product development, once these manufacturing costs have been incurred the money has gone, so stringent budgeting will help ensure you at least stand a chance of making a profit.

There are many costs involved in arranging for a CD to be pressed, beyond those associated with the purely mechanical process of stamping out a number of CDs. These additional costs include everything from preparing glass masters from which the stamp (that is used to stamp the CD) is prepared to preparing the casing and the artwork.

The costs will vary depending on a range of factors; however, the costs of pressing are generally very controllable. Assuming you are going down the glass master route, there are some fixed setup costs, but after that most of the costs are dependent on the numbers of CDs pressed. The more CDs that are pressed, the higher your costs will be (since you will be buying a greater number). However, with greater numbers you will probably be quoted a cheaper per-unit cost.

The key mechanism for controlling costs (for CD reproduction) is to control the number of CDs that are pressed. By controlling the number of CDs you order, you can also control your cash flow. If you split one large CD run into two smaller batches, then you will probably increase your overall cost. However, by following this course, you can use income generated from selling the first batch to fund the costs for the second batch.

There are, of course, many different products you can offer, and for each product there will be a different and unique manufacturing process. For instance, if the product you will be offering is a live show, then the manufacturing process will revolve around pulling the show together and rehearsing the musicians, and so on.

Marketing Expenses

Marketing is the process by which you make potential purchasers aware of your product. Marketing costs can vary hugely. However, if you've been paying attention in the earlier chapters of this book, then you will have built up a database of your fans and you will know how to contact these people directly (whether by SMS message, email, snail mail, or some other system). If you are using email, then marketing costs are negligible (a bit of time preparing and sending the communication and some electricity).

However, if you feel your database doesn't include all of your fans (and there is a good chance that it won't), or you want to expand the size of your fan base, then you may decide on a more elaborate marketing campaign. This may involve advertising and promotion work. In crude terms, advertising will cost you money while promotion work will take your time (and need you to spend money getting to the location of the promotion).

The amount of marketing you do is likely to have a very direct effect on the success of your product. It should also have an indirect effect of growing your fan base (that is, growing your database of known fans) over time.

Provided you have a database of fans to in effect guarantee a certain level of sales, you can have a successful product without spending significant amounts on marketing. Beyond that point, your marketing budget can be controlled quite tightly, but once you do start spending on marketing, there is always the temptation to spend "just a little bit more" to get a slightly better result.

You will also find, as for manufacturing, that you can spend a certain amount on marketing and then wait for the product to generate some income, which can then be applied to fund more marketing. However, if you are marketing an event that is fixed in time (such as a gig), you will not have this luxury because any delay in marketing the event could lead to failure.

Distribution and Delivery Costs

Distribution and delivery are about getting the product to the purchaser. This is a simple matter of logistics. However, when you include the human factor and multiply the possibilities for unintended errors by a whole fan base, you will understand why this can be one of the most frustrating parts of the process from a fan's perspective.

You are likely to get your products to people in different ways. Here are some examples of the means of distribution and the costs that will affect your pricing:

- If you send CDs and DVDs by mail, then the costs will include the postage, the packaging, and the human costs involved in processing the order and preparing the package to be mailed. You will also incur costs in processing payments. Typically, if you receive money by credit card, then you will receive an amount equal to the price of the product less a credit card processing fee.

  With mail order the customer will usually be charged for post and packaging, so you may not see this as something that should be included when you are thinking about pricing your product. However, if you don't get your mail order pricing right, you will incur a loss, and that loss will need to be funded from somewhere, so I recommend you get the pricing right before you start sending out products. And if you do find that you have got the mail order pricing wrong, then change it at the earliest opportunity.

- If your CDs and DVDs are distributed by a fulfillment company, then they will also charge a fee for post, packaging, processing, and the humans involved in their process. There will also be the cost of getting your CDs/DVDs to the fulfillment service. A whole stack of CDs can be quite heavy, and this can make courier charges quite steep (especially if your fulfillment service is overseas).

- If you sell CDs/DVDs at gigs, then you will need to keep a certain level of stock, and the storage space may cost (even if that cost only appears to be the stress of having your stock sitting around at home).

- If you sell CDs/DVDs through record stores, then there will be a cost of physically getting the product to the record stores. There will be another hidden cost in that the record store may not pay you for a while (perhaps not for several months). In this situation, while not an explicit cost, there is a price that you will pay for effectively giving the record store a loan.

- If your product is a live show, then you will have a large number of expenses associated with putting on the show. These could include the cost of the venue, security staff, getting equipment to the show and getting it set up, as well as transportation and accommodations for everyone involved.

After-Sales Service: The Hidden Costs

After-sales service may not be something you think about—it's not as if you're selling a toaster. However, this is an area you will have to consider even if it is virtually impossible to accurately budget for it. For instance, what happens if a CD you have sold doesn't play? Or what happens if the mug your on-demand supplier sells is chipped or has a blurred photo?

In many cases, after-sales service will not cost very much money; however, it will take an awful lot of time and may divert you from other activities from which you could be generating income. That being said, replacing one or two CDs may not cost much, but replacing a whole batch of 25,000 could have a significant impact on your profitability if you have to pack and mail each CD out.

Shoddy goods and failure to attend to after-sales service also have the possibility to do a lot of damage to your reputation.

Making Money from Products

The purpose of a product is to sell it in order to make money. The amount of money you can make from your products is determined by a range of factors:

- The number of products you sell
- The profit you make on each product

The Number of Products You Sell

There are two factors determining the number of products you can sell:

- The number of people who will buy your product
- The number of products you have available for sale

It may sound simple, but the more people you can sell to, the higher your income will be. However, although you may have an excellent product, if your market is limited (for example, taking the illustration I used in Chapter 7, if you are a classical guitarist), then there will be a ceiling on the number of people who are likely to buy your product. Therefore, to generate more interest, you need more products (so your income per fan rises).

Only you will know your particular situation and your fan base. In light of this knowledge, you will need to decide whether you should spend more time marketing or more time developing a wider product range if you want to positively influence your income stream.

As a side note, do remember that the rule that selling more products leads to more income is only true if you are making a profit. If you have priced your product at a level that creates a loss, then higher sales equate to greater losses.

The Profit per Product

Another control you have over the income that flows from each product is your profit margin. However, irrespective of the cost of production, many products will have a maximum price above which no one (or only a few people) will buy the product. For instance, if you are selling a CD, most people might expect to pay in the range of $8 to $15, and you will only find a few who would be prepared to pay more than $20.

Sometimes you can't break the ceiling price for a product. However, at other times you can. For instance, if you are playing a gig, then there is probably a ceiling on the maximum price you can charge for tickets. The solution to generating more income in this situation is to sell more tickets, which you can do by using a bigger venue. Obviously, a bigger venue will lead to higher costs, but you should be able to factor these in to ensure that you make greater profits.

Profit Levels

In broad terms, the profit you will make from any product is the income from sales, less the costs. However, some of your costs will be fixed; for instance, once you have recorded an album, any studio costs that need to be recouped through the project will be fixed. As we have also seen, other costs can be managed on an ongoing basis—for instance, the cost of CD duplication can be controlled by limiting the CD run.

The difficulty with costs is that they tend to be big numbers—they're usually followed by three zeros, denoting amounts in the thousands. By contrast, income tends to come in small amounts. This disparity means that it can take a long time to recoup your investment in a project. If you don't have any money to fund yourself until you are making a profit, you run the risk of bankruptcy.

I will look at some of the ways you can finance your career and your products while you are waiting for your income to start flowing in the next chapter, as well as consider the wider issue of income and profitability.

At this point I want to illustrate the costs and potential income from a product with the example of a CD project. For this example I have invented numbers to illustrate my point. You should not assume these numbers are anything realistic. More realistic numbers will be discussed in the next chapter. Also, to make this example easier, I have assumed that the CD is sent out by mail order and all distribution costs were calculated perfectly (and have therefore been excluded from the calculation). My final main assumption is that you have a source of income to fund your project.

For this project, I am assuming we have an established band of four members who each draw living expenses from band funds of $2,500 per month (in other words, $10,000 per month for the whole band or $30,000 per year per band member—no one is going to buy a Rolls Royce on that salary).

I will assume that the time spent during the development phase and the recording phase (up to the point that the CD can be released) is 12 months. In other words, the band's living expenses will have reached $120,000 over that period.

I am assuming that the band has a reasonable following and that there is a manager who will take 20% of the net income (which I am defining as the income less the recording costs, but not including the band's living expenses). I will talk more about managers in Chapter 10, "Building the Team around You." There will probably also be office staff (running the website and so on) and other miscellaneous unaccounted-for expenses, but let's not get too detailed yet.

Anyway, for this album project, let us assume that:

- The recording studio plus engineer costs $50,000.

- The producer costs $35,000.

- Mastering costs are $5,000.

- The artwork costs $2,000.

- There were miscellaneous costs of $8,000 (such as pizzas and beer for everyone when the recording sessions ran over).

In total the recording costs come to $100,000. This figure has to be recouped before the band can see any income.

For the manufacturing costs, let's assume that the band gets the CD pressed in batches with the following costs (including shipping from the plant to the band's distribution center):

- The cost for the first 10,000 CDs comes in at $10,000.

- The next 15,000 CDs cost $10,000.

- Subsequent batches of 25,000 CDs come in at $16,000.

We'll assume each CD is sold for $10, and as I've said, we're also assuming the fan will pay for postage and packing. Let's assume that there is a credit card charge of 60 cents for each sale, meaning that each CD will bring in $9.40. To make things simple, I am not making any allowance for sales tax (such a VAT or any state or national equivalent).

Before a single CD can be sold, the recording costs have come in at $100,000, and the first batch of 10,000 CDs has cost $10,000. Added to this, there is the expense of running the band, which came in at

$120,000, so the total spent before any money has been earned is $230,000 (see Table 8.3).

Table 8.3 The Costs of Recording a CD
and Getting the First Pressing

	Income	Expenditure	Total
Earnings during recording	$0		
Band expenses during recording		$120,000	
Recording studio plus engineer		$50,000	
Producer's fee		$35,000	
Mastering costs		$5,000	
Artwork		$2,000	
Miscellaneous expenses		$8,000	
Pressing the first 10,000 CDs		$10,000	
Total expenses to date			–$230,000

Assuming the first 10,000 CDs can be sold at $10 (bringing in $9.40 after credit card charges), this will generate $94,000. From this, the manager will take nothing because the recording costs have yet to be recouped. After the sale of 10,000 CDs, the project is running at a loss of $136,000.

With the pressing of the next 15,000 CDs, a further $10,000 will be spent, giving a total loss for the project of $146,000 (see Table 8.4).

When this batch of 15,000 CDs is sold, they will generate an income of $141,000. At this stage, the recording and CD pressing costs will come to $120,000 ($100,000 recording costs, plus $20,000 for pressing 25,000 CDs to date), so the manager will start taking his or her fee. In this instance, the manager's fee is 20% of the income above recording costs (in other words, $94,000 + $141,000 – $120,000).

Table 8.4 The Costs Incurred after Selling 10,000 CDs and Arranging for a Second Pressing

	Income	Expenditure	Total
Loss on recording (see Table 8.3)			−$230,000
Cash generated from selling 10,000 CDs (income after credit card charges)	$94,000		
Pressing next 15,000 CDs		$10,000	
Profit generated by project to date			−$146,000

After deducting the manager's fee of $23,000, the project is still running at a loss of $28,000. This means that after 25,000 CDs have been sold, each CD now equates to just over $1.00 lost. To generate more income, more CDs need to be pressed. This time 25,000 will be pressed at a cost of $16,000, leading to a total loss to date of $44,000 (see Table 8.5).

Table 8.5 The Costs after Selling 25,000 CDs and Arranging for a Further 25,000 CDs to Be Pressed*

	Income	Expenditure	Total
Losses to date (see Table 8.4)			−$146,000
Cash generated from selling next 15,000 CDs (income after credit card charges)	$141,000		
Manager's fee (20% on income over $120,000)			$23,000
Pressing next 25,000 CDs		$16,000	
Profit generated by project to date			−$44,000

* Note that the manager is taking his/her fee while the project is still running at a loss.

If this next batch of 25,000 CD is all sold (making total sales of 50,000), it will generate $235,000, from which the manager will take $43,800 (in other words, 20% of the income from the sales less the production cost).

The breakeven point is when the expenses have been recouped and therefore any further income is profit (refer to Figure 8.3). At the point that the project sells 29,095 CDs, it will break even, and the band will start to make a profit (in other words, they will start to generate some income for themselves). However, due to the nature of the product that is being sold here, there is a cost associated with each CD (for instance, the cost of manufacture and the credit card charge). Accordingly, the breakeven point is not as simple as Figure 8.3 may suggest. A more detailed explanation of the breakeven point is contained later in this section.

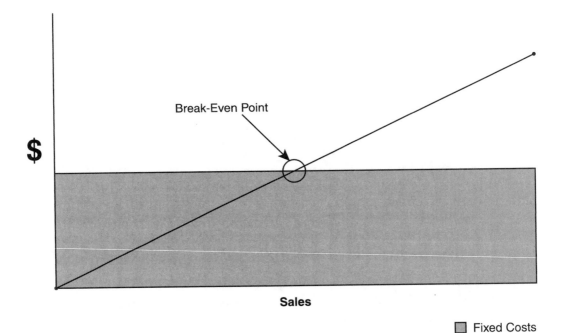

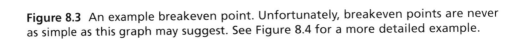

Figure 8.3 An example breakeven point. Unfortunately, breakeven points are never as simple as this graph may suggest. See Figure 8.4 for a more detailed example.

Having sold 50,000, the CD has now made a profit of $147,200 for the band members—in other words, $36,800 per member (see Table 8.6).

Table 8.6 The Project Finally Moves into Profit

	Income	Expenditure	Total
Losses to date (see Table 8.5)			−$44,000
Cash generated from selling next 25,000 CDs (income after credit card charges)	$235,000		
Manager's fee (taking account of the cost of pressing 25,000 CDs)		$43,800	
Profit generated by project to date			$147,200

This implies an income for each member of the band of around $66,000 for just over a year's work. However, let me add some caveats here.

First, there will be more expenses—for instance, accounting costs, warehousing costs for storing the CDs, and insurance, to give three examples. There could be quite large expenses, such as hotel costs and transportation for the band and their equipment (with roadies) while working at the studio. Second, the band is likely to have to tour extensively to support this album and generate this level of sales. At this level, the income from touring may be quite volatile.

Added to this, it may be two years before the next album is released, which implies the profit would need to be split over two years, giving an income (including the money used to fund living expenses) in the region of $33,000 to $48,000 (depending on how much income the band members draw).

Perhaps the most significant caveat is that it is really hard work to sell 50,000 CDs. However, I wouldn't wish to discourage you from your aim. In fact, why not work even harder and try to sell 100,000? Look at Table 8.7 for an illustration of the income that this sales figure could generate.

Table 8.7 The Project Reaches the Level Where Band Members Can Generate a Healthy Income

	Income	Expenditure	Total
Profits to date (see Table 8.6)			$147,200
Pressing next 50,000 CDs		$32,000	
Cash generated from selling next 50,000 CDs (income after credit card charges)	$470,000		
Manager's fee (taking account of cost of pressing 50,000 CDs)		$87,600	
Profit generated by project to date			$497,600

As Table 8.7 shows for this example, selling 100,000 CDs could generate a profit for each band member of $124,400, which equates to $62,200 per year if it is split over two years. However, do remember that you may not sell all of your CDs immediately once they have been pressed.

At the start of this example, I put in an allowance for band living expenses during recording of $2,500 per month. If this amount is removed to show the total profit for the project, then the total profit on the project would amount to $617,600. If this figure is split over two years for each band member, it equates to a monthly income of just under $6,500 (before taxes, savings, or any other deductions).

I will discuss the level of earnings you need to achieve to live on in greater detail in Chapter 11, "Your Pay Packet." I will also discuss the comparative income you could generate under a typical contract with a record company.

Expenditure
Before we move on, I want to draw to your attention some of the large amounts that have been spent in this project. Some of these charges are explicit (the band has to pay them directly—an example of this would be the studio costs), and others are implicit (and cause a reduction in the band's income—an example of these would be the credit card charges).

Selling 100,000 CDs at $10 should have generated an income of $1 million. However, the band only received $497,600—in other words, half of the income. Let's have a look at where the rest went.

- $120,000 (12% of the income) was drawn by the band as living expenses.

- $100,000 (10% of the income) was spent on recording costs.

- $154,400 (15% of the income) was charged as the manager's fee.

- $52,000 (5% of the income) was spent on CD manufacturing.

- $60,000 (6% of the income) was spent on credit card fees.

Because the respective proportions vary according to the number of CDs sold, I am not going to show these elements as a pie chart (because that could only show a snapshot at a certain level of sales). Instead, refer to Figure 8.5 later in this chapter for an illustration of the proportion that each party takes.

The figure that leaps out here is the charge by the manager, which accounts for 15% of the income (although, do remember that the manager's charge is 20%—the discrepancy arises because some expenses have been set against the income before the fee is calculated). However, before you judge the manager too harshly, remember that this is not straight profit for the manager. From this figure, the manager will need to fund his or her office and many of the costs of running the band. Also remember that in this example the manager doesn't take a cent until the recording costs have been recouped, so there is a risk that the manager may not generate any income.

You should also note that in some ways this is a slightly unrealistic number. Conventionally, a manager will take around 20% of gross earnings (that is, earnings before any deduction). However, that figure is set when a band may be on a royalty of 18% to 23% of the price that the CD is sold to a dealer. In other words, if a CD is sold into a shop at $6.00, then the band might receive $1.20 (before the manager's cut) and the manager would take $0.24 per CD sold.

By contrast, under the business model set out here, the manager could be taking $1.79 per CD sold. This may sound like a large number until you remember that calculated on the same basis, the band could be taking $7.17 per CD *after* the manager has taken his or her cut.

If you are going to adopt this business model, you may want to have a discussion with your manager about what expenses should be included or excluded when calculating his or her fee.

Just to close off this discussion, if the manager were looking after a band with a major recording company, then he or she could expect perhaps 1 million albums to be sold, generating a fee of $240,000. However, using this business model, we have assumed that 100,000 CDs are sold, which will generate a fee of $179,000. Although $61,000 isn't an amount to be sneezed at, the fees for the manager in both scenarios are in the same ballpark, suggesting that the fee level may be reasonable.

I will talk more about manager in Chapter 10.

For me, the next charge that leaps out is the cost of the credit card company. You will see that the credit card charges exceed the cost of manufacturing the CDs. This is not an abnormally high fee (although I did round it up). For illustration, a credit card company may charge 2.9% of the purchase price plus $0.30 per transaction. If the CD had been priced at $14, then the credit card fee would have been $0.70. Unfortunately, this is one of the charges you have to accept because there really isn't a viable alternative.

As you read earlier in this book, one of the benefits of running your own career is that you can retain control. To a large extent you can decide who you work with and how much money you want to spend. This example has illustrated the costs for producing and selling a CD. However, many of the expenses could have been managed in a different way.

For instance, if you had recorded the album in your own studio, you could have cut approximately $100,000 from the budget (although there will be a cost associated with setting up and running your own studio). By contrast, you could have chosen to work with a producer with a world-class reputation and paid $1 million plus for his or her services.

Breakeven Point on a Project

One of the most important factors in the project I have just illustrated is the breakeven point. This is the point at which the project ceases to make a loss and starts to generate a profit.

In simplistic terms, once you have covered the expenses, then the project will move into profit. (This principle was illustrated in Figure 8.3.) However, in reality, the breakeven point is actually a moving target because the expenses get larger over time. This is particularly so in two areas:

- Each time a new consignment of CD is pressed, there is an expense.

- The manager takes a cut of the profit once the cost of producing the recording and pressing the CDs has been met.

You will also have noticed from this example that there was no way that costs would be covered with the first consignment of CDs. Indeed, costs were not covered with the second consignment. It was only after the delivery of the third batch of CDs that the project moved into profit.

There was a logic for this action: controlling cash flow (in other words, not spending more money than was at hand so that as much money could be retained in the business as possible). Keeping a tight reign on spending also has the effect of controlling potential losses. If all of the CDs had been purchased in one lump, it would have cost an additional $42,000 (or perhaps slightly less with a discount for bulk). This would have made a total expenditure of $52,000 on the CDs. Splitting the purchases meant that the band was not left with $52,000 worth of unsold stock.

As a side note, you should also remember that there are other sources of income that could be derived from the music (for instance, online sales, licensing for inclusion on compilation albums, and licensing for use in film and television). All of these additional sources of income could be used to offset any losses.

To return to the subject of the breakeven point, this is probably best illustrated by the graph set out in Figure 8.4.

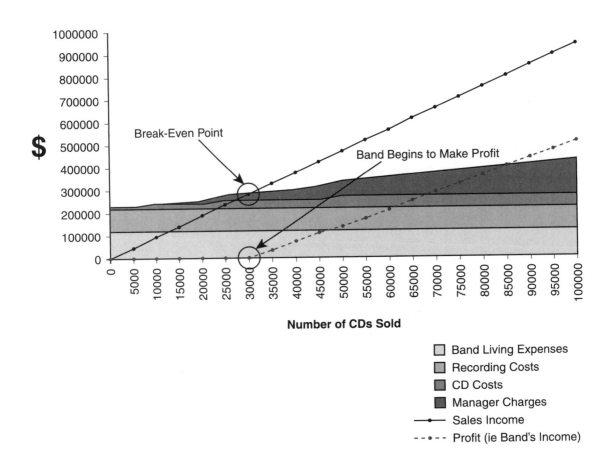

Figure 8.4 This graph shows how the breakeven point is a moving target due to the increasing level of expenses. When sales income exceeds expenses, then the band starts to generate some income.

As you can see:

- The recording costs and the band expenses are fixed, as is the cost of the first CD pressing.

- The costs rise after 10,000 sales when the second batch of CDs is ordered. In reality, this second batch of CDs would be ordered before 10,000 sales had been achieved in order to ensure that the product was always available.

- The manager's fee kicks in at 12,766 CD sales when the costs of recording (excluding the band expenses) and the costs of the CD pressings have been recouped.

- The costs rise again after 25,000 CD sales when the third batch of CDs is ordered.

- There are no profits until the income exceeds the expenses (which, as we have seen, continue to rise). This occurs when the project has sold 29,095 CDs. This is the breakeven point. If we had ordered, for instance, 100,000 CDs at the start of the project, then the breakeven point would have been much later.

- Although the breakeven point has been passed, expenses continue to be incurred, which is why the profits increase at a lesser rate than the income.

Lastly, do remember that some expenses are included by way of a reduction to income (specifically credit card charges, which are not explicitly shown in Figure 8.4).

Profitability

In Figure 8.4, it may look like the band doesn't fare particularly well. In this business model the band takes the greatest risk and finances the project. Unlike under a conventional recording contract, the band will also get the greatest reward. Figure 8.5 illustrates this point.

This graph shows how significant each financial element is as sales increase. You will see that initially, all of the income is dedicated to meeting the costs. As the income grows, the manager's charges are also paid. When the project has broken even, then profits are generated, and the band can share in the gains.

However, you will see that as sales continue to increase, the profits increase considerably too. If you were to extrapolate this graph, you would see that the fixed recording costs (including the band expenses) would become comparatively tiny, and the band's profitability would increase further. Indeed, as the sales increase, the band's profits tend toward 80% of the net income (but will not reach that figure because there is always the expense of pressing further CDs to meet increased demand). The band will never reach 100% income because the manager will always take 20%.

One point you should note about Figure 8.5 is that the graph is intended to show the main proportions and does not show (for instance) the expense of credit card transactions. Also, until the breakeven point, remember that the expenses will exceed income. Until this point, the graph illustrates the relative proportions of the losses.

As a last point, could I remind you that this is a book about building a career in music, not a manual about releasing your own CD? If you are going to release your own CD, then you will need to undertake considerable research (and hopefully this chapter gave you some pointers about some of the financial aspects that you should be considering).

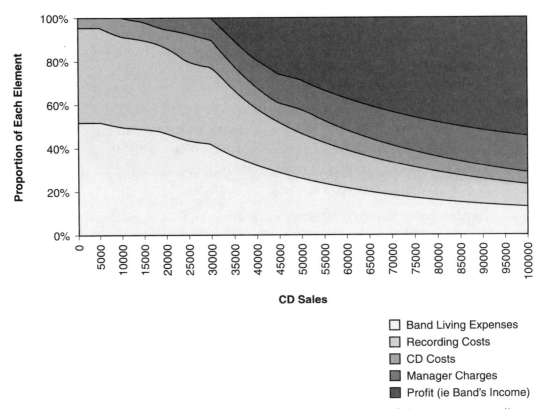

Figure 8.5 This chart shows how the respective proportions of the income are split as sales increase. With greater sales, the fixed costs become less significant and the band's profits increase.

The Nasty Commercial Bits

9 Economics 101

As I have discussed throughout this book, the musician looking to build a successful career in the 21st century has many more options than were available in the last century.

One of the key differences between the old approach and the new approach is that before, the musician could have expected his or her income to come from one or two sources, and now there are many more possible sources of income. However, although the sources are more numerous, each source is likely to produce less income.

On their own, many of these sources will not appear to be viable. However, the musician has the opportunity to aggregate these sources and to increase the period over which the income is received and so can obtain maximum value from each product. In this way, the musician can develop a sustainable career.

I have spent a lot of time focusing on the proactive actions that musicians can take. I have advocated this approach for a number of reasons:

- Major corporations have major overheads. Although there may be efficiencies that the majors can negotiate, you can often earn more money (as a percentage of each product sold) if you take a proactive approach. (For instance, a self-released CD can generate more income than the royalties paid by a major label if it releases your CD.)

- A self-managed approach gives more people an opportunity to have a viable music career. This should have the effect of making music more diverse and less driven by the commercial imperative (not that I have any problems with commercial and popular music).

- You learn and understand the business.

- Your career begins immediately, and your career is a long-term undertaking, not something that will end when you cease to be flavor of the month.

- You keep control of every aspect (from financial to artistic).

- This is simply a better way to promote yourself if you want to deal with the majors. They come to you because you have something highly valuable to offer.

- Fans are treated with respect.

However, this approach is not the only way, and I would not wish you to think that you shouldn't deal with the major entertainment companies. Just deal with them from a point of strength!

Having control and having negotiating power means you can start your career in a self-managed fashion. Once you reach a certain level of success, it may be in your interest to work with a major record label—only you can make that decision.

However, if you do decide to deal with a major, don't abandon the principles set out in this book. There will almost certainly come a time when both you and the record company want to end the deal. If you don't have a direct relationship with your fan base, then you may not be able to sustain a career after the deal ends.

Sources of Income: How Much Can I Earn?

We've already looked at the economics of releasing your own CD in the context of how you can create a product. In this chapter I'm going to go further and look in more detail at the economics of more products. In doing this I will try to compare the income you can generate by taking different approaches. For instance, I will compare the income you could expect if you release a CD through an on-demand service, on your own, or with a record label.

In illustrating each option, I will use figures that are within the bounds of reasonableness at the date of writing. Although reasonable, they are definitely not the lowest cost/highest income figures you would be able to find after commercial negotiation. You should not regard these figures as accurate because they will be out of date by the time you read them, and local conditions (including local taxation) will almost certainly affect your position if and when you are in a position to undertake any of these activities.

In Chapter 11, "Your Pay Packet," I will look at how much you need to earn to sustain your lifestyle. This may influence the amount you feel you need to earn.

Before we go any further, I want to warn you about many of these figures. This warning is especially relevant if you are selling in the European Union.

Many jurisdictions, particularly within the European Union, have purchase taxes (a tax levied on the sale of goods). In the EU, this tax is value added tax (VAT). The rates of VAT vary, but they are generally around 20% of the purchase price. To give an example of how VAT works in the UK (where VAT stands at 17.5%), if you sell a CD for £10, then after you have accounted for VAT you will receive £8.51 (£8.51 + 17.5% = £10).

Your credit card processor will charge its fee based on the full selling price (in other words, what you receive and VAT), so this can be something of a double-whammy: As well as paying tax, you will be charged to collect tax on the government's behalf.

The figures in this section do not (except where specifically noted) take any account of VAT, so you are getting an inflated idea of potential earnings in jurisdictions where this tax is payable. However, where you are looking at royalties, VAT will have been dealt with at the retail level, and you do not need to worry about having to further account for VAT. This means that some of the figures shown here may not be comparing similar situations.

Earnings from CD Sales

A CD release perhaps gives one of the best illustrations of how your income (and your cost control) can change depending on how you produce the product. For instance, your income will differ hugely depending on whether you release the CD yourself or it is released by a major record company. Although your income can vary, so can the financial risks you are taking.

You should note that in all of these examples, I am not comparing (I cannot compare) like with like. Again, look at a self-released CD compared to a CD released through a major. On your own, you could take 100% of the profit, where with a major you might get 15% of the list price. 100% may look better than 15%, but if you don't recoup your costs, then you are getting 100% of nothing.

You should also note that the charts I am using here illustrate proportions. (Broadly, they illustrate what proportion of the income from a CD's sales translates into profit, or income, for you.) They do not illustrate how much income you can make from each source. So if you're looking at how much income you can generate (and trying to calculate whether it will be enough to live on), remember that 100% of $1 is a lot less than 1% of $1 million.

To see the significance of the proportions, you have to multiply the proportion, by the number of sales, by the price of the CD (or whatever other product you are selling). The benefit of being able to take a greater proportion of the revenue means you need far fewer sales to generate sufficient income to sustain your lifestyle.

However, when you start scaling up your operations (in other words, when you start selling sufficient quantities of product to earn a living for yourself and everyone else involved in the project), then you may find that administration and logistics become far more significant. You may end up spending all of your time fulfilling orders. This will stop you from making music, so the only option that will be left to you is to take on staff. When you take on staff, your costs will rise, so you will need to sell more product. You will find it becomes a fine balancing act to make money.

On-Demand CDs

Let's start by looking at on-demand CD production, since this is one area where you can generate immediate profits (once you have met your recording costs). For the musician, this offers the nearest thing you will find to a zero-risk self-released CD.

Let me just be clear about the term "profit": What I am implying here is that you *can* set up an on-demand CD without costs, so you can start selling without having to buy stock. All costs of the service would be implicit and charged on each CD purchased, so there will be little benefit to be gained from scale. You may want to go with a service that charges a setup fee if this gives a better profit.

To give an example of a price being quoted by an on-demand delivery service today (with no setup costs for you), if you sell a CD for $10 using this service (direct mail order from the service—your customer pays for postage), then for each sale, you would generate a profit of $3.60.

There is a very modest benefit from scale. Larger orders (more than 11 CDs) could generate a slightly higher profit of $4.40.

There are many reasons not to go with an on-demand service. For instance, the CDs will be produced on CD-R discs (in other words, the same sort of disc that you would burn in your computer's CD drive). This may not give quite the professional image you are after, although I would guess that not many people will notice or care.

However, on-demand delivery gives you a way to get your CDs out very quickly and with little cost.

You should also remember that sales tax (such as VAT) may be payable on CDs, depending on the jurisdiction. If you are offering your CD at a price that includes VAT, then (using an example VAT rate of 20%), you could see your profit from a $10 CD drop from $3.60 to $2.26.

Figure 9.1 shows the respective proportions relating to the production, sales tax, and profit for an on-demand CD sold for $10. If the price were to be raised, then the VAT would increase (since it is price-related), so would the production costs (that's how the on-demand service makes its profits), and so would your income. The proportions would remain broadly similar (unless you increased the price significantly).

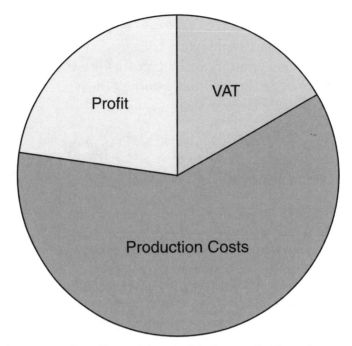

Figure 9.1 The costs and profits associated with the production of an on-demand CD (including VAT).

Pressing Your Own CDs

I looked at the economics of arranging for pressing of your own CD in Chapter 8. I will repeat the comment that I mentioned then: This is not a book about pressing your own CDs. If that is a route you wish to follow, you should remember that there are many issues involved. (For instance, if you want your CD to show up in the charts, you are likely to need a barcode.) I would suggest you seek advice from a local expert about the requirements in your jurisdiction if this is an option you intend to follow.

One of the key features of this option is that you have to make an investment—you have to purchase your initial stock before you can sell it. As I noted in the earlier chapter, you don't need to buy all of your stock immediately; however, you will probably be able to negotiate better discounts with larger orders.

If you are getting your CDs pressed (rather than getting a number of CD-Rs reproduced, which you might do for short runs), then there is the upfront cost of a glass master. Many pressing plants will factor this cost into their quote.

Another factor to bear in mind is that once you have your product you will need to store it and insure it. (Most household insurance policies would not cover this sort of commercial activity.) In addition, there would be a cost associated with the distribution of the product—this cost would be in terms of physical distribution (in other words, paying a courier/postage) and, assuming your sales are sufficient, human fees (in other words, paying someone to undertake the work—if you sell 100,000 CDs, you probably won't want to send them all out yourself).

I have not added these additional costs in this illustration. You should make an appropriate allowance before you make any price comparisons with other methods of CD production.

For this example, I asked for a quote for 25,000 CDs to be produced in the UK. The price I was given was £8,555 (including VAT on the purchase of the CDs), or roughly $16,500, which equates to 66 cents per CD. At this US price, if each CD is sold for $10, then you would make a profit of $9.34 per CD. However, as illustrated in the earlier chapter, there are a lot of other charges that could reduce that apparently large profit by a considerable amount.

If we take the effect of VAT on the sale of the CD into account (you have to pay VAT if you sell in Europe—for this example I've assumed VAT is 20%) and add in the credit card processing charges, then you could reduce your profit to $7.49. I do realize I'm mixing apples and oranges by applying a European tax to a US dollar amount; however, I want to illustrate how VAT can chew into your earnings.

If you're trying to follow these figures, then you may have difficulties because I have offset VAT inputs and outputs (to give the technical term to the VAT you pay and the VAT you must charge). This is a practice so that you don't pay VAT twice. This is not a book about tax, so for once may I ask that you trust me on this number without further explanation?

Also, you have to actually sell your CDs to make that profit. If you don't, then you've wasted $16,500. If you are intending to sell your CD through record stores, then, as an example, you are likely to find your distribution costs are disproportionately high when compared to those of the majors, who will have quite a slick distribution operation in place and will be able to negotiate much better deals than you can.

The chart in Figure 9.2 illustrates the proportions of income that would be attributable to the costs of producing and selling 25,000 CDs. This chart also shows the proportion that would be profit. To add some realism, the chart shows an allowance (of 15% of the sale price) for distribution expenses. I will talk more about distribution costs in a moment. I have also added in an allowance for a manager to take his or her cut because you may well have a manager involved by the time you are selling this number of CDs.

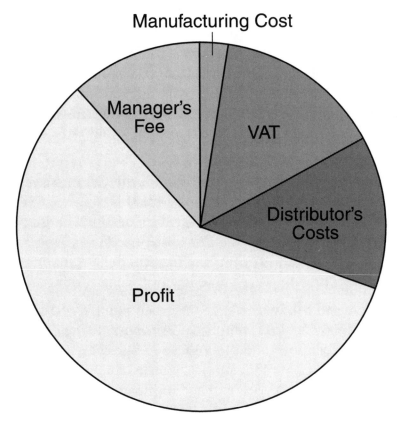

Figure 9.2 The costs and profits associated with pressing your own CD.

Before you get carried away looking at the profit, remember that to make this proportion of profit, you have to sell 25,000 CDs. That is a huge number of CDs to sell. If you don't sell that number, then you could make a loss. Let me show the graph again (see Figure 9.3), but this time I have assumed that you get 1,000 CDs pressed (which will obviously cost a lot less than getting 25,000 pressed), and then you only sell only 800 of them. In this scenario, I have removed the distribution cost and replaced it with the expense of storing CDs for a year. I have also removed the manager's fee because you're unlikely to have a manager if you're selling only 800 CDs. As you can see, the profit is very healthy, but it is still considerably less than the proportion of profit if you sell large numbers of CDs.

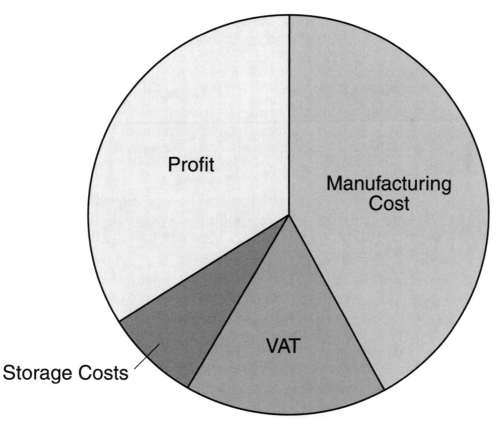

Figure 9.3 The costs and profits associated with pressing a small number of CDs and then selling 80% of the batch.

I said I would mention distribution costs. If you're going to get 1,000 CDs pressed, then you are unlikely to be at a level at which the major record stores will pay any attention to you. That probably won't concern you because you would probably be selling CDs to friends and at gigs. Even at 25,000 CDs, the national record store chains are unlikely to be interested in you; however, this number does vary depending on your jurisdiction and the market for which you are aiming.

When you start selling in big numbers, then you will probably need a distributor because you're not going to be able to pack the number of CDs you want to sell into the back of your car and deliver them all by hand—take some time to think about the logistics of distributing 1 million CDs by hand. Unfortunately, when you get other people involved, huge chunks of your profit get swallowed up, as we will see when we look at the income you can generate by releasing a record with a major record label.

One form of distribution that is likely to be appealing to you is mail order; this is perhaps the only practical way (until you are a very well-established artist) to get a CD to a fan base that is spread over a very wide geographical area. If you want proof that mail order is a viable option, look at how Amazon (and the like) continue to grow while the number of record stores is decreasing.

To give you an idea about distribution costs for mail order, let me talk about CD Baby (cdbaby.com) for a moment. For a one-off setup fee of $35 per CD and a fee of $4 per CD sold, CD Baby will handle your mail order distribution. You set the price, and CD Baby will take orders and send out the CD and charge you $4 for each transaction. As far as fulfillment of the order goes, all you have to do is sit back and wait for payment (which comes every week).

The other expense you will incur in using a service like this is the cost associated with delivering your CDs to CD Baby. However, when you order your CDs from the pressing plant, you can always arrange for the plant to deliver the CDs directly to CD Baby. This won't cut costs, but it will ensure that you are not charged twice for delivery.

Using CD Baby (but ignoring the cost of getting your CDs to CD Baby), each $10 CD would generate $6.00 for you. If you then deduct the manufacturing costs (based on 25,000 CDs being pressed), that would give you a net income of $5.34 per CD.

Record Label Deal

The income you may be able to generate from a deal with a record company depends very much on the nature of any particular deal, your status as a recording artist, and the type of label with which you are dealing. However, there are certain characteristics of different types of deals, and I have used these characteristics to give an illustration of the different royalties that you could expect in different situations.

I have given a few brief pointers about the different sorts of deals and the different commercial considerations that may apply; however, for details about the nature of the different types of recording deals and the financial expectations under each, I suggest you check out *All You Need to Know About the Music Business* by Donald Passman and *Music—The Business: The Essential Guide to the Law and the Deals* by Ann Harrison. (Links to both of these books are included on my website at www.noisesculpture.com/c21.)

When trying to make a comparisons—particularly when trying to compare the apparently generous levels of profit you can generate by pressing your own CD—remember that record companies have very large expenses associated with the release of a CD (and those expenses are mostly not related to funding the record executive's lifestyle). In particular, the label will handle the publicity for your CD, which may be the single largest cost that the label meets.

In addition, record companies will usually pay some sort of advance. I will look at alternative ways of raising financing later in this chapter. These alternate forms of funding could replace an advance and fund a project—including the marketing and distribution cost—if you would still prefer to release a CD on your own terms.

Size of Record Label and Your Status in the Industry

Two factors that will have a considerable bearing on the deal you can negotiate are:

- The size of the record label you are dealing with

- Your status (and therefore negotiating power) within the industry

With a smaller label, you may be able to negotiate a better deal, perhaps even a profit-sharing deal, which may be beneficial to you in certain circumstances. In this context, when I talk about a "better" deal, I mean one with higher percentages and more artistic control. However, the downsides to dealing with a smaller record label are that they are likely to have less money to pay an advance and to fund marketing activities.

You may also find that although the label you are dealing with is smaller, it will have done a deal with a larger label. This may arise when you are signing with a production company of some sort, rather than a record label. Some more of the detail of this kind of deal is discussed under the section headed "Production Deals," later in this chapter.

The other side of the coin when looking at deals is your clout. Your status is likely to fall into one of three groupings:

- A new act with little negotiating power. If you're at this stage, then you probably haven't read the rest of this book (or if you have, you haven't acted upon it). If you don't have a fan base and you have no proven track record of generating income, then you have little clout and will probably take any deal that is offered to you because it is your only way of getting money. Unless you are a very lucky person, you could end up disappointed by this deal.

- An act with some clout. In this situation you could be an act looking for your first deal with a record company or an existing act looking to re-sign. Either way, if you are bringing something to the party, then you stand a much better chance of negotiating a satisfactory deal, provided you have the right team around you to guide you. See Chapter 10, "Building the Team around You," for further details about getting the right team.

- An established star/superstar. If you fall into this category, you're probably too busy/famous/rich to read this book, although you may find that one of your "people" has read it. Given that this category of artists is unlikely to be reading this book, I won't focus on them too much.

As I've already discussed, negotiating power comes through having the option to walk away. If you have your own fan base and you are already making a living in the music industry, then you are in a position to walk away from an unfavorable deal. This gives you huge negotiating clout.

Another factor giving you clout is whether anyone else is bidding to sign you. In competitive bidding situations, people are likely to pay more to ensure they sign you. This may be good for you (because you can negotiate more money and better terms), but it may also be bad. For instance, you may negotiate yourself into a position where you will never live up to your own hype, so the relationship will go sour when expectations (on both sides) cannot be met.

You are most likely to find yourself with several bids if you are a proven commercial proposition (in other words, you can demonstrate that you have a fan base and you have a proven track record of selling CDs).

Type of Deal

There are many different forms of deals that may be on offer to you. All of these deals are likely to involve you selling your copyright to the sound recordings to the record label. Some deals where you may not need to assign your copyright are considered under the heading "Other Types of Deals," which follows this section.

Don't get too hung up on the differences between these deals. The differences are not always as black and white as this section may suggest. What is important is that you understand the nature of any deal that is offered to you, and you understand (in minute detail) what this deal means for you both financially and in terms of your career.

Exclusive Recording Contract

For many musicians, the exclusive recording contract is the Holy Grail and is regarded as the first step to superstardom.

An exclusive recording contract is what most people understand (or think they understand) when they talk about a recording contract: The act signs with a record label, who then funds several albums. The reality is, of course, somewhat different.

In practice, the record company is likely to fund a few singles or an album. Depending on the success of the recording, the label will then decide whether to release the product—often the label will be under no legal obligation to release. However, if it does and the recording sells well, then the record company will exercise its options.

Often, the most that a record company will commit to is to release an album (if even that). If that album is seen as not being a commercial success, then the act may be dropped. When an act is dropped, the record company rarely breaks its contract. Instead, it simply decides not to exercise its option to commission another album. In effect, the future contract simply lapses.

Generally, you would only expect to take another form of deal (one that isn't a long-term exclusive recording contract) if no other deal is on the table. If no other deal is available, then you probably haven't made yourself sufficiently attractive. If this is the case, then I suggest you walk away. I suggest this not because the deal will be bad (although it is unlikely to be the best deal that you will ever see), but because you don't have the fan base that is necessary to make your career work. Go back and build the fan base, and then approach the record label when you have proved your commercial worth.

Production Deals

A production deal is similar to an exclusive recording contract. The key difference relates to the record company with which you are signing. Typically, the record company will be owned by a manager, producer, or even a recording studio. In reality, therefore, the "record company" is a production company rather than a record company. Sometimes these production companies will be funded by a larger record company and will act as a talent scout for that label, bringing them finished "product" that can be launched without any significant investment in developing the artist on the part of the larger label.

For the production company, this is often a very attractive deal. The company gets to do what it wants to do and what it does best: develop talent. Even better, this is funded by someone else. The company then has a guaranteed outlet for its product. The company can choose to work with artists it likes and believes in. These are all positives for the artist.

However, the profit that the production company generates is based on the fee that it is paid by the larger label, less an amount to fund the production company's expenses and also less some profit for the production company. The net result of this may be that you will usually generate less income by signing with a production company than you would if you signed directly with the larger label, and you may also miss out on the larger label's marketing muscle.

If you have a fan base and some success behind you, then a production deal may not be the most enticing deal for you. You should have already done a lot of your own development and will already know what your fan base wants. However, there are features of this style of deal that may be appealing.

Primarily, this form of deal may be interesting if the production company is your own company. In this case, the deal would probably work more like a licensing deal (which is discussed in the "Other Types of Deals" section). You may also find this sort of deal appealing if you are using your infrastructure to promote another act (in other words, you are starting to act as a record/production company). Some more of these options are discussed later in this chapter, under the section "Income from Your Infrastructure."

Demo Deal

With a demo deal, a record company (or production company) will pay for you to record some demos in a professional studio, with a professional producer. This sounds good, but the downside is that you are actually entering into a recording contract. The record company will own your recordings and will probably want the right to release those recordings if they see fit.

In many ways, a demo deal is a cheap way to get you under contract.

Other Types of Deals

The next three types of deal have, at various times, had a bad press. However, for the self-promoting musician, these deals may be very attractive, especially since you can maintain high levels of control and you may be able to either keep your copyrights or get them back after a set period.

Licensing Deal

With a licensing deal, you grant a record company permission to release and market your product. In return, they will pay a license fee, which may be similar to the royalty you could expect under an exclusive recording contract. However, since you will be meeting the development costs and the cost of recording and then presenting the final product to the record company, who can decide whether to license the product, the record company's risk will be greatly reduced. This may mean that you can expect a better percentage than would otherwise be payable.

Under a licensing deal, you may be able to retain your copyrights. However, you would likely have to enter into an agreement that would tie up your copyright on an exclusive basis for a number of years (usually between five and ten). At the end of the license period, you may get full use of your copyrights; so for instance, you could re-release an album or enter into another licensing agreement with your music.

Joint Venture

With a joint venture, the artist and the record label create a separate business entity (its precise legal structure is irrelevant). This entity is a joint venture owned by the artist and the label. The joint venture will generate income and will have costs. Once the costs have been met and the profits calculated, these are then shared between the artist and the record company.

Joint venture arrangements are usually more favorable to:

- The record label when sales are modest.

- The artist when sales are higher. However, in this case, the record label is less likely to be concerned about what it is paying you since it will be generating a healthy income itself.

Pressing and Distribution Agreement

As its name suggests, a pressing and distribution deal is an arrangement where you can tap into a record label's logistical expertise.

Under these arrangements, you give your finished masters to the label/distributor, and in return they will get your CDs pressed and into the shops. All you then have to do is promote your CD! In many ways, this arrangement is very similar to a self-pressing setup, but instead of you getting your CD pressed, you are using the record company's expertise. You are also avoiding the hassles of distribution, which, if you are intending to play on an international stage, will save you from considerable stress.

Typically with pressing and distribution deals, the record label will charge a percentage for distribution (perhaps 20%), and production costs will then be deducted. The profit is the wholesale cost, less the distribution charge and less the production cost. As you can see, this is likely to give you the highest proportion of income for any of the deals that may be available with a record label.

However, this option also gives you the highest risk. CDs are generally sold on a sale or return basis. If your CDs don't sell and they are returned to you, then you will be charged for the distribution and return costs (as well as the production cost), but you will have no sales to fund those expenses. You will also have a lot of unwanted CDs to store.

The nature of pressing and distribution deals is different in different territories. As an example, the practices in the UK and the US differ. In the US, the big distributors are the record labels, so you would make a pressing and distribution deal with one of these labels. In the UK, the labels contract out their distribution to specialist firms, so you would likely make a pressing and distribution deal with one of these special-ist companies.

Clawbacks under Recording Contracts

For anyone not familiar with the term *clawback*, let me explain it. A clawback is a way to take money back from people that has been given in another way. So for instance, a record label may say, "We'll pay you $1 million," and then find a way to clawback most of this and only pay you (for instance) $10.

Once you have your deal with a record label, you will find that while you are getting creative with your music, the record label is getting creative with ways to keep hold of the money and avoid paying it to you. In addition to what you'll read in the following subsections, you will find there are many other ways the record label can keep hold of your money—for instance, by keeping a reserve against any returned CDs (a practice that is adopted because all record companies allow dealers to return unsold CDs).

Advances

One of the main reasons to take a deal with a record label is the advance that will often be paid. An advance is an immediate chunk of money that you can spend as you want, but from a practical point of view it is intended to pay for necessities, such as food and accommo-dations, until you receive your royalties.

An advance is like a loan. However, unlike a loan, there is no interest payable. Also, unlike a loan, the record label can't usually ask for an advance to be repaid. Instead, it takes the advance out of the artist's royalties, and artists do not receive royalties until the advance has been fully recouped. For this reason, one of the most significant clawbacks from royalties is the repayment of this advance.

You will see that in this book I don't outline the level of advances you can expect. My reasons for this are twofold. First, the amount you can expect is highly dependent on your situation. Second, advances are not real money. Now, this is a slightly rash statement—many times, all an artist will receive under a recording contract is an advance—so let me explain. Ninety-five percent of artists don't recoup their advance, so the royalties on offer are just an illusion. The advance is an amount of money designed to get an artist into debt with the record label and then to keep the artist working for the label.

Hopefully this section of the book goes a long way to explaining many of the factors behind the failure of 95% of artists. One thing I want everyone who reads this book to achieve is to recoup any advances he or she receives, which would be good for the artist and is also good for the record company (because they will be shifting a lot of product).

Advances tend to come in two flavors: one that includes the cost of recording (often called a *recording fund*) and another that doesn't (*personal advances*). Including the cost of recording a CD gives the artist a certain degree of control. However, any overspends will cut directly into any money that the artist would have used to fund day-to-day living expenses (such as food). Recording fund deals tend to be less generous when compared to personal advances plus the associated cost of recording a CD.

One of the main reasons why artists look for a deal with a major record label is to secure an advance to provide income and to fund the recording of a CD. As you will see later in this chapter (in the "Sources of Finance" section), there are other options instead of an advance, and you don't need an advance to kick start your career. However, these other options may include an expectation of interest and repayment.

Producer and Recording Costs

The cost of recording an album will be met by the artist. The cost of the album has many factors; as you might expect, the largest costs are people and places.

The people are the engineer(s) and the producer. In particular, producers are often paid an advance and also receive a percentage. The producer's percentage is nearly always met from the artist's royalties, so if you're on a 16% royalty and the producer gets 3 points (in other words, 3%), then your royalties will be cut to 13%.

The places that cost money are recording studios and any accommodations that are used during the recording process (such as hotels or properties that may be rented in the vicinity of the studio to house the artists during the recording). These expenses are all recouped before royalties are paid.

Usually the costs of the studio will need to be met before the facility will release the master tape. The deals for producers usually provide that unlike the artist's royalty, the producer's royalty will not take account of recording costs. This can mean that a producer starts to earn his or her royalties before the act does.

Overseas Sales

You might think you're signing to a global entity when you sign with a multinational record company. Actually, these businesses are managed as group of individual businesses, and hence, each separate business has to make its own profit. This means that each overseas company will take its own cut. For you, the artist, this means you can expect a reduced royalty rate from overseas income.

Another downside to having each territory working as a separate entity is that you usually won't be able to force an overseas arm of the company to release your product. However, this is an issue that goes beyond the scope of this chapter.

You may find that in overseas territories, your royalties are cut to around 75% of the royalty in your home country. Sometimes the royalty can go as low as 50% of your home country royalty (so if you have a home country royalty of 16%, then you may only get an 8% royalty for overseas earnings).

Sometimes, particularly when you are dealing with a smaller label, there will not be an overseas office. In this case your label will often license your music to a local label in each territory. Sometimes this licensing can generate an advance (which the record label will be keen to snaffle up). When tracks are licensed, it is unlikely that you will make as much money as you could if there were a local arm of your label.

Container Charges

A significant deduction from an artist's royalties will be container charges. This is an amount intended to cover the packaging of CDs (the argument being you get your royalties on the CD, not on the packaging) and is usually set between 15% and 25%. This charge is usually levied before the royalty is calculated, so if you have a 20% royalty based on a CD price of $15 and a 25% packaging deduction is applied, you can expect to receive $2.25 per CD sold (before the other deductions that I discuss in this section).

Breakages

Until the 1950s, records were made out of shellac. These discs were comparatively fragile and were liable to break. Due to the high number of breakages, it was assumed that a certain number of discs would break, so a discount was given. A conventional discount to allow for breakages was 10%.

In these days of CDs and downloads, breakages are comparatively rare. However, the practice of giving a 10% discount for breakages still remains with certain labels (and the breakages allowance can even be applied to downloads).

New Technologies

Historically, record contracts have had a provision for new technologies. Essentially the provision works so that a reduced royalty rate is paid for any releases that use new technology. Typically, the royalty paid will be 75% of the full royalty. (For instance, if the full royalty is 16%, the new technology royalty will be 12%.)

Depending on the nature of the deal, new technologies may include CDs (the technology may be over 25 years old, but some record companies still regard it as new) and digital downloads (where there is no cost to physically manufacture the product).

Promotional and Free Copies

Record labels legitimately need to give away a number of free copies of the CDs they are promoting. If they don't give CDs to radio stations, then the music won't be heard on the radio. Equally, it can be helpful for record stores to have a copy of the music to play for their customers.

However, labels go further than giving away a few free copies here and there. Often they will give away a large number of CDs (perhaps 5% or more of a total order) to retailers. The effect of this practice is to give retailers a discount, and because the CDs are given away, no royalties are paid on them. This discount won't particularly hurt the label's income (it's a marketing expense), but it will hit the artist's royalties because the artist won't get paid on these CDs if they are sold.

Cross-Collateralization

Under a cross-collateralization arrangement, a record label may take a profit you have made in one area to fund a loss you have made in another area. So for instance, if you don't recoup your advance on your first CD but your second CD propels you into the stratosphere, the record label may use your earnings from the second CD to fund your loss on the first CD.

In practice, this means you won't see any royalties from your second CD until the debt on your first CD has been met.

Videos

For many artists, videos are an integral part of marketing their music. However, videos are a very expensive luxury—some cost more than $1 million to make—and videos don't usually generate any significant income.

Although videos fall under the marketing budget and therefore the costs would usually be met by the record label, very often the label will split the cost with the artist, or sometimes, especially when a budget exceeds a predetermined limit, they may charge the whole cost of the video to the artist.

When the artist is charged for the video, the cost is met by the record label, and this cost is then recouped from the artist's earnings.

Independent Promotion and Other Specialized Marketing Activities

Most record companies have their own promotions department. The cost of promotion by a record label's in-house promotions department is usually met by the label as part of its business cost.

Labels will also hire promotions specialists who will be paid a large chunk of money to get your record played (usually on the radio). Often the fee that the promotion firm will be paid will be linked to the record's chart success.

Unlike the in-house promotion department, the cost of independent promotion specialists is usually met by the artist, although like the situation for videos, the cost will be met by the label and recouped from the artist's earnings.

Independent promotion is also sometimes a euphemism for payola-style practices (that is, the practice where, bluntly, a record is played in return for an inducement, which may be financial or otherwise). Using independent promotions services removes the record label from the grubby business of bribing people and allows the record labels to deny that they are aware of the practice.

Tour Support

Touring is another one of those highly expensive activities with which musicians get involved. Conventionally, until you reach superstar status and can sell out a tour and bolster your income with merchandising and sponsorship, touring results in a loss.

Although touring often results in a loss, it is often encouraged because it is a great way to build a fan base. However, if you build your fan base slowly and progressively and interact directly with your fans, then you can tour in a small-scale manner without incurring a loss.

For acts that don't have an established fan base, record labels will often underwrite tour losses to a certain predetermined level. Anything beyond the agreed level of loss will usually be met directly by the artist. Again, although the cost will be met by the record label, any spending will be charged straight back to the artist as a deduction from royalties.

So What Will I Actually Get Paid under a Recording Contract?

If you take a couple of moments to search the internet, you will find many explanations about how record contracts work to the detriment of artists. You will find comments on this situation by many people, including individuals who have reached a certain status in the industry (some of the most vocal individuals on this topic are Don Henley from the Eagles, Courtney Love from the band Hole, and the record producer Steve Albini).

Much of this disquiet arises because artists generate very large sums of money and create wealth throughout the music industry and yet end up with very little income for themselves. I will illustrate just how little they could end up with in a moment.

Royalty Percentage: Percentage of What?

Once you've generated some income, and the record label has clawed back as much as it can, then you can start looking at your percentage. Unfortunately, the figure on which your percentage will be based is not necessarily a straightforward figure.

In most of Europe, royalty percentages are usually calculated as a percentage of the price that the dealer pays for a CD (in other words, the wholesale price). In the US and some other territories, the percentage is driven off a suggested retail list price (usually called the *SRLP*). Ironically, the SRLP is often not the recommended list price, but the wholesale price increased by 30%.

Royalty rates will differ depending on your status and depending on what the royalty is based. When royalties are based on the suggested retail price, they will be lower than if they were based on wholesale prices.

For artists whose royalties are based on suggested retail prices, royalties are usually in the region of 10% to 20%. For artists whose royalties are based on retail prices, royalties are usually in the region of 15% to 30%. The lower amounts are for new artists signed to a smaller label, and the higher amounts are payable to more successful artists with a track record of success.

Example of Possible Royalties

Here's an example of earnings from a CD release with a record label. For this example, I'm going to make some assumptions.

- Number of CDs sold: 250,000. (This would represent a low number of sales for a record label; however, it would also take a lot of work to reach this number.)

- Suggested retail price of CD: $18.

- Artist's royalty rate: 15%.

- Container charges: 20%.

- Breakages: 10%.

- Free CDs: 10%.

- New technology: 100%. (In other words, there is no clawback.)

- Recording costs: $100,000.

- Video costs: $250,000.

- Producer's royalty rate: 3%.

Take a look at Table 9.1 to see how this income translates to income for the artist.

So after selling 250,000 CDs, the artist is still in debt to the tune of $4,400. This is probably a highly unrealistic figure—you will see that many costs have not been included. For instance, there is no fee included for the manager, and the artist is likely to have had an advance that would also be recouped from royalties.

Let's take the same figures, but assume:

- The artist had an advance of $100,000 (which does not cover recording costs—in other words, recording costs plus the advance equals $200,000).

- Five-hundred thousand CDs were sold.

- An independent promoter was paid $200,000. (Without the promoter, sales of 500,000 would be unlikely.)

- The manager charges a fee of 20%.

Table 9.1 An Example of Earnings from a CD Release

Item	Calculation	Cost
Royalty base		$14.40
Suggested retail price, less	$18	
20% container charge	– $3.60	
CDs on which royalties are based		200,000
Number of CDs sold	250,000	
Less free CDs	– 10%	
Less breakages	– 10%	
Artist royalty		12%
Royalty rate, less	15%	
Producer's royalty rate	– 3%	
Income from CD sales for royalty calculation purposes	$14.40 × 200,000	$2,880,000
Artist's royalty	12% of $2,880,000	$345,600
Less		$350,000
Recording, and	$100,000	
Video costs	$250,000	
Total income for the artist		–$4,400

Table 9.2 shows what the position could look like.

Again, this figure may not be realistic because it does not include any costs incurred in touring. However, you can see that although the artist has sold a lot of CDs, he is still in the same position as when he started (that is, owing the record label nearly $100,000).

I don't like unhappy endings, so let's take the last scenario and assume that instead of selling 500,000 CDs, the artist sold 600,000. This would be enough to give a modest profit, as Table 9.3 shows.

Now let's have a look at the proportions shown in Table 9.3. These are set out in Figure 9.4. For this chart, I am assuming that the wholesale price is $6 and distribution costs make up $2.50 of that $6.

Table 9.2 A Slightly More Realistic Illustration of Possible Earnings from a CD Release with a Major Record Label

Item	Calculation	Cost
Royalty base		$14.40
Suggested retail price,	$18	
Less 20% container charge	– $3.60	
CDs on which royalties are based		400,000
Number of CDs sold	500,000	
Less free CDs	– 10%	
Less breakages	– 10%	
Artist royalty		12%
Royalty rate, less	15%	
Producer's royalty rate	– 3%	
Income from CD sales for royalty calculation purposes	$14.40×400,000	$5,760,000
Artist's royalty	12% of $5,760,000	$691,200
Less		$788,240
Recording costs	$100,000	
Video costs	$250,000	
Advance	$100,000	
Manager's fee	$138,240	
Promoter's fee	$200,000	
Total income for the artist		–$97,040

As you can see in Figure 9.4, the artist's earnings account for nearly one quarter of the income that arises from the sale of each CD. If an artist could take one quarter of the income, he or she would become very rich very quickly. However, as you can see, there are costs that are taken from the artist's royalty. Figure 9.5 shows how the artist's royalty is spent (in other words, how the costs that are charged against the artist's royalties eat into those earnings).

Table 9.3 After Selling 600,000 CDs, the Artist Finally Shows a (Very) Modest Profit

Item	Calculation	Cost
Royalty base		$14.40
Suggested retail price, less	$18	
20% container charge	– $3.60	
CDs on which royalties are based		480,000
Number of CDs sold	600,000	
Less free CDs	– 10%	
Less breakages	– 10%	
Artist royalty		12%
Royalty rate, less	15%	
Producer's royalty rate	– 3%	
Income from CD sales for royalty calculation purposes	$14.40 × 480,000	$6,912,000
Artist's royalty	12% of $5,760,000	$829,440
Less		$788,240
Recording costs	$100,000	
Video costs	$250,000	
Advance	$100,000	
Manager's fee, and	$138,240	
Independent promoter's fee	$200,000	
Total income for the artist		$41,300

So there you have it. If each CD was sold for $15 (in other words, at a discount against the suggested retail price of $18), then the artist will have generated income of $9 million, but will see only $141,300 (including the advance). In other words, a 15% royalty will have equated to 1.5%. And as I keep belaboring, that is after selling 600,000 CDs, which is a large number to sell.

Looked at another way, the record company will have generated income of $2,880,000 (480,000 × $6). The artist will see 4.9% of this figure in this highly favorable example. In the real world, the artist would be much more likely to still be in debt after selling 600,000 CDs. As a general rule of thumb, an artist will start to make a profit under a recording contract after selling more than 1.5 million CDs.

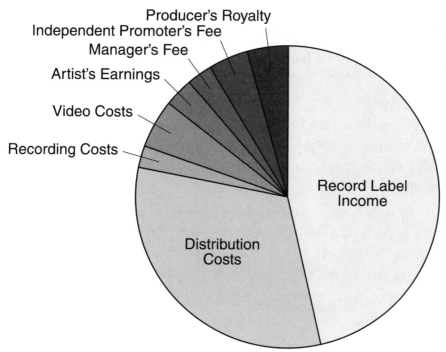

Figure 9.4 How the income is split for a successful CD.

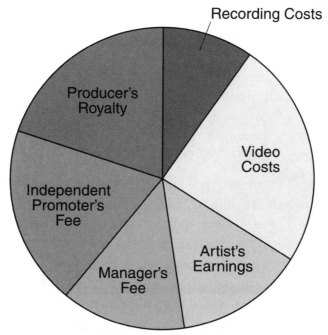

Figure 9.5 How the artist's income from a CD is spent.

I hope this illustrates why the likes of Don Henley, Courtney Love, and Steve Albini rage against current business practices. I also hope this explains why you may be better off following your own path.

Downloads

Although they represent only a small proportion of the market, downloads (such as those available through iTunes) are a valuable source of income and are likely to represent an increasing proportion of an artist's income.

With so many download services (there were more than 350 legal services at the last count), there are many different deals. Perhaps the most significant deal is that offered by iTunes, which pays 65 cents on each 99-cent download (in other words, there is a deduction of 34 cents).

However, as an artist you may not receive 65 cents for each download. First you need to get your music onto the system for each of the download services. You can do this yourself, but it's likely to take time to get all 350 services sorted out. Each will have different requirements (for instance, different encoding standards). However, you can do it if you're keen to keep the full 65 cents.

Alternatively, you could use a provider such as CD Baby, who will arrange for your music to be encoded and placed on all of their partner download services (which includes iTunes). They do this as part of their service and do not raise an additional setup fee. CD Baby will then charge you 9% on all download income, so this will give you an income of 59 cents for each 99-cent download (99cents – 34cents – 6cents; in other words, 9% of 65 cents), which is still a pretty reasonable income.

However, if you have a deal with a record company, you are likely to receive considerably less. Sales on iTunes are (presently) regarded by many labels in the same manner as sales from record stores. In other words, iTunes buys the track wholesale (for 65 cents) and then sells it at whatever price it wants. The record company will then treat that 65-cent income in the same manner as if it had sold a physical product and will make the same deductions as if a product had been sold (for instance, for container charges, even though there was no packaging) and will then pay a royalty on the income. This could give an income of around 10 cents.

As you would expect, there are other deals out there. For instance, some download services treat tracks as if they had been licensed, so a license fee can be paid. However, since some labels have figured this may generate more money for the artist, these deals are becoming less common. There are other methods of calculation—see the "Future Sources of Income" section later in this chapter for some discussion about the other main options.

You can also be sure that with the release of Microsoft's Zune players and Microsoft entering the market, it is likely that there will be many new developments over the next few years.

Moving Images

You can make money from putting your music with moving images in a number of ways. The two main options are putting out your own video and allowing your music to be used as part of a soundtrack. Songwriters can also make money from royalties generated from video sources. Songwriting royalties are considered in greater depth later in this chapter, in the "Songwriting Royalties" section.

DVD (and Video)

If you are signed to a record label, then your video rights will almost certainly be signed up too. In this case, if you release a DVD (or a VHS cassette)—for instance, of your recent live tour—you can expect a royalty (perhaps up to 20% of the wholesale price) in a similar way to how you get a royalty on CDs.

Alternatively, you (or your label) could license someone to create a DVD and generate income in that manner. If a record company licenses the creation of a DVD, then your royalty would usually be based on the income that the record company generates.

By contrast, if you are running your own show, then you could get 30,000 DVDs pressed for around $60,000 (in other words, about $2 per DVD). This might sound good, but remember, there are considerable costs in the production of a DVD (such as the camera crew costs and editing). You are unlikely to have the expertise (or sufficient number of talented friends) to be able to create a video of merchantable quality without making a significant investment. How much you then spend on production is really up to you.

Also remember that 30,000 DVDs is a large number. It could be really hard work to sell this number of DVDs, and if you don't sell them you're going to need a lot of storage space. This was the lowest quote (in terms of numbers to be pressed) that I could readily find for pressing from a glass master. You may find quotes for DVD-R duplication, but the unit cost is likely to be higher.

Synchronization Fees

Another source of income in connection with moving pictures comes from what is called a *synchronization license*. This is, quite literally, a license to add your original sound recording to a soundtrack of a video, film, TV show, corporate video, game, and so on.

The license fee is dependent on a number of factors, largely your negotiating clout and the ability of the licensor to pay. The amount the licensor will want to pay is likely to depend on the use of the music. For instance, an advertiser who wants to feature your song in a global advertising campaign (think "Start Me Up" by the Rolling Stones when Microsoft launched Windows 95) will pay much more than a TV company producing a daytime soap in which your music is playing on a radio in the background. The fee is also likely to be governed by local agreements and practices.

Merchandising

Merchandising is an area where the costs and possible income are ever variable. The notion of what actually constitutes merchandising is quite tough, but in practice, it can cover a wide range of products branded with your logo (or other image), including:

- Clothing, such as T-shirts, sweatshirts, hoodies, jackets, caps, and so on

- Printed materials, such as calendars, books, photos, posters, and programs

- Stationery, such as pens, pencils, paper, rulers, and erasers

- Dolls and other figures

- Chinaware, such as mugs and plates

- Bags, buttons (that is, badges if you speak English English), fridge magnets, clocks, coasters, mouse pads, pillows, and candles

- Anything else your creative mind can come up with and for which you believe there is a market

You have three main choices if you want to generate income from merchandising:

- Use an on-demand service that can create a product when it is ordered by the customer. (This is the same principle as applies for on-demand CDs.)

- Create and sell your own product (which probably means you need to commission someone else to produce the product for you).

- License someone else to create and sell your branded merchandise.

As always, you can mix and match these options. However, if you license a third party to create and sell merchandising, that party is likely to expect an exclusive contract (even if only for a limited territory). This requirement may constrain your more entrepreneurial merchandising avenues.

As you may expect, as a general rule of thumb an on-demand service will have the advantage of allowing you to create a range of products at a one-stop shop. By contrast, creating your own product may give higher profits, but you will have to find product suppliers, spend money up front, store the goods, sell the goods, and then deliver them to your customer. For both of these routes, you will have to commission or create your own artwork.

With a licensing deal, all you have to do is sit back and wait for the money to roll in—it will be in your licensor's interest to proactively sell as much product as possible. This is obviously an oversimplification of the position; however, the work involved is much reduced. For instance, you may not have to create your own artwork. If you follow this route, you will need to spend more time approving the quality of the products you are licensing your images to.

When you license the production of merchandising, you can expect a royalty of between 50% and 80% of the profit. The licensor is likely to be able to obtain the raw materials and create the product for a far lower cost than you can, so you may find this share of profit exceeds the profit you could make by creating your own products. You may also find a licensor will pay you an advance.

Whether you go down the on-demand service route or arrange for printing yourself, T-shirts tend to come out between about $5.80 and $6.80 once you order around 100. This is a very rough pricing based on my local sources—in your market you may find a better price with some work. If you order fewer, the price per unit goes up, and again there's little to separate the prices. If you obtain the T-shirts yourself, you can probably get the cost down, but the setup costs for screen printing are fixed. For anything greater than 100, screen printing tends to be cheaper.

You may be wondering why I showed a price for 30,000 DVDs but only considered a run of 100 T-shirts. This is largely because the markets for DVDs and T-shirts are influenced by different factors. There are many reasons why you are likely to purchase T-shirts in smaller numbers.

- First, the minimum run of DVDs using a glass master that I could find was 30,000.

- Although T-shirts are not perishable, they are less easy to store than DVDs. For instance, T-shirts can rot and go moldy if kept in an inappropriate storage facility. Also, DVDs are less likely to be eaten by mice. Hence, you can order more DVDs.

- Styles and fashions change, so the lifespan of a T-shirt design is shorter than the lifespan of a DVD (or a CD for that matter). Added to this, T-shirts are often linked to certain events (for example, World Tour of Iceland 1993).

- You may be able to produce one or two new T-shirt designs each year, whereas you can only get an album or DVD out every other year.

- Fans may well buy your whole album collection. They are far less likely to want to buy your entire selection of T-shirts (although some may).

In practice, you will probably find that a sensible approach is to use an on-demand service to provide your mail-order T-shirts. For gigs, you may be able to get a supply of T-shirts more cheaply. Alternatively, you could bulk buy (which usually means more than 100, but can mean as few as 25) from your on-demand provider.

Ideally, you will probably want to do a deal to license someone to provide your merchandise because this is likely to generate the most income for you. If you do, then ensure that you get commission on any sales you generate (for instance, any sales generated or initiated from your website).

Live Performances

You have two main choices for putting on a live performance:

- Hire the venue yourself and take all of the risk.

- Get hired by a promoter who will put on the gig.

As a general rule, you are only likely to hire the venue and put on your own gigs when:

- You are first starting out.

- You reach superstar level.

Apart from that, the benefits of using a booking agent and promoter are likely to outweigh the effort, risk, and difficulty in putting on your own gigs. However, don't let me stop you putting on your own gigs (and acting as the promoter), especially in your own territory. For an explanation about the roles of booking agents and promoters, see Chapter 10.

If you are going to act as the promoter for your gigs, then you need to be reasonably certain about the numbers who may come; otherwise, your economic plans may be thrown into disarray. Also, you must have the logistical infrastructure in place to be able to put on a gig at a particular venue in a particular territory.

So for instance, you may be a band based in Paris and have a large fan base in Japan. However, do you know where all of these people are? Are they all in Tokyo or are they spread over the country? Suppose you choose to put on a gig in Tokyo—do you have the necessary skills to put on a gig? Can you speak the language? Do you know the level at which tickets should be priced? Do you know where to hire a PA system? Are you aware of any local legislation that may impinge on the gig?

If you're going to go the booking agent/promoter route, then you will probably find that the agent will take somewhere between 15% and 20% of your income. The amount you can squeeze out of the promoter will vary depending on the size of the venue and your negotiating power. You may find a promoter will pay a fixed fee—this is particularly likely when you have less pulling power. When you can guarantee an audience, you may be able to negotiate a profit split with the promoter. You may even be able to negotiate a share of the profit and a guarantee (which, like an advance from a record label, is non-returnable).

Touring also provides an excellent outlet for selling your merchandising. If you have appointed a merchandising firm, then they will expect to be able to sell at your gigs (however, your promoter may want a cut of this income).

You should also remember that each time a song is performed, it generates performance royalties for the songwriter, which may be another stream of income for the artist.

However, although there are many opportunities for generating income from touring, there are even more opportunities to lose a lot of money. The drains on your finances while you are touring arise in the following areas. All of these expenses can be controlled to a certain extent; however, they are unfortunately expenses that do need to be incurred.

- Travel, which is mostly the cost of transportation between each gig. At one extreme, you can hitchhike to gigs, but this may prove impractical, especially if you are the drummer. At the other extreme, you can have a private chauffeur for each musician, some helicopters, and a private jet. From a practical perspective, you are likely to have a van or bus. The time when you switch from a van to a bus, and the size and luxury of the bus, will vary depending on your finances.

- You may be able to avoid hotel costs by sleeping in your van or sleeping on friends' and fans' floors. However, you are more likely to need some form of hotel accommodation, which could be a cheap motel or a suite in a five-star hotel. When looking at hotel costs, remember that you need a bed for every member of the tour, not just the musicians.

- Staff, in the broadest sense, cost money. Except when you are on the tightest budget, you will need a road crew (technicians to look after the equipment) and possibly other musicians who will all need paying. As your act grows, so will your entourage grow to encompass caterers, wardrobe people, stylists, as well as personal gurus.

- An army marches on its stomach, and every member of your tour will need feeding (probably several times a day). Even if you're only eating cheap takeout (which is not a healthy diet!), those costs could still mount. Ten people on a 45-day tour, each eating a $5 meal three times a day, would cost nearly $7,000 for the tour.

- Insurance. I'm sorry to be tedious, but you're going to need insurance. In some areas you may feel you can take a gamble. If someone steals your favorite stage hat, then you may just have to swallow that cost. However, there are areas in which you cannot gamble, particularly with public liability and third-party insurances. These insure against any liability that arises against you for any injury suffered by another person—for instance, if the tour bus runs someone over or someone gets injured at a gig. You need insurance, so go find a specialized music industry insurance broker who can help you get the right coverage.

As I have said—and hopefully the outline of the main costs illustrates—the costs of touring can be considerable. Most artists do not make any profit from touring until they get to the superstar level. Instead, they regard touring as a way to build up a fan base. It is for this reason that record labels have historically been agreeable to providing tour support (in other words, meeting some of the losses you incur while touring). Any tour support expenses are then deducted from future royalties, so think of this as a further advance.

There are, of course, other options. If you know where your fans are, and they will come to your shows, then you can be more selective about which gigs you play. If you only play gigs where you are going to make a profit or break even, then you won't incur a loss from touring. However, it is difficult to take this approach.

For instance, if you're a band from London and you know that you are big in New York, Seattle, and Wichita, then it may not be practical to "tour" the US, just to play three cities. Equally, you would probably find the hassle of arranging a tour of three US cities plus the cost of shipping your gear to the US would far outweigh the benefit of playing three gigs. Also, by limiting the geographical spread of your tour, you are limiting your opportunities for reaching a wider fan base.

For these reasons (and because you're a musician whose role is defined by being on the road), you may decide to take the short-term loss on touring for the long-term gain. If you do that, in addition to the sources of income I have already discussed, look at opportunities for using your fan base to offset some of your losses. Some more thoughts about how you can marshal your fan base to come to your aid are discussed under the "Commission" section later in this chapter.

Sponsorship/Endorsements

When I mention sponsorship, my first thought is always about gigs. Gigs are perhaps your most visible public appearances and so are one of the easiest ways for a product or brand to associate itself with you.

Sponsors want to be associated with you because they believe the demographic of your fan base is the same demographic at which they are aiming their product. So for instance, if you are a female singer whose fan base is predominately younger teenage girls, then you may find that a makeup firm wants to be associated with you. Alternatively, if you are a hard-rock band with a reputation for raucous hard living, then you may find that a hard-liquor firm wants to be associated with you. You're unlikely to find a teen princess sponsored by a whiskey brand or some hard rockers advertising mascara (unless 1970s glam makes another return). You get the idea.

You should remember that sponsorship deals are not simply a case of someone giving you money for free (although it may feel like that at times). Sponsors are going to want something in return. The nature of the something may be the subject of negotiation. Naturally, if your tour is sponsored, then the sponsor is going to want to see its name on the advertising and on the tickets. It is also going to want to see its banners strung liberally around the venue.

However, a sponsor may want more than that. For instance, it may want a block of tickets to give to staff as a reward or to impress clients (thereby filling your gig with corporate stiffs). A sponsor may want you to meet some competition winners, or it may want you to meet some of its key executives. The sponsor may want to go further and gain access to backstage areas before and after the gig. Some executives from potential sponsors may want to be your friend. These are usually sad, lonely, deluded people you should run away from. Seriously, you do need to think about what you are giving up in order to get money.

As for the amount of money, as you would expect, it is very much dependent on your status and the marketing budget of your sponsor. This is one reason to use a sponsorship agent (discussed in a moment). These are the people who know and understand the deals that have been done and should be able to find you the best sponsors and squeeze the most financially rewarding deals out of them.

Endorsements take the idea further. Instead of simply associating a product with you, you will be asked to imply that you use a certain product. For musicians, the most obvious form of endorsement is when you state your use of a certain musical instrument and allow photos of you using the instrument to be included in advertising for the product. However, this practice can go much further. When you reach the superstar level, you will find people endorsing clothing, fragrances, cars, alcoholic and non-alcoholic beverages, food (and restaurants), as well as personal care items, such as razors.

There are two ways to find sponsorship and endorsements. First, go out and find it. Second, wait for the advertisers to come knocking. They're only likely to come knocking when you're a megastar and your brand has reached the consciousness of the mass media.

When you do not figure on most people's radars, then you will have to find your own deals. You can either do this by knocking on doors yourself (or getting your manager to do some knocking) or by using an agent who specializes in arranging sponsorship. These people will usually work for a percentage, anything up to 20%.

If you are going to knock on doors yourself, then you need to have a strong reason why the potential sponsor would be interested in sponsoring you and what the benefit would be to their business—this will be the business proposition that any sponsorship agent would be putting to potential sponsors.

Just because you are a lower-profile act, don't think there are no opportunities for you. There will be—it's just that the potential sponsors are (like you) likely to be slightly lower down in the hierarchy. This means you may need to look to local sponsors and specialized niche sponsors.

Commission

There is a wide range of commissions you can capture to generate income. Some of these sources are formal arrangements, and the details are published. For others, you'll have to ask and negotiate a deal. You are likely to find that the formal arrangements are with larger organizations, and you won't be able to negotiate a specific deal for yourself or your fans. Instead, you will be able to take commission, and the commission won't affect the price that your fans pay.

With the individually negotiated arrangements, you will sometimes be able to negotiate discounts for your fans (which won't do anything directly for your income, but might encourage more people to spend money, which will help your cash flow indirectly).

Perhaps the most widespread commission arrangement is the Amazon Associates arrangement. Under this plan, you can direct people from your website to specific products on the Amazon website through customized links. (It's all very easy—Amazon will give you the HTML code for this.) If the person you have directed to Amazon then spends money, you get a commission. Better still, the commission is based on all products the person purchases at Amazon after following one of your links.

The rates payable vary depending on the Amazon to which you are linking. For instance, Amazon.com (Amazon US) has rates between 4% and 8.5% depending on the volume of sales you generate, while Amazon.co.uk rates are between 5% and 7.5% (and up to 10% in certain circumstances). These are percentages of the Amazon selling price. The breakpoints at which you qualify for higher rates differ by location too. These are just two Amazon examples; each separate Amazon has its own rates.

The one downside to this arrangement with Amazon is that you need to provide a link for each separate Amazon, so if you want (for instance) to get credit for sales with Amazon US, UK, and Canada, then you need to provide a separate link for each of the Amazons.

Once you have signed up as an associate, it really is very quick to set up the links. (As I said, Amazon will generate the HTML code for you.) All you have to do is drop the code into your website, then sit back and wait for the commission to roll in. Clearly, you won't become a millionaire from this arrangement; however, you may generate more income from an Amazon sale of your CD than you would generate from royalties from a record label. Ten percent of the Amazon retail price for a CD could be more than 20% of the wholesale price that a record label may pay you.

Amazon is just one of the organizations that has an associates arrangement. Also, as noted in Chapter 3, you don't just have to create links to your own products. You can link to other merchandise that may be of interest to your fan base and other people who browse your website. So, for instance, if you are a death-metal band, you could include links to books about serial killers.

Thinking about some of the commissions that you could generate yourself, this is where you need to bring your creative skills and negotiating power to the fore. Perhaps the most obvious commission you should generate is anything that you can sell through your website. So, for instance, if you have licensed your merchandising to someone else, then any sales through your website should generate commission.

Equally, if you are not promoting your own gigs, then you get a commission on all ticket sales that you generate. Ticket agencies would take a cut, so why shouldn't you? Perhaps you could go further and arrange accommodations and transportation to and from the gig. You could then take a cut of each element that you have organized.

I am sure there are many other activities that you can think of that could generate commission by leveraging the spending power of your fan base. All you have to do is figure out what these opportunities are and negotiate a cut of the action (or rather, get your manager, who will be taking 20% of all your income anyway, to negotiate a cut of the action).

Songwriting Royalties

If you write a song, and it is used (that is, recorded or performed), then you are due royalties from a number of areas. In particular, you are due:

- Mechanical royalties, which are royalties from sales of CDs, DVDs, and the like

- Performance royalties when your music is performed live or broadcast

The amount of the royalties depends on the territory, the type of license that is issued for the use of your music, and whether you have entered into any deals to share your income with anyone else or to allow them to pay you less than the going rate.

You've probably heard many urban myths about songwriters making a fortune. Although not necessarily based on fact, there is a potential for songwriters to make a lot of money. Two of the main reasons for the earning capacity of songwriters are:

- There are many outlets (for instance, there are many radio stations that play records).

- With certain exceptions, there are no clawbacks against songwriting earnings. The main clawback is a practice adopted in the US called *controlled composition clauses*, whereby record labels restrict the amount of earnings a songwriter can make from releasing his or her own songs.

Let's look at songwriting royalties in a bit more detail, starting with mechanical royalties.

How Much Do I Get from Writing Songs? Mechanical Royalties

There are two main approaches to calculating mechanical songwriting royalties (royalties that arise from CDs, DVDs, and other sound recordings of your songs). In very broad terms, there is one approach taken in the US and Canada and another approach taken in the rest of the world. Naturally, each separate jurisdiction will have its own quirks.

US and Canada Mechanical Royalties

I'll use US figures for this example and will ignore the effects of controlled composition clauses. If you want to know more about this clawback, then check out Donald Passman's book. (If you haven't already seen the references to this book, then check out the links on my website.)

In the US the songwriter (or writers) may get paid 9.1 cents per track on a CD. This royalty is paid for each CD sold. Therefore, if you have written songs on a CD that sells 100,000, you will get paid $72,800 (100,000 × 8 × $0.091). I say "may" get paid, not "will" get paid because this is the statutory (compulsory) rate.

The statutory rate is payable in certain circumstances. One of those circumstances is *not* the first recording of a song. Therefore, on first recording, the record label can negotiate a separate deal and screw you to the ground. However, the statutory rate does give you a yardstick to see how much you aren't being paid.

Video royalties can be individually negotiated (although again, controlled composition clauses do come into play).

Rest-of-the-World Mechanical Royalties

Much of the rest of the world operates a system in which royalties are paid on the sale price of the CD or DVD. Let me use the UK as an example.

In the UK, songwriting royalties at the rate of 8.5% of wholesale (or 6.5% of retail) price are paid to songwriters. Where the CD contains more than one song, each song gets a pro-rata share (so if there are 10 tracks, then each song gets 0.85% of wholesale (or 0.65% of retail).

The rates are the same for videos and DVDs, although there are some rate reductions in certain circumstances, depending on the nature of the content of the DVD. For details of the varying rates, check to the website of the Mechanical-Copyright Protection Society (www.mcps.co.uk).

How Much Do I Get from Writing Songs? Performance Royalties

Performance royalties arise when your music is performed or played in public. There are many sources of performance royalties; the main sources are:

- Radio
- Television
- Internet
- Live performances
- Public playing of your music (for instance, if your CD is played in a bar)

The amount you get paid from each of these sources will depend on the venue of the performance. With most sources, there is a vaguely scientific attempt to attribute the extent to which your music has been played. The income this will generate will then depend on how that source pays royalties.

Some sources pay a set fee according to how many minutes of music are used—this fee can then be allocated to give you a share of the distributed income. Other sources pay a more generalized license. Again, this license fee can be allocated to give each songwriter a share of the income that relates to songs that he or she has written.

To put it bluntly, someone somewhere does a calculation and pays you money. Unless you are very wealthy, you are going to be hard-pressed to challenge the payment that you receive.

Collecting Songwriting Royalties

Songwriting royalties are collected by a range of collection societies. Most of these societies relate to a specific territory, and some relate only to certain income streams within their territory—for instance, the Performing Right Society in the UK collects income in the UK relating to performed music. The collection societies then remit their payments to music publishers.

It should go without saying that music publishers will then take their cut. Typically, a publisher may take 25%, but they could take anything between 10% and 40%. There are other options—for instance, you can cut out the middleman completely and join each collection society yourself, so royalties will be paid directly to you. Alternatively, you could appoint a collection agent (who, for a fee usually in the region of 10% to 15%, will collect your royalties).

You may also find that if you are using a publisher, your overseas earnings are reduced still further as the publisher will subcontract the collection of publishing rights to a publisher in each jurisdiction. The overseas (in relation to you) publisher will take a share of the income it collects before sending the money to your publisher, who will take another cut and then pay you.

In Chapter 10, I will look at some of the options for collecting royalties with a lesser percentage being deducted. However, don't go leaping ahead expecting a panacea: Music publishers tend to take much less than their record-label counterparts. Also, if you are looking to have your song placed with other artists, then you will probably need someone to go out and find those other artists to record your songs. This is a service where a music publisher really will earn their fees.

There is one other wrinkle you should be aware of: If you are self-releasing your own CD/DVD, then depending on the restrictions in the territory where you are releasing, you may not have to pay yourself. In certain territories (such as the UK), you can avoid paying royalties to yourself by confirming that you are the copyright holder and that you do not require royalties (which will be the case if you are receiving all of the profits from the release). Usually the paperwork to regularize this process needs to be put into place before a license can be granted for the production of the CD (assuming that a license is necessary).

Future Sources of Songwriting Royalties

In the "Future Sources of Income" section later in this chapter, I will look at some of the developing income sources—primarily the income that can be generated from downloads. At the time of writing, this is a developing area. However, one principle seems to be quite clear: The songwriter should also get paid for any downloads.

The major players (iTunes and Napster) as well as some of the other download services have entered into agreements to pay royalties to songwriters in connection with their services. These deals are being reached between the collection societies and the download services on a service-by-service, territory-by-territory basis. To give you an indication of the level of deal that is being struck in the UK, a fairly typical rate is a royalty of 8% (of retail price, less VAT—in other words, sales tax). We will have to see whether this rate holds over the longer term and becomes applicable within other territories around the world.

Gifts

I went to a seminar a few weeks ago. All of the attendees were given goodie bags as we left. Among other things, the bag contained a CD.

There is a market out there for gifts. These may be gifts to customers or these may be gifts to staff. Most of the people who are buying are corporate buyers. These are not people looking to buy a single CD, who will worry about whether it is priced at $14.99 or $15. Typically these are people who have budgets of thousands of dollars who want a lot of your product.

The hard work is finding these people. Needless to say, if you can find an agent to look for opportunities, your life may be easier. However, even with an agent you're going to need to understand the market in which the potential purchaser works. So, for instance, if you produce ambient music, then you may be able to sell your CDs to a health food store to offer as a special gift to their customers. If you're a hard-living heavy-metal band, then the health food store is probably less likely to be interested in your CD.

As well as finding these people, you'll also have to figure out what else you may be able to sell them. For instance, someone in a corporation may be keener to purchase a job lot of your CD if he or she also sees you perform. The idea of a corporate gig may not appeal, but it will provide reasonable money where you can have a fair expectation of being paid.

Income from Your Infrastructure

I briefly want to talk about an area where you can make comparatively easy money. However, this is an area where you can lose your fan base very quickly through greed and crass stupidity. It is also an area where your business practices will be indistinguishable from those of the record companies from whom you have so cleverly run away.

If you have been following some of the suggestions I have set out in this book and have pursued your own course into the music industry, then you will have two things:

- A fan base

- An infrastructure (that is, a means by which you can create product and get that product to your fan base)

These are two highly valuable business assets. However, you may find that these two business assets are being underutilized. *Underutilized* is a business term which broadly translated means "somewhere where we can easily earn more money."

Before we go any further, let me refer you back to Chapter 4 and remind you about the expectations of your fan base.

Okay. If you've read and have heeded the messages of the earlier chapter, then I'll continue.

One way you can make more money is by selling more things to your fan base. You will find that you can only create a finite amount of product (and there is a point at which most of your reasonable fans will feel that they have enough of your stuff). However, your fan base will be open to purchasing music and merchandise from other people.

So, for instance, here are some of the things you could do to generate income from your fan base:

- Sell CDs made by other artists. For instance, if you swap gigs with another act, you could also swap CDs. If you give each other a certain number of (non-returnable) CDs, any you sell would then be direct profit for you. Done with some care, this could also work as a service for your fan base.

- You could help other acts to record and release their own CDs. The risk and the reward you take for being involved in this activity would be up to you. However, you have a range of options, from working as a purely benevolent facilitator to becoming a record label releasing other people's product.

- Alternatively, you could find other acts who have recorded and pressed their own CDs and help them with distribution and order fulfillment.

When you start looking at the options, you will find that there are many ways you can generate income from your infrastructure. However, before you move ahead too quickly, do remember that you are taking very different sorts of risks and risks that you may not fully understand, so please proceed with caution.

Future Sources of Income

I've looked at the main sources of income that are available now. However, we are living in a changing world in which new sources of income are becoming available.

I am always deeply skeptical of any predictions of the future because they will always be wrong, but I do want to look at one or two areas where there is pressure for change at the time of writing, which may have significant implications for musicians' incomes. In particular, I want to look at the source of income from downloads (both conventional downloads and cell (mobile) phone ringtone downloads). This is particularly important for the musician who does not have a contract with a major record label, because it is an area where the independent musician can compete on a similar basis.

It looks likely that CD sales will continue to fall, and online distribution will become an increasingly significant source of income. However, there are many different ways that people could pay for the music that they receive over the internet. As the online market becomes more dominant, there will be a lot more arguments, with companies looking to take any action they can to increase market share and cut out competitors.

There are probably four possible outcomes. A final solution may contain a combination of one or more of these options.

Paid Downloads

An example of a business that works with paid downloads is iTunes. The process is simple: You are charged for each track you download (sometimes with a discount for albums). Once the track has been downloaded, you can upload it to your iPod, and you are permanently licensed to listen to the track. The process is very simple and straightforward. iTunes charges a fee of approximately 34% for sales through its store; the balance is paid directly to the record label. In addition, a royalty of 8% is paid to publishers in respect of songwriting royalties. (This 8% is deducted from the earnings retained by Apple.)

However, everything may not be well in the world of iTunes. For a start, apparently Apple doesn't make profits on iTunes. In many ways, this is not surprising. iTunes was set up to provide a source of material for iPods, and in this respect, it has worked very well. Apple was rather surprised that iTunes has become as popular as it is.

Although iTunes does not generate much revenue, Apple is being challenged on a number of fronts. iTunes is currently in a monopoly position in a number of areas—for instance, you can only purchase iPod downloads from iTunes store. No other downloads are compatible with iPods. This practice is being challenged under European and US competition (anti-trust) laws in a number of areas. There is also the problem of pricing discrepancies. For instance, downloads are currently more expensive in the UK than they are in France, so this practice is being investigated by the European Union.

I'm not sure how this will end up, but history teaches us that monopolies do tend to get broken up, so I'm sure there will be some loosening in the market. A more flexible approach may give more opportunities, but is also likely to shave margins even thinner.

Subscription Services

Now that it has been reborn as a legal download service, Napster is offering all the downloads you could want—currently you can download around 2,000,000 tracks. There is, of course, a catch: You have to pay a monthly subscription fee (currently $9.95 to download to a PC only or $14.95 to also be able to load onto an MP3 player), and if your subscription lapses, you can't access your music.

Napster is not the only subscription service, but it is one of the market leaders, and it does offer many other services (such as the facility to burn tracks to CD so you can access them after your subscription ends). You can also buy individual tracks with Napster (in the same manner that you can with iTunes).

One downside to all of these services is that they are not compatible with iPods. However, as noted a moment ago, this is due to restrictions imposed by Apple. I'm sure Napster and the like would love to provide iPod-compatible content.

At the time of writing, Napster had recently secured a deal with publishers in the UK to pay songwriting royalties. There is a similar arrangement in the US. The fees for tracks that are sold (through Napster Lite) are similar to those that are paid by Apple and other iTunes-style services.

The fees can vary depending on a number of factors (and several of these factors can affect income arising from Napster Lite and iTunes-style paid download services too).

- As exchange rates fluctuate, the fees remitted from overseas services will vary.

- There are different fee rates for streaming and conditional/tethered downloads (downloads that take place while a subscription is being paid but which are not accessible if the subscription is cancelled).

- Napster offers free web-streaming service, which is limited to five listens by any particular user. This service generates lower fees (usually a fraction of a cent).

In broad terms, the income from Napster usually works out at around one or two cents per listen or stream. However, the fees for conditional downloads under their subscription services are somewhat more complicated.

To calculate the fee that is paid to the holder of the sound recording copyright, Napster creates a pool of money. This is essentially its income over a period less its expenses (for instance, the expenses of running the business, including credit card fees, the cost of paying the songwriter levies, plus an element of profit). This pool of money is then shared between everyone whose track is downloaded over the period that the pool of money has been earned.

All conditional downloads or streams (regardless of how or where they originate) are paid based on a proportion of that record company's artists' plays in relation to all of the streams that took place through the Napster service. In other words, the payout budget is set on the basis of Napster's income over a period, and all that then fluctuates is the proportion of that pool of money to which you may be entitled.

Free Downloads, Advertising Funded

At the time of writing, I am unaware of a fully operational arrangement where downloads are free and are funded by advertising. However, SpiralFrog (www.spiralfrog.com) has announced it is going to start offering this service. As yet, it is not clear how the advertising content will be delivered to the listeners. Nor is it clear what revenues will be paid to the copyright holders. Hopefully by the time this book is published, the service will be live, and all of these questions can be answered.

The notion of free music is appealing. In particular, this notion may be appealing to younger music fans who do not have a credit card. (Access to a credit card is a prerequisite for buying music legally over the internet.) I am sure that SpiralFrog will not be the only company offering this form of service.

"Free" Downloads with a Levy

Several jurisdictions around the world have implemented, or have considered implementing, a levy on blank tapes and/or blank CDs. The logic for this levy is that the only purpose that a purchaser of the blank media would realistically put the tape/CD to would be to copy copyright material. The levy is then distributed by the collection societies.

Many people have advocated a similar levy being raised in the digital age. Two targets have been suggested for this levy:

- Internet service providers (ISPs)
- Digital playback devices (such as iPods and MP3 playback devices)

These two targets are commonly identified since it is perceived that their businesses have grown rich on the back of illegal downloads. (Indeed, many see that these companies use illegal downloads as a marketing tool.)

Although a levy on ISPs and hardware is attractive for many reasons, it is questionable whether it will happen. If nothing else, there will be strong resistance from the ISPs and hardware manufacturers. Added to this, the notion of getting every major jurisdiction to implement legislation to ensure that this form of levy could be raised seems quite unlikely. (Just think how difficult it is to get international cooperation on matters of terrorism—do you think governments are going to work hard to get cooperation on music use?)

Due to the digital nature of the product, without an international solution, this route is unlikely to be workable. For instance, if Germany were to adopt this form of levy, and therefore all music in Germany were to effectively become "free" (subject to an ISP/hardware levy), then logically, German citizens would buy their hardware outside of Germany, and the rest of the world would try to source their downloads from Germany (because they would be free).

Your Own Download Solution

Just because there are many commercial download services, that doesn't mean you shouldn't adopt your own system. You could adopt an off-the-shelf solution for selling digital goods. For instance, the provider PayLoadz (www.payloadz.com) offers a simple way to sell digital goods online. This approach can be readily integrated into your website and works well with PayPal.

Alternatively, you could commission some custom programming on your website and come up with your own arrangement for selling your tracks and for ensuring that you get paid immediately.

Ringtones

I've already mentioned that I find this market a highly bizarre one. However, my views probably tell you more about my innate conservatism than they do about market economics. Whatever my views, we must accept the phenomenon of cell (mobile) phone ringtones where customers are happy to pay two, three, or even four times more for a short clip that plays when someone calls them on their phone than they would pay for a download that can be played on their iPod or MP3 player.

Many people believe that royalties from cell (mobile) phone ringtones will replace CD sales as the main source of income for music makers around the world.

One other aspect that should be acknowledged is that ringtones are becoming popular in markets that are not traditional music markets. For instance, India has approximately 50 million phone subscribers. However, it has a population of 1 billion people, which, to put it in context, makes it three times the size of the US and 16 times the size of UK.

By the way, when I talk about India as being a nontraditional music market, please do not misconstrue my comment. Music is an important and significant part of Indian culture, especially through its gift to the world: Bollywood cinema. The only point I am trying to make is that to date, it has not necessarily been a country where non-Indian artists would look to sell their music.

At the moment, the royalties generated from ringtones are a bit of a mishmash of arrangements. Some royalties are negotiated on a license-by-license basis. In other territories, there is a prescribed rate. For instance, in the UK, the MCPS (*Mechanical-Copyright Protection Society*) has set a rate for the use of music on mobile phones. This rate is the greater of:

- 10% of the gross revenue received by the licensee

- 10 pence (approximately 20 cents)

Under the first option, a fee of 45 pence (90 cents) could be generated on a ringtone costing £4.50 ($9). That compares well with the income that could be generated from a download from iTunes, where a royalty of just over 50 pence ($1) may be paid. Indeed, if you convert sales from iTunes' US store to sterling, then the ringtone will make more than the income from iTunes.

However, much like the income from iTunes and the other download sites, the record labels are treating ringtone sales as if a physical product has been sold. As with downloads, many labels are making the same deductions as if a physical product had been sold (for instance, for container charges, even though there was no packaging) and will then pay a royalty on the income.

However, this is a growing market and a developing source of income. As the cost of entry to the market continues to decrease, I am sure that there will be more competitive ways for musicians to get their music out to this market.

Sources of Finance

If you were thinking about opening a sweet shop, you would probably consider getting a loan. So if you're going to run your music career as a business, why not raise some finance to fund it?

If you genuinely believe in what you're doing, then it would be a reasonable business decision to finance your business with a loan. However, many banks may perceive that you are too much of a risk and so would decline your application. I now want to look at some of the options for raising money and some of the practicalities around this action.

If you are going to borrow money, then the person you borrow from will want to make a profit. This is not an unreasonable attitude. Therefore, to borrow money you are going to have to put a business proposition to the other party that explains how you will make money and, therefore, how they will make money. In putting forth this proposition, it is important that you understand how the lender's/investor's business is structured and how they make money.

What Are You Getting? What Are You Giving Up?

There are two main forms of finance:

- Loans
- Equity

The difference between the two is significant.

Loans

With a loan, you borrow money. Your only obligation is to pay back the money that you have borrowed, with interest. Typically the lender will not have anything to do with the running of your business—all they will want from you is timely repayment.

A lender may ask for security (particularly if you are perceived as a high risk, which you are almost certain to be). The purpose of the security is to give the lender an asset that it can sell to raise money if you do not repay your loan. The security may be a business asset (which could include your copyrights) or a personal asset (such as your home).

A lender will make money by charging interest on the loan.

Equity

When you sell the equity in your business to an investor, you sell part (or all) of your business.

As a creative person, there are huge implications in selling part of your business. You will be selling rights to the income that arises from your copyrights. In addition, your investor will then have same rights as the other shareholders and so, for instance, will be able to influence strategy.

To sell equity, you would probably need to structure your business as a company with shares (although this may not be necessary). This company would then need to become the legal owner of the rights to your income—I would expect the investor would want this to be *all* sources of income (including recordings, publishing, merchandising, and so on) or as many sources as possible. You would hold some shares, and the investor would hold some shares.

An equity investor will make money by selling his shares in your business. In essence, the investor will not expect to make any money until he sells his shares. When he does sell his shares, he will look to get back his original investment and some profit. Typically, the level of profit will be much higher than the level of interest that you would pay on a loan.

You will hear equity investors talking about their "exit strategy." This strategy is the process by which they will sell their shares (hopefully for a profit). A concern for the equity investors is who will buy their shares. Unless the potential investor can see that there will be a reasonable prospect that someone will buy their shares when they want to get out and leave your business, then they are unlikely to invest.

Although you are selling rights to the income that derives from your copyrights, equity investors differ from record companies and music publishers in a significant way: The equity investor will always look for a time when the deal ends and he can sell his shares. Record companies and music publishers will often hold the copyright until the end of the copyright period (which, in the case of certain copyrights, can be 70 years after the death of the creator).

Initial Financing

When you are first starting out, you are unlikely to find any bank or other financial institution that will lend you money. This is not unreasonable—you have no track record and probably have no assets to offer as security to back any loan.

Accordingly, if you need money you will need to raise it from:

- Your own resources (so if you're not independently wealthy, you will need to get a job, even if that means flipping burgers at McDonald's)

- Family

- Friends

This may sound like a fearfully unscientific way to raise capital. However, this is the way that many businesses start.

Taking money from family and friends should make you aware of the risks you are taking. If you can't repay your debts, then it will be your family and your friends who are out of pocket due to your stupidity.

Initial financing of this form can take the form of loans (where repayment may or may not be demanded) or equity.

The Fan Base as a Source of Finance

A unique source of financing could be your fan base.

Marillion (who are featured in Chapter 14) borrowed money from their fans to finance an album. The band was smart and didn't structure the borrowing as a loan. Instead, they asked fans to preorder the album 12 months before release. (Note: The band was quite honest about what they were doing. Fans weren't left expecting a CD to turn up any day when, in fact, it had yet to be recorded.) Using their loyal fan base, the band encouraged 12,000 fans to preorder the CD. At the current CD price, this number of sales could generate income of around £100,000 or $200,000.

Banks

Once you have a viable business, banks will consider loaning you money. In addition to its conventional form, in which a bank will lend you money, loans can take many different forms, which may include an overdraft facility and factoring (where the bank will advance you against invoices you are waiting to be paid).

If you want a loan, don't just go to your nearest branch and ask for a loan. Instead, you need to find a bank with a specialized creative industries department, where there are people who will understand your business. While your business is small (in the bank's eyes), a specialized creative industries department may not want to deal with you. If this is the case, they should be able to recommend another part of the bank that can deal with you more sympathetically.

Banks provide loans and do not make equity investments.

Business Angels and Private Investors

Business angels and private investors are essentially the same beast, although they may behave slightly differently. Try not to get too hung up on the terminology since anyone can apply either of these labels to themselves. People who apply an "angel" tag to themselves usually like to be thought of as being more benevolent and less money-grabbing. For this section, I will use the term "private investor" to refer to both types of investors.

Private investors are individuals who are happy to buy equity in small companies and to support the companies in other more practical ways—for instance, by helping with the finances or marketing. These investors do not necessarily expect to see a return on their investment in the short term but will usually hope to sell their shares at some point. However, they may also be interested in the business and enjoy the kudos that come from being associated with their investment.

Accordingly, they may not be quite so aggressive and demanding about their exit strategy.

You may also find some private investors who are companies. It's unlikely that many companies would want to invest in your business; however, I am mentioning this for completeness.

Venture Capital

Venture capitalists are equity investors who specialize in investing in higher risk businesses that often do not have a long track record.

Venture capitalists will expect to make a return that is a multiple of their original investment and will expect to see this return over a comparatively short period of time (perhaps three to seven years). Unlike some private investors, venture capitalists will need a very definite exit strategy.

Venture capitalists look for businesses that have very good growth potential and that can produce an ongoing stream of income. The chances of getting an investment from a venture capitalist are practically nonexistent, but don't let that stop you if you have a solid business. However, unless you can demonstrate that your business has immense growth potential, you will not get any venture capital interest.

Business Partners

You may well find that your business partners can be a useful form of finance; however, this will very much depend on the nature of your business. For instance, a record company may be interested in investing in your business in order to gain a share of your income from areas where it may not usually receive income (such as merchandising).

When you first start your business, you are unlikely to have any business partners, so this will not be a useful avenue for you to pursue. However, as your business grows and you develop more business relationships, you should look for financing opportunities. It should go without saying that if you sell your rights (for instance as part of a record deal or a publishing deal), then a large part of your business will already have gone, and you won't be able to sell an interest to another business partner.

What Sort of Investment Should I Go For?

You may have finished reading the last section and be sitting there scratching your head, not really knowing how to go forward. Raising financing is a highly complex subject, so let me give you my overly simplistic view about the options you should consider.

- First (with thanks to Polonius), neither a borrower nor a lender be. If you are able to survive without borrowing, do. Borrowing costs money and so reduces your income. (The same principle is also true for investment.)

- If you need to raise financing, then follow the simplest course. This will usually involve taking out a loan of some variety. If you take out a loan, then get the smallest loan you can and combine it with more flexible sources of income (such as an overdraft or money borrowed from family and friends).

- Be very wary about any equity investment. You are selling something very valuable (which, if you make it to the big time, will be worth an awful lot more). If you are dealing with private investors, they understand a lot about investment and very little about the music business.

- The Marillion idea of seeking funding from the fan base is interesting and may be appealing. However, you need a very loyal fan base to raise sufficient funds, and then you need to deliver a truly remarkable product. Marillion did this; not everyone can. If you get it wrong, you'll probably never see any of your fan base ever again.

Also, take some time to consider the situation from the investor's/lender's perspective and look at the returns they will be expecting. Take a look at Figure 9.6. This graph shows how over time the value of a typical growing business and the risk associated with a business may change.

At different stages of a company's development, the different growth/risk profiles will make your business attractive to different investors/lenders. As far as your career goes, you are unlikely to form a company that goes on to be traded on a recognized stock exchange. However, if your business grows, especially if you leverage the benefits of your infra-structure, you may find yourself listed on a recognized stock exchange one day.

You are also unlikely to be able to sustain the level of growth that will make you attractive to venture capitalists. Therefore, this source of financing is unlikely to be of interest to you. However, this may not be a bad thing because you may find that getting involved with this sort of business doesn't fit well with a music career.

You are likely to stay in the area where you want loans and perhaps some private equity. This is not a bad thing: Many businesses remain at this level, especially when the owners want to stay involved and live a certain "non-corporate" lifestyle, and they can make a comfortable living. (Indeed, you may often hear these businesses referred to as "lifestyle" businesses.)

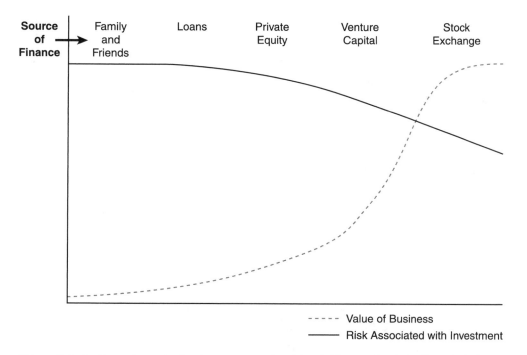

Figure 9.6 As the value of a business grows, its risk profile tends to decline slightly, and the form of investment that would be suitable changes.

Drawing Up a Business Plan

If you are going to borrow money from anyone or seek an investment, then you will need a business plan.

The point of the business plan is to demonstrate:

- How you intend to run your business

- How the lender/investor is going to make money from his participation in your business

Main Headings in Your Business Plan

The main headings you are likely to see in a business plan include:

- An executive summary. This is your opportunity to explain (in less than a page—lenders/investors lose interest quickly) why a lender should lend or an investor should consider investing. The one thing you don't need to do is tell them anything about your business—just focus on the profit they can make!

- A description of your business. This is your chance to set out who you are and what you do, and to describe the products you offer and plan to offer.

- The marketing and sales strategy. This is your opportunity to talk about your fan base and how this group of people can be (and are being) converted into an income stream. You should talk about how you nurture and grow your fan base.

- The team running your business. Here you need to set out the credentials of the people who are running the business and your business partners. You should also mention your future plans for other people you want to work with to further your business objectives.

- Your operations—in other words, the details of how you run your business. Here you should include details of your premises, how your products are produced, and how your products are sold and delivered to your customers/fan base.

- Financial forecasts. As you might expect, this is one of the key aspects of your business plan and is your opportunity to bring all of the strands of your business together to paint a picture of your financial status and projected financial status.

Assumptions

In any business plan, you'll have to make assumptions. It stands to reason—you're looking into the future.

Most investors expect a business plan to look forward five years. The projections about the first two years should be as realistic as possible. It is understood that the next three years are based on educated guesses, and you have to use certain assumptions.

Whatever assumptions you use, these should be documented and justified. This serves two purposes. First, it allows the potential investor to understand the basis of the projections you are giving him. Second, it is your opportunity to demonstrate your grasp on your business.

If you put in dodgy, unsubstantiated assumptions, you'll make yourself into a laughingstock. For instance, if you're selling CDs to 1,000 fans per year, then some increase may be acceptable. If you suggest that in year four you'll sell 1 million CDs (in other words, sales will increase a thousand-fold by the fourth year), then you'll just look stupid and/or money-grabbing, unless you have some real evidence to back these claims.

The Need to Suffer Pain

Anyone looking to invest in your business will need to know that you are committed. Not only will they need to know, but they will need this demonstrated through your actions. There are two things you can do here.

First, you can demonstrate that you have invested heavily in the business, so you will take a substantial loss if it fails. (Potential investors will see this, rightly, as a very strong motivator for you.) Second, you will need to minimize the amount of earnings you are drawing from the business. If it looks like you need an investment to fund your lifestyle, then the investors will get nervous and walk away.

Costs

One of the advantages of the conventional route in the music business (in other words, signing up with a manager, publishing company, and major record label) is that everything is done for you. All you have to do is focus on your music (and the associated duties, such as writing music, recording music, and promoting your music). If you need a present for your husband/wife/girlfriend/boyfriend/son/daughter and so on, then you will probably have "people" who will do this for you (at least once you reach a certain level). If you need transportation, then a limousine will be provided. You will find that you can live a very pampered life.

The downside to this pampered lifestyle is that you will be paying a lot of money for it. Not only that, but you will have virtually no control over the costs that are being incurred in your name. As most of the examples in this chapter have demonstrated, when you are on a royalty, all of the expenses are taken out, and then you get what's left.

This is one of the reasons for the clichéd situation in which a successful musician is living an extravagant lifestyle one day, and then is destitute the next.

Much of the money that is deducted from the income generated by a musician, before the musician receives his of her royalty (if any), is used to meet expenses at various points down the chain. For instance, it may look as if a record label takes a huge chunk of an artist's earnings (and it does); however, the record company will have made a huge investment and will have considerable expenses that need to be met, and these expenses need to be paid from somewhere. The only source of income is the earnings you generate, so the expenses will be met from there. Unfortunately, that is the way of the world. You can rail against the capitalist system all you like, but until someone comes up with a better solution, that's what we're stuck with.

The costs a record company has to meet are significant. I want to look at these in more detail. I want to focus on these costs for two reasons:

- First, so you can understand some of the expenses that a record company may incur to get your CD into the stores (and then into your fans' homes).

- Second, if you are going to follow your own path and release your own CDs, then you will have to incur many of these costs, although hopefully you will be more modest in your spending.

Record Label Expenses

One of the most significant costs a record label will have is its staffing cost. A&R people need bonuses for luring you, executives need bonuses for seeing your project through, and the chief financial officer needs a bonus because of the work he or she will have done keeping track of everyone else's bonus. Seriously, people cost a lot of money, so I have separated out this topic in the next section ("The Cost of Hiring Staff").

Before we leave the subject of people costs, let me remind you of one thing. In large, multinational corporations (which many record labels are), executives' bonuses are based on financial results, not on artistic endeavors. Therefore, any executive is going to have his or her bonus based on how much money he or she can squeeze out of your product, not on whether your new CD (or whatever you are producing) is any good. The only time an executive will genuinely be worried about the quality of your product will be when he or she assesses whether it will sell (since a product that doesn't sell won't generate any income).

Please don't look at these comments as a damning indictment of the record industry. This is how all large corporations work: The music industry is no better and no worse than any other industry (although as you have seen, it does have some particularly archaic practices).

Property Costs

Picture the situation: You're a hot new band, and you have two record labels interested in you. One has its offices in the heart of town. These are the plushest offices you could imagine—the latest designer furniture in the lobby, hand-stitched carpets, and receptionists manicured to within an inch of their lives.

When you get through to the meeting rooms, the tables are inlaid with hand-carved detail, and the chairs are covered in the softest leather you have ever felt. Needless to say, the audio-visual facilities are to die for.

The executives who show up to meet you are dressed in smart (but casual) expensive designer suits. Their jewelry (both the men and the women) is discreet, but you know it is about as expensive as you can get.

Now think about another label with its offices about an hour out of town. Unfortunately, you're an hour out of town too, but in the other direction. When you get to the offices, you find that the street on which they are located was recently used as a set in a film about a Victorian strangler.

Inside, the offices are painted white, and the carpets have seen better days, showing signs of wear. There are no meeting rooms, so you all congregate in the A&R guy's office, which is a mess, piled high with demo CDs from other acts. The A&R guy apologizes for the mess, but doesn't apologize for the state of his Metallica 1997 tour T-shirt.

Okay, which of these two labels impresses you more? Which label says "success?"

You might lie to yourself and say you won't be impressed by the flashy offices. However, when you have been in a position to make a side-by-side comparison, you will always find that the plush office leaves an impression.

Record labels know this and know that they can intimidate artists and their managers with impressive offices—think of it as the building equivalent of power dressing. Accordingly, record labels will always spend money on their premises.

Even if you don't want to have the most impressive office in town, if you are going to follow your own course, you will need some premises, and premises come with a lot of expenses. At a minimum, you are likely to have to incur the following expenses in connection with any property that you use for your business:

- The cost of purchase or renting (including taxes and lawyers' fees)
- Local property taxes
- The cost of amenities, such as water and electricity

- Insurance costs, both for the property itself and against anyone injuring himself or herself while in the property

- Maintenance costs, which may be as low as a door hinge or a coat or two of paint, but could get as high as extending or rebuilding part of the building

Computer Costs

Record labels spend a lot of money on their computer systems. There are many elements to these systems, including the computers themselves (both desktop computers and servers), licenses for the software that runs on the computers, cabling and network gizmos, a bomb-proof backup system that cannot fail, staff to run all of this stuff, and training for all of the staff on how to work the computers. This is before a cent has been spent on customized programming for the accounting and royalty payment systems.

Even using free software (such as Linux), you're going to have to spend money installing and running a computer system.

Taxes

Record labels get hit with a range of taxes. These include taxes on the profits that the label makes, employment/social taxes (such as National Insurance Contributions in the UK, which are mentioned in greater detail in Chapter 11), and sales taxes (such as VAT). Some of these charges get levied on a regular basis (for instance, corporate taxes and employment taxes), while others (such as sales taxes) are incurred as part of the daily business of the label. (For instance, manufacturing costs will include sales tax if this is charged in the jurisdiction within which the record label is operating.)

There's an old cliché that the three certainties in life are birth, death, and taxes. However, this is only partially true. At the time of writing, birth and death are both certain, and while the need to pay taxes is absolute, the amount that will be paid in taxes is far from certain. If you are smart, there's a lot you can do to avoid taxes.

At this point, let me add a few caveats and some other more general warnings. First the caveat: This is a book that offers some ideas about building a successful music career in the 21st century. It is most definitely not a tax-planning manual, and it does not seek to offer any advice on matters of tax. If you are looking for tax advice, then talk to a suitably qualified professional who actively practices in this area.

Second, a more general warning: There is a difference between tax avoidance and tax evasion. Let me look at the position in the UK for a moment, where tax avoidance is legal. However, tax evasion is not. With tax avoidance, you arrange your affairs in a manner that provides the most favorable tax position to you. With tax evasion, you lie and cheat and generally break the law. Similar principles apply in most jurisdictions around the globe.

The line between tax avoidance and tax evasion is a fine one (and can sometimes be quite blurred), so again, I recommend you talk to a suitably qualified professional in the jurisdiction in which you will be generating income. You should also note that there will be consequences if you restructure your affairs to avoid tax. A professional adviser will be able to tell you about the consequences and discuss whether they are significant for you.

So with the warnings out of the way, here are some of the things you can do to avoid taxes (and these are things that companies do in practice):

- Reduce profits. This may seem bizarre; however, it is quite logical. With lower profits, there will be less tax. There are several ways to reduce profits; the main one is to spend more money, which you can do by paying shareholders a dividend, paying expenses, or paying staff more. There are some corporations who will set up an intricate web of intra-company charges, the effect of which is to leave any profit in a jurisdiction which has a very low tax rate.

- Pay people less. You may not think that employers need an excuse to pay their staff less. However, given the level of employment-related taxes, employers do have a legitimate interest in minimizing their payroll costs. However, sometimes the reduction in salary can be balanced by paying staff in other ways.

For instance, if you reduce someone's wages in the UK and then give them goods to the value of the reduction in their salary (or to a similar value), you can (in certain limited circumstances) avoid employment taxes.

Dividends

I briefly mentioned shareholders. By their nature, corporations have shareholders (people who own the business). Shareholders tend to come in two forms:

- People and institutions (such as banks, insurance contributions, and retirement funds) who own shares in companies

- Other companies, where one company will be a subsidiary of another company

Whatever the nature of the shareholders, they have one thing in common: They want to be paid for owning shares in the company. The way that companies pay their shareholders is by distributing an element of their profits. This distribution is usually called a *dividend*, and its amount is determined by the executives of the company. (You can guess what the shareholders do to any executives who do not provide a suitable dividend.) Shareholders also expect to see the value of their holding go up, so that when they come to sell their shares, the shares will be worth more than the shareholders paid for them.

If you set up your own business, then you will have shareholders implicitly or explicitly. You will be one of the key shareholders. Although you will probably (at least initially) be saved from the rapacious greed of external shareholders, you will need to extract money from the business (if nothing else to pay for things such as food and shelter). How you extract the money (for instance, whether you take a salary or a dividend) will have implications for you and your business. I've said it before and I'll say it again: You need to talk to someone about the significance of those implications for your personal situation.

Getting the Product to the Customer

There are other costs that a record label will incur that are directly related to your product. The main costs are manufacturing, distribution, and marketing. If you self-release a CD, you will incur these costs too, although you may want to spend less than a record label would, and you are likely to employ other distribution options (such as mail order) to a greater extent.

A record label will probably be able to get your CD produced for a lower unit cost than you can. This is because a label will put far more business with a pressing plant than you will and so can negotiate much better deals. Also, a label will expect to sell a lot more CDs than you could and so will get many more CDs pressed. Unless these CDs sell, the record company will not generate any income, so the next step is to get the CDs to a place where they can be sold.

The process by which CDs get from the pressing plant into the stores (whether bricks and mortar or online) is called *distribution*. Distribution always seems such a simple task—you give someone a CD, they sell it—however, there are many factors to be considered. As a first step, a decision needs to be made about the number of CDs to be pressed and how many CDs will be sent to each outlet.

Usually a decision about numbers is driven by the orders received; however, if the label doesn't press enough CDs to meet demand, then it may not be able to get a second order in quickly enough. Conversely, if it presses too many, then it will need to find an outlet to sell its unwanted stock.

Once the numbers have been sorted, the CDs need to be physically transferred. This is partly a logistical exercise and partly a paperwork exercise. For you, the musician, the paperwork is crucial: Each CD that goes into a store constitutes a sale for you. For each sale, you get a royalty. If someone doesn't keep track of the sales, then you won't get what is due to you. The other aspect of distribution is returns. All CDs are 100% returnable. Again, it is crucial that proper records are kept because returned CDs reduce the amount of royalties you will receive.

Advertising

Once your CDs are in the stores, then they need to sell. If they don't sell, they will be returned.

If you're lucky, some people will buy your CD on the basis of the cover. However, how often do you walk into a record store and buy a CD by an artist you've never heard of? My hunch is not very often. If you, as a musician, don't buy other musicians' products without hearing them, what expectation can you have that an average punter will go into a record store and buy your music? It is for this reason that you need a marketing campaign.

Major labels can spend huge amounts on marketing. If TV advertising is involved, it is not unheard of for a label to spend more than 50% of the cost of putting out the CD on advertising. There are, of course, cheaper options, but these may not be as effective as TV advertising. Also, the form of marketing will be largely determined by your audience: If you're a pop act, then TV advertising may be a reasonable choice. However, if you're a heavy metal band, then TV advertising may not work, but touring is far more likely to generate interest.

If you're only intending to sell your CD directly to your fan base (in other words, you are intending to avoid the retailers, whether bricks and mortar or online), then your marketing costs can be contained. However, if you are looking for sales from a wider base and you are hoping to sell your CD through the retailers, then you will need to do some marketing to ensure that your CDs are not all returned.

The Cost of Hiring Staff

There will come a time when you need people to help you in your endeavor. This is good if you like to brag because you will then be able to say, "I'll get my people to call your people." However, in all other ways, hiring people is a really tough thing to do.

Although this chapter is about the economic aspects of the music business, please indulge me for a moment as I mention some of the human aspects.

Most people take up employment because they need money. That is not to say that they can't or don't enjoy their work, or that they wouldn't do some work if they weren't paid. However, on balance, given the choice between working and not working, many people would choose not to work.

Some people will work for you for free because they want to get close to you as a musician, but on the whole, if someone is going to work for you, then they will expect to get paid. They will use the money you pay them to provide for themselves and their family, and they will make plans for their life on the assumption that you will be a fair employer and the employment relationship will continue.

Their plans may not be big plans—in fact, they are probably going to be very average sorts of plans (perhaps taking the kids to the cinema or going on holiday with the family). There will also be more serious plans, such as paying the mortgage or saving for their retirement.

In return for their service and loyalty, these people will be relying on you to continue to provide a source of income. If this income stops, the knock on effect for your employees and their families could be catastrophic. The impact will be the same, regardless of whether the income stops due to your fault.

Before you hire anybody, please ensure you are confident that you will treat that person as fairly as you can because, quite literally, you will be playing with his or her life.

Hiring people and keeping them on your payroll is a costly exercise and a logistical nightmare. The rest of this section deals with some of the costs you will incur. These are costs that involve direct expense (for instance, paying your staff); indirect expense (for instance, the time you have to spend each month to process paychecks); and your time, which you could otherwise spend making music.

Employment expenses vary according to territory. For instance, in some jurisdictions you are required to provide a certain level of pension contribution in respect of your employees. However, this is not a requirement in all jurisdictions. If you're looking at hiring people and you want to know what requirements apply in your jurisdiction, I suggest you talk to an employment lawyer.

As a general rule of thumb, you should expect any employee's work to generate income for your business of at least three times that employee's pay. The reason for this multiple is that salary only constitutes one third of the expense of employing somebody. Let me elaborate with a more complete list of the expenses of employment:

- The largest expense of hiring someone is likely to be his or her pay. The amount you will need to pay someone is likely to depend on the skills he or she brings. For instance, if you are hiring someone to package up your orders and send them out, you will probably be able to pay less than you would if you were hiring an accountant to work as your business manager.

  At the end of the day, wages are generally set by market conditions, so if you work in a high-wage area (for instance, a capital city), you are likely to have to pay higher wages than you would if you set up in a backwoods area. At the bottom end of the wage scale, you may find yourself caught by the minimum wage that applies in some jurisdictions.

- Coupled with wages, you may have to pay employment taxes or social charges. I have already mentioned National Insurance Contributions, which are the UK's equivalent of these costs. They hit both employees and employers, with employers paying up to 12.8% of earnings as (Secondary) National Insurance Contributions. You can see that when employer's contributions are added to the 11% of earnings that employees pay as (Primary) National Insurance Contributions, this is quite a significant tax.

- In addition to an employee's direct earnings, you will usually also have to pay the employee indirectly by way of benefits. The benefits you have to provide will differ according to the custom and law of the marketplace in which you are operating, as well as the seniority of the employee and the level of desperation you have to hire them. However, other benefits you may have to provide could include a car, pension savings, death benefits, and health insurance.

In addition to the obvious benefits, there are some less obvious benefits that may not have a monetary value for your employee, but will cost you. These include sick leave and holiday vacation.

If you want an illustration of how expensive pension benefits can be, check out the "Pensions and Retirement Funds" section in Chapter 11.

- Another considerable expense associated with employees is the space within which they work. Even if they only have a workspace that is the size of their desk with a bit of room to get a chair in and out, you will find that employees take up a lot of space. This means you will need premises of some sort. Once you get premises, you get a whole heap of new costs (including maintenance and insurance), as well as a whole heap of time wasted (for instance, getting a maintenance person to deal with the blocked sinks in the restrooms).

- As well as needing a space to work, staff will also need tools. The tools they need will depend on the task they are asked to perform. However, it is likely that the tools will include a desk, a computer, a phone, pens, paper, and so on. When you start adding up these costs (along with the training costs to use the tools), and then multiplying them by a number of staff, you will see your costs rise rapidly.

- You will find there is a lot of administration associated with having staff. In fact, you may even find out why corporations have Human Resources departments. When you get to a certain size, then you are likely to have to pay people to look after the other people you have hired.

The sort of administration you are likely to come across includes running a payroll for your staff, so you will have to calculate how much to pay people, deduct their tax and social contributions, deduct anything else you are required to deduct (for instance, child support or a court-imposed payment), and then calculate how much you have to pay in social costs. When tax rates change or you give a pay raise, you will find your administration systems will temporarily be thrown into disarray.

There are many other pieces of administration in which you could get involved. Let me give you one more example of an area that will swallow up time and money: recruitment. You first need to define the task you want undertaken, agree on the role with anyone else who needs to be involved (such as band mates), and agree on the salary, and then you need to look for the person to fulfill the role. In this quest, you may well interview a number of people. The whole process can waste days of your time.

- Having people around will lead to other costs, such as theft and damage caused by your staff. You may also be vicariously liable for the actions of your staff. For instance, if a member of your staff working on your business harms someone else, that person may sue you.

- To cover the financial risk related to the injuries staff may suffer and the damage they may cause while working for you, you may want to take out (and indeed, you may be obliged to carry) insurance against these risks. As you would expect, this is a cost you will have to meet as the employer.

- You may also find there are costs if the relationship with any employee goes sour or his or her performance is simply not up to scratch. If you terminate the employment relationship, you may be obliged to pay a lump sum termination payment, or you may be sued for damages. Sometimes you will find that the cost of hiring a lawyer to fight claims against you exceeds the cost of damages that are being sought, so it may be easier to simply pay the claimant.

This list is not complete; however, I hope it does go some way to illustrating the costs of staffing your operation. It should also explain another reason why it is so expensive to run record labels, publishing houses, and the other businesses associated with the music industry.

10 Building the Team around You

You may be wondering why it has taken so long for me to get to the chapter about building your team. After all, I have mentioned many of the people who will be on your team in several places throughout the book. Added to that, you have probably already figured that one person who can really help take your career to the next level is a manager.

Let me explain by adding one detail that I have yet to explain explicitly. So far I have suggested that you take a businesslike approach to your career in the music industry. However, I am actually going further than that and advocating that you establish your own business. I'm less concerned about whether you decide that the right course for you is to self-release a CD or to go with a major record label. Whatever choice you make for how you get your product to your fan base, I am concerned that you treat your business as a business and ensure it is properly managed.

That doesn't mean you have to become a businessman or business-woman and turn up for work at 9 a.m. every morning (in a suit with a freshly laundered shirt and your umbrella under your arm) and then leave at 5 p.m. It does mean that you need the right attitude, and you need to ensure that if you don't look after the business, then someone else (whom you trust completely) is attending to these details.

Structure of Your Business

There are many ways that you can legally structure your business—for instance, as a sole trader, a partnership, a partnership with limited liability, or a limited liability company. I'm not going to talk about these options here because they are irrelevant to the subject of your career.

Another reason I am not going to talk about the structure of your business is that the options open to you will differ according to your jurisdiction.

If you are serious about your business, then I recommend you get legal and other professional advice because there are many other implications that flow from the decisions you make about structure. In particular, there are issues of tax and personal liability. I will talk more about getting professional advice later in this chapter.

However, I do want to talk about how you structure your business in terms of the roles and responsibilities that people will play in driving your career forward.

Key Functions That Need to Be Performed

Any business has a range of people who will do different things to help the business. Take a look at any business and you will probably find most of these people performing the following functions in one way or another (see Figure 10.1):

- The shareholders (or partners) own the business and are responsible for appointing the board.

- The board sets the strategy for the business.

- The management team implements the strategy set by the board, and each member of the board is accountable for his or her own performance.

- The workforce undertakes the work that makes the money for the business.

- Advisers (such as lawyers or business consultants) offer advice to the board and the management as it is needed. This advice could be on a range of issues, from legal points to matters of strategy.

- Agents are appointed to undertake specific tasks on behalf of a business (for instance, to look after the business's computers).

So how does this apply to you, and where do you fit in?

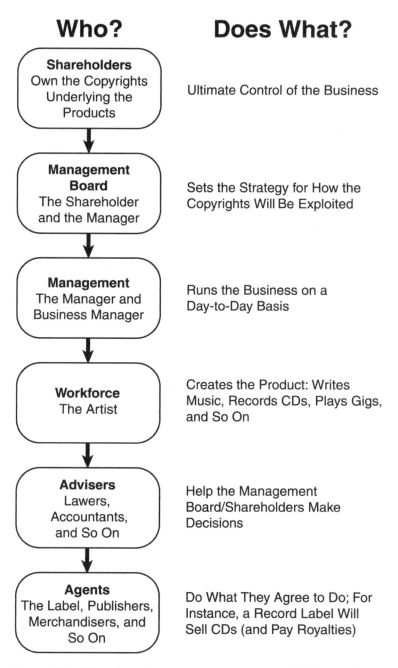

Who?	Does What?
Shareholders Own the Copyrights Underlying the Products	Ultimate Control of the Business
Management Board The Shareholder and the Manager	Sets the Strategy for How the Copyrights Will Be Exploited
Management The Manager and Business Manager	Runs the Business on a Day-to-Day Basis
Workforce The Artist	Creates the Product: Writes Music, Records CDs, Plays Gigs, and So On
Advisers Lawers, Accountants, and So On	Help the Management Board/Shareholders Make Decisions
Agents The Label, Publishers, Merchandisers, and So On	Do What They Agree to Do; For Instance, a Record Label Will Sell CDs (and Pay Royalties)

Figure 10.1 Who does what in your organization? This is a simple structure for organizing a business. See Figure 10.2 for an explanation of how this becomes a practical reality.

Most importantly, you, the musician, are the workforce. As with any business, it is the workforce who will make the money. The function of the management is to ensure that the product created by the workforce is sold for the best possible price and that the systems for selling the product are as efficient as possible to ensure that profits are maximized.

However, you are also the shareholder of the business—this is your business, after all. You should therefore also be an active member of the board setting a strategy to propel your career forward.

Separate the Goals to Be Achieved from How You Achieve Your Goals

Before we go too much further in thinking about the team of people, I want to remind you about the range of choices you have.

There are many different things you can do in many different ways. Your focus should be on what you are trying to achieve financially, as well as from an artistic and marketing perspective. For instance, if you are thinking about producing T-shirts, you may have several aims. These could include:

- Making money from the sale of T-shirts
- Getting as many people as possible wearing your T-shirt in order to raise your profile

There are many ways you could achieve this aim. These options include:

- Ordering some T-shirts printed with your design. (If you like hard work, you can order the stock and printing from different suppliers.) Sell the final product to your fan base directly.
- Using an on-demand service and marketing the T-shirts to your fan base. You may also find that the on-demand service generates a number of sales.
- Ordering some T-shirts and then supplying them to a range of outlets (primarily clothes stores).
- Licensing someone else to produce T-shirts with your logo and to sell the clothing.

Each of the different options will produce different results in terms of financial return to you and the size of the population that is reached with the T-shirts. Some options will realistically only reach your fan base; others are likely to reach lots of people who are not in your fan base.

The options also have differing financial risks from your perspective. As you increase the amount of stock you are holding without having firm orders, you will be increasing your financial risks and increasing the likely costs from storage and other associated costs.

So if you are looking for the lowest financial risk and the widest geographic coverage, you may want to consider licensing, although that option may not be the most immediately appealing. However, do remember that just because you have chosen one option, that doesn't close off the other options—for instance, you could license your product and sell a product directly. (You may even be able to sell your licensee's stock and generate more income than would be generated from the license fee alone.)

The key issue in this example is that the goal (for instance, to get as many people as possible wearing your T-shirt) is different from the method by which the goal is achieved (for instance, licensing). Remember, to have a valid career, you don't have to do everything yourself.

The Right People at the Right Time

Any business will need to expand or contract depending on various factors. For instance, if you run a toy shop, then you may need more staff during the Christmas season. By contrast, if you run a seaside hotel, you could probably need a lot less staff during the winter period (clearly, the staff who aren't wanted in the hotel should go and work at the toy shop).

As a musician with your own business, you don't necessarily need to have staff (that is, people whom you directly employ and for whom you need to deduct tax and social costs from their wages). However, you will probably want a permanent relationship with certain people. For instance, you will want a permanent relationship with your manager— a manager's job should not be seasonal.

Then there are people whose services you will only want on a temporary basis. For instance, if you are going on tour, then you may need to hire a sound engineer for that tour. At the end of the tour the sound engineer would then effectively cease to be an employee. When you next tour, you may hire the same sound engineer again, but the contract would still only last for the length of the tour.

As well as hiring people directly, you may outsource some of your tasks. In this instance, you pay someone else to do something for you. The benefit to you is that you don't have to find someone to undertake the task and, provided you find a suitable service provider, you will be looked after by people whose business is dedicated to performing that task, so you may be able to expect a higher service than if you undertook the task yourself. An example of this arrangement could be if you use a third party to mail out your CDs.

As you will understand, one of the key challenges to running a business is ensuring you bring in the right people for the business needs and that appropriate service providers are appointed. This coordination is one of the key tasks that a manager will perform. If you don't have a manager (or someone fulfilling that function), then much of your day will be spent organizing other people.

First, I want to give an overview of who the team could be. I then want to look at some of the details of what you could expect from your team members and what they can expect from you (in other words, what you are likely to have to pay them).

One point you should note is that you don't necessarily need a separate person to fulfill each of these functions—you just need to ensure that someone has responsibility for ensuring all of the necessary tasks are undertaken.

So Who Does What?

It is crucial to the success of your business that everyone knows what they are meant to be doing and understands what constitutes success.

If you hire a manager, then there is no point in you trying to undertake the functions the manager should be performing. However, although you shouldn't try to do his or her job, you should ensure that the manager does perform as expected. If performance is not up to standard, then you should end the relationship. Think about a business: If an executive isn't performing, he or she gets fired. Why should a manager be any different?

So who should be doing what? Take a look at Figure 10.2 for an example of how the parties work together.

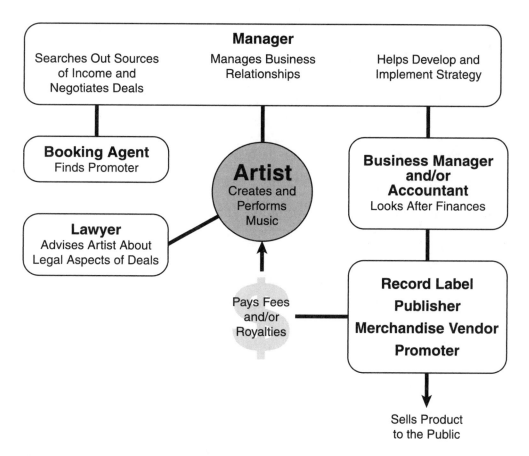

Figure 10.2 The working relationship between the main parties involved in an artist's career.

The Shareholders and the Board

In legal terms, the shareholders (in the broadest sense) are the people who hold the copyrights underlying the products being marketed. So for instance, if you are a band and you all own the copyright to a sound recording (that is marketed as a CD and a download or may be licensed for use as a cell phone ring tone), then you would be a shareholder.

The board is there to represent the interests of the shareholders and to set the strategy for the business. You probably don't need the formality of many corporate board meetings; however, it is important that there is a forum for strategy to be discussed and agreed upon.

The board meeting should be open to more than just shareholders. For instance, your manager should have a lot to say about your strategy. (If he/she doesn't, why did you hire him/her?) You should ensure that he or she is present whenever strategy is being discussed—first for his or her input, and second because this is the person whose role it is to ensure that the strategy is implemented successfully.

The Management Team

The management team will implement the strategy set by the board and will be accountable for their performance to the board. There are two key players whom you need:

- A chief executive. This is the person who is in charge of running your business on a day-to-day basis while you are getting on with making music. This role would usually be filled by your manager (sometimes called a *personal manager*).

- A chief financial officer. This is the person who looks after the commercial aspects of your business and is often called a *business manager*. This person will ensure that you get paid and that you get paid the right amount. Many artists do not have a separate business manager—they leave the function to their personal manager.

I will talk more about managers later in this chapter.

The Workforce

The workforce undertakes the work that makes the money for the business. As a musician, you are the workforce. The creation of music is a pure blue-collar occupation. Each day you will be working at the factory; whether your task is songwriting or playing a gig, your role is to manufacture the product that is then sold.

Advisers

You will need several key advisers to assist you in your career.

Perhaps the first adviser you will need is a lawyer. I am sure you have heard countless tales of young, naïve bands who get ripped off. This tends to happen for two reasons: First, they have little negotiating power, and second, they haven't taken appropriate advice.

Half of this problem is dealt with by finding a lawyer. The other half of the problem is addressed by ensuring you have as much negotiating power as possible. If you are running your career as a business, adopting many of the principles set out in this book, then you will have much more negotiating clout than the average musician.

The other advisers you are likely to need early in your career will include:

- An accountant to advise you on finance and tax matters
- A banker to help provide funds to run your business

Picking the Team

I've outlined the various elements of the team. When building your team, there are several things you need to think about.

Does the Team Work Together?

You need to make sure all of the people in your team work together. You need to ensure that everyone gets along—you don't want two advisers working for you who are suing each other. You also need to ensure that everyone understands the extent of their role—you don't want to pay for two people to perform the same task, and equally you don't want any gaps in responsibilities so that two people can say, "It wasn't my fault," when something goes wrong.

Hiring the Right People

You need to make sure you get the right people. Finding the people is hard enough—making sure you've got the right people when you've found them is even harder. When you're looking for people, ask around and get any recommendations. (If possible, the first people you should talk to are the people who have been recommended more than once.) Don't just look in a directory and hope to pick the right person because you like his or her name.

Once you've got a shortlist, then get references on those people. Talk to their existing clients (and if possible former clients) to get a well-rounded picture of these people's business sense.

Finding the Person Who Actually Does the Work

When you are looking to build a team around you, you may not always be hiring a single person. For instance, if you are taking on a manager, then the manager may have associates. Equally, if you hire a lawyer, then you are probably actually hiring a firm of lawyers. This is a good thing. You want to know that there are other people around to support the person who is working for you.

However, you should be cautious. Many firms will put up a salesperson to bring in new business, and then once your account has been won, they let someone far more junior run the account. Again, this may not be a bad thing—the junior person may be very keen, very talented, and able to dedicate all of his or her waking hours to your business, plus he or she will have the resources of the bigger firm and more experienced colleagues to call upon. However, it may be a bad thing. The junior may be an inept fool.

Whenever you are looking to appoint a new team member, ask who will be working for you. Get to meet that person and make sure he or she is the sort of person you want to work with. If he or she is not, but you still like the organization, then ask to meet someone else who may fit better with you.

Errors and Omissions

What happens if someone else gets something wrong?

For instance, what happens if your accountant makes an error in calculating your tax figures, so you make an incorrect tax return? Nothing, you may think, until your tax authority fines you and audits your books. This is a comparatively minor problem—there could be much bigger problems.

One way to protect yourself against any financial cost is to ensure that your advisers have errors and omissions insurance (often called *E&O insurance* for obvious reasons). This is insurance to protect their business in case they make mistakes. This is good for you because first, they will have funds to be able to compensate you for their mistakes, and second, their business will not collapse if you raise an errors and omissions claim.

It may seem odd to want to ensure that their business does not go down the tubes. If you find any errors, you may want to take your business elsewhere; however, you probably want to ensure that you can extract yourself in a businesslike manner, rather than losing everything because their business has gone into liquidation.

You can expect professional advisers (such as your accountant and your lawyer) to carry errors and omissions insurance. However, you should confirm this. Some of the other parties you deal with may have some form of insurance, but it is unlikely to be as rigorous as that carried by your advisers.

The Shareholders

I want to look at the shareholders. As I indicated earlier, I am using the term "shareholder" in its broadest sense to mean anyone who owns the copyright that underlies a product that is created and anyone who may earn royalties through having sold/licensed their copyright. I am not intending this term to only mean those people who own part of the company if your business is incorporated.

The people who are most likely to be shareholders are:

- The songwriter(s).

- The artist(s)/band members who each own part of the copyright of a sound recording (or visual performance). Clearly if you have signed with a major record company, you are unlikely to own your sound recordings; however, you will have an interest in the royalties generated from these recordings.

You may have other shareholders—for instance, the person who designed your artwork. To run your business efficiently, you may want to buy out other copyrights (such as the artwork).

The nature of music is such that you will almost never create a product on your own without any involvement from another person. You may write a composition with someone else, or you may perform with other musicians who have equal rights to you. Whenever you are collaborating, it is important that all of the shareholders work together. For instance, if you co-write a song and your writing partner then seeks to block its release, not only is this frustrating, but it will stop both of you from earning money.

For this reason, it is important that all shareholders have a common understanding of how their assets are going to be exploited (for the benefit of all shareholders). The most straightforward way to establish and document this understanding is through a written agreement between the shareholders. This could take the form of a band agreement or similar document.

Perhaps the hardest challenge you will face with your co-shareholders is recognizing that you can't fire these people. These will be people with whom you will always have some link (like two divorced parents), so think hard before you go into business with someone else.

The Manager

In the conventional way of thinking, you want to find an experienced manager because these people know the key executives at several record labels and will have credibility with those people. The supposed benefit for you is that the manager can walk into the record label with your demo, and you stand a really good chance of being signed. There's no need to worry that you're a bit of a rough diamond; your manager will be able to help the record company see what they are signing.

There is a lot of truth in this view—or rather, there *was* a lot of truth.

As you might expect, in a changing world, managers are changing too. Many are getting more entrepreneurial rather than being pugnacious bruisers. Recognizing that major record companies are signing less talent and that due to the increasing number of small labels, they can't have a relationship with everyone, managers are now putting a greater emphasis on artist development.

Instead of approaching record companies with a diamond in the rough, managers are approaching record companies with a polished product (an act with an image, a professionally recorded and produced CD, a video, and so on). By taking the development risk and presenting a record company with a product that is ready to be launched, managers are helping recording companies to significantly reduce their risks.

Another reason that the relationship between managers and record companies is now much less significant is that the income artists generate from record companies (as a percentage of total earnings) is now less significant (although you do still need the central product—the music— from which to generate the spin-offs). As we have already seen, there are many more sources of income from which a manager can negotiate deals. This also means that there is much more a manager needs to understand (and, of course, far more for a manager to get wrong).

So that explains something of what managers can do for themselves. What could a manager do to help you?

What Can a Manager Do to Help You?

There are several main areas where a manager can help you. It is easy to suggest that any one of these areas may be more important than the other; however, in practice, when you are looking for a manager, you want someone who can bring all of these strands together (whether on his own or through bringing together a team of people).

Strategy

You may not believe it, but you do need a strategy. You need to understand:

- Where you are going
- How you are going to get there

Strategy in the broadest sense should be discussed and agreed upon at board meetings, and your manager should be there, giving his or her view about the strategies you should be following. However, strategy then needs to be implemented on a day-to-day basis and refined for a particular situation. Your manager should have a firm grasp of this aspect of your business.

Business Administration

You are running a business. Someone should make sure everything that is meant to be happening is.

This means you need someone who understands how business works. That person will need to understand how your income from each and every one of your income source is calculated and when payment can be expected. He or she will also need to take action if the money is not forthcoming. Once you have been in business for a while, you may have hundreds, if not thousands, of sources, so your manager must have robust systems (computer databases, paper filing, and so on) or else you will lose money.

You may well use a business manager (and the role of the business manager is discussed in a moment). If you are using a business manager, then your manager should ensure that the business manager is on top of his job.

Representation

You need someone to go out and find deals and/or create income for you. Your manager should be the person who finds deals, brings them to you, and negotiates the deal. This may be a deal with a record company; it may be a deal with a publisher; it may be a deal with a CD pressing plant; it may be a deal with a merchandiser. It doesn't matter who the deal is with. Your concern is that:

- The deal is good for you (both financially and for your reputation).

- You are being represented in the best light. You don't want a manager who makes promises and threats that may be embarrassing to you.

- There are no side deals that benefit your manager but not you. He or she may have negotiated a good deal for you; however, this counts for nothing if he or she should have negotiated a great deal.

Who Should You Get as a Manager?

Artists often have a dilemma when they consider a manager—whether to go with a more experienced or a less experienced manager.

The advantage of a more experienced manager is, well, experience. You can expect this person to know the business and to be competent. However, if a manager is competent and experienced, then he or she will have other clients, and so the question for you is whether this manager will give you the time you need in order to help you develop your career (if he or she will even consider signing you).

You may also find that, since the experienced manager already has a perfectly adequate source of income, he or she may take a rather laid-back approach to your career. After all, the manager won't starve if you don't get a deal.

The advantage of a less experienced manager is that he or she has everything to prove and everything to lose. You can therefore expect this person to work every hour of every day to further your career. The disadvantage is obvious: A less (or zero) experienced manager has less (or zero) experience.

However, don't dismiss a less experienced manager. If he or she has bucket loads of get-up-and-go and really *can* make things happen, then that person might be just what you need to kick-start your career. If your manager believes in you, then he or she is likely to be happy to work for a greatly reduced fee while you have minimal earnings. If your manager genuinely has the business chutzpah, then he or she will help you to start earning money. If he or she doesn't, then you may wish to end the relationship.

Between the two extremes you will find a range of people. My only suggestion in dealing with these people is beware of anyone whose business and acts are mediocre. Some people can see the good in others, some can see the bad: These people can see mediocrity. They will find the mediocrity in you and convince you that it is what you wanted. If you want a career that is, at best, adequate, knock on these people's door. If you want more, then run screaming if you ever find these people.

What Does a Manager Charge?

Each deal will be different, but as a general rule of thumb, a manager will charge 20% of your gross earnings (that is, 20% of what you earn before any expenses). You may find that there is a commonly accepted figure in your jurisdiction. You shouldn't simply accept any figure, but rather seek to set a figure that is right for you.

Some managers charge less (for instance, 15%), and some will try to charge more. If you have huge earning potential, then you may be able to negotiate below the 15% figure. However, if your earning potential is that great, you've probably got a very successful career already, and you may feel you don't need to read this book.

Many artists have perished on the rock of not understanding the difference between net and gross. These are two technical terms that you must understand because the implications are so significant. As a start, gross is usually a big number, and net is a smaller number (hence managers want their fees calculated on gross figures).

Your gross earnings are your earnings before any deductions. Your net earnings are what you are left with after all deductions (you may even be left with a net loss).

Say you have a tour, and the income it generates is $1 million. In this case, your gross earnings would be $1 million. If your manager takes 20% of your gross earnings, then his or her fee would be $200,000.

Now, say you had costs associated with the tour of $1.1 million. In this case, your net loss would be $100,000. However, it gets worse if your manager is on a gross earnings deal because you will have paid him or her $200,000, giving you a net loss of $300,000 (while your manager still gets paid).

It is for this reason that many artists do not like their managers getting paid on gross (especially for touring income).

However, the manager's counterargument to this is that many tour expenses can be constrained. Taking this example further, the $1,100,000 spent on the tour may, to a great extent, be directly attributable to the artist's insistence that the whole of the band and the crew stay in five-star hotels and drink the most expensive champagne every night. Perhaps without those extravagant expenses, the tour could have made a profit.

Accordingly, if a manager is going to take a percentage of a non-gross figure, he or she will probably want to constrain certain expenses—for instance, the manager may limit hotel expenses to a certain figure.

One area to pay careful attention is what the manager's fee is a percentage of. This is something you should ask your lawyer to look at in detail.

Historically, managers' fees have been in the 15% to 20% range because the manager is running his or her own business. The manager has an office to pay for, staff to pay for, and so on. However, if you are expecting a manager to run your office with your business, then it may not be necessary for your manager to have his or her own separate overhead. This would imply that you may be able to negotiate a lower fee.

You may also find that a manager doesn't want a percentage of gross earnings; instead he or she wants a share of the profits. This is much riskier, so it is likely that the share of profits (that is, net profits) will be much higher. A manager may particularly want this kind of deal if he is being more entrepreneurial and developing the act himself. If the manager is taking more risk, then he will expect more reward.

One last thing to think about when deciding on your manager's remuneration is the issue of post-term commission. In other words, how much are you going to continue to pay your manager after his or her contract has ended? For instance, if the manager negotiates a record deal, then he or she may expect some payment for this work. However, if the contract ends before the first payment under the deal is made, you may not want to pay (especially if you have got a new manager in place who is taking a percentage).

Clearly, this could lead to much unhappiness on all sides, so you may want to think about the point sooner rather than later. Again, this is an area where your lawyer will be able to give you some very useful advice.

The Business Manager

The nature of business managers can vary greatly according to the requirements of the act and local custom. The identity of the business manager and the manner in which the functions are carried out are irrelevant. For an act running its business on a sound footing, it is important that someone undertake the functions of the business manager. This someone could be the act's manager, or it could be an accountant. It doesn't matter who, as long as the functions are undertaken.

What Does a Business Manager Do?

The nature of what a business manager does will vary depending on your needs. However, the main functions you can expect a business manager to perform are:

- Monitoring money received and money paid. This may sound simple, but remember that you may have hundreds of sources of income that each need to be individually monitored, verified, and accounted for.

- Agreeing on budgets, which may include budgets for recording, making videos, or tour support.

In some jurisdictions (such as the US), it is quite common for a business manager to also act as a financial adviser and advise about investments. In other jurisdictions this practice is uncommon (for instance, in the UK financial advisers need to be regulated, so it is uncommon for business managers to perform this function).

What Does a Business Manager Charge?

There are many different ways that business managers will be paid. The fee structure usually depends on the nature of the relationship.

- Some business managers are paid a salary. You may expect to pay a salary (which may be broadly comparable to what the person could earn if he or she worked for, say, an accounting firm) if you employ someone directly. One advantage of having a business manager on the payroll is that he or she may also be able to act in other functions (for instance, he or she may be able to also work as your tour accountant).

- Some business managers expect to be paid an hourly rate (in other words, you pay X for each hour the business manager spends working on your account). This is the kind of arrangement you may expect if you hire a firm of accountants to perform the functions of a business manager.

- Other business managers may charge a percentage of (gross) earnings. A typical indicative percentage may be around 10%. The business managers who are most likely to look for this sort of fee arrangement are those whose business is being a business manager. These are often accountants who set up their own businesses (as opposed to their own accountancy practices).

One of the most influential factors determining a business manager's fee is the manager's fee. If you are paying your manager 20%, then it may not be unreasonable to expect that he or she will provide (or procure) the services of a business manager. It would certainly be regarded as expensive to pay 30% in management fees (20% to your manager and 10% to your business manager).

Risks in Hiring a Business Manager

There are risks in hiring a business manager, in the same way that there are risks in hiring a manager. One of the biggest risks may be your assumptions. Just because someone holds himself or herself out as a business manager, that does not mean he or she is an accountant (it does not even mean that the person is competent).

It is not necessary for your business manager to be an accountant, nor is it mandatory that your business manager be regulated by an accountancy body. However, if you are considering working with someone who is not regulated, then you should consider the level of risk you are taking with your business. See the "Errors and Omissions" section earlier in this chapter.

Lawyers

As I've already mentioned, you have probably heard countless tales of young artists being ripped off. The simplest way to reduce your risk of being treated shabbily is to find a good lawyer.

As good lawyer will do several things for you:

- Explain what each legal document actually means. You can probably read a contract and understand what each word means. Your lawyer should be able to take that concept forward and explain what the contract (or other document) means in terms of your income (in particular, how much and when) and your obligations (for instance, you may be entering a deal that will take up the next 15 years of your life).

- As well as explaining what each contract means, your lawyer should be able to give you some sense about whether you are entering a good deal or a bad deal. The lawyer will have experience in the area in which the deal is being done (if he or she doesn't, then run away) and so will be able to tell you about similar deals he or she has come across.

A lawyer cannot guarantee you will get a good deal. If there is only one deal on the table, and it is a take-it-or-leave-it deal, then all your lawyer will be able to do is warn you about the risks. In this case, the lawyer cannot make the deal financially better, although he or she may warn you away from disaster.

Which Lawyer Should You Appoint?

As with appointing any professional adviser, you should always look for personal recommendations when appointing a lawyer.

When you do appoint a lawyer, it is particularly important to find one who has experience in the music industry and music industry practices. Given the long-term nature of deals within the industry, advice from a less than competent lawyer can cause you problems over a very long period. Indeed, poor legal advice may end your career.

Ideally, you should appoint a lawyer you trust and respect and with whom you can develop a long-term, mutually beneficial relationship.

How Much Do Lawyers Charge?

Lawyers' charges depend on the jurisdiction within which the lawyer is operating and the rules of the body that regulates the lawyer (assuming the lawyer is regulated).

In the UK, lawyers are typically paid on an hourly basis, so you will pay an agreed-upon fee for each hour that a lawyer works on your account. Subject to appropriate disclosures and client agreement, fees can be adjusted for other contingencies (essentially success-based criteria); however, this practice is quite unusual in the UK.

In the US, hourly rates are still used, but they may be less common. Some lawyers are kept on a retainer, so the client pays a monthly fee, and the lawyer advises as necessary. Other lawyers charge a percentage of the deal on which they are working. A typical percentage may be around 5%. A third option that some lawyers adopt is value billing, which is where a fee is charged according to how much value a lawyer feels he or she has added to a deal. This is likely to be a percentage of any increase to the financial terms of the deal.

However you remunerate your lawyer, you should have a clear indication of how his or her fees will be calculated before you instruct the lawyer to start work for you. Ideally, you will have the fee agreed upon up front. If this is not possible, then you should aim to set a limit on the fee that the lawyer cannot exceed without your agreement.

On the subject of lawyers and fees, I would add a word of caution: Always pay your lawyer. Lawyers know how to sue people—there are many lawyers who spend the whole of their professional lives suing people for their clients. If you don't pay your lawyer, he or she will sue you, and this will be an easy and cheap thing for the lawyer to do. And don't think you can fight lawyers by taking them to court. You are likely to find it very hard to find another lawyer who will help you take legal action against your lawyer.

Accountants

The main function of accountants is, as the name suggests, to account for things. In other words, they count and make a record of everything.

Your accountant will be able to tell you how much income you have received and how much you have spent. He or she will also be able to tell you what you have not received that you should have. Many accountants will also advise you on tax-related matters (including VAT and purchase taxes) and will help you structure your business in a way that is most efficient from a tax perspective.

As with lawyers, you should look to appoint an accountant who has experience in the music industry. There are several practices in the music industry (which are quite legitimate) that may cause confusion for accountants who are not aware of the practices. For instance, it can take a long time to receive your earnings—possibly even years. Accountants without the necessary experience may have difficulty giving you a true understanding of your financial position.

Most accountants will charge an hourly fee. However, as with lawyers, you will find other accountants whose fees can be calculated in other (legitimate) manners.

Bankers

We've already looked at some of the role of banks in the "Sources of Finance" section in Chapter 9.

In short, there are three things you can expect your bank to do:

- Receive money of your behalf (whether in the form of cash, checks, direct credit transfers, or credit cards) and then look after that money for you.

- Pay money on your behalf. (Again, this may be by direct credit transfer, check, or some other form of transfer.)

- Loan money to you. These loans may take several forms, including an overdraft facility or a loan made directly to you.

One other thing you can expect from a bank is to be closed down if you don't pay back money you borrow.

You can find banks in your local neighborhood that will provide basic banking facilities. When you are first starting, these banks may be ideal for your purposes. However, you are likely to be treated like any other customer and will probably find that any loan applications are decided according to criteria that are applied by a central loans department. The result of this may be that you are seen as a high risk (and face it, music is a high-risk business), so you will be turned down.

Once you reach a certain level of success and income, you will be able to make use of more specialized banking sections. You should look for a bank with a department that specializes in creative industries. Once you get hooked in with these people, you will find you are treated much more like a regular business customer.

Basic banking services are usually quite cheap (some may even be free). As you borrow money, you will find you start to pay interest and arrangement fees. Interest is often calculated according to the bank's perception of the risk you pose.

Booking Agents/Promoters

There are several ways to get gigs. When you first start off, you will probably arrange your own gigs and will take whatever you can take as a fee. This may be a couple of beers and a small amount of cash to cover gas; it may be less. If you have a manager, then he or she will spend a large part of his or her time trying to find gigs for you until you become an established act (when hopefully you have something of a following, and so gigs are easier to book).

Booking Agents

As you start to develop a reputation, you may find that you can use the services of a booking agent who will find gigs for you. The main advantages of a booking agent are:

- He or she will have a range of contacts and so should be able to get you more gigs over a wider geographical area.

- He or she should be able to get better fees (since he or she takes a percentage).

- He or she will free your and your manager's time (as well as cutting phone bills).

For this, the booking agent may take a fee in the range of 10% to 15% of the gross figure negotiated for the gig (and often the manager's fee will then be calculated on the gross figure less the agent's fee). Usually a booking agent will expect exclusivity from their client. This exclusivity may be limited to a geographic region.

Promoters

The role of the promoter is more venue-specific than a booking agent. A promoter is the person who arranges the entertainment at the venue for the night when you are playing. He or she will hire the venue and sell the tickets. In other words, this is the person who is hiring you and the person who will be responsible for making sure all of your riders are met (which can range from requiring certain equipment be provided or certain food be made available to insisting that the dressing rooms are painted with green, pink, and purple stripes).

Some promoters will work with just one venue, others with a range, and some work nationally.

The artist and the booking agent are both dependent on the promoter for their income. The promoter will be reliant on ticket sales and other income that can be generated (for instance, from advertising/sponsorship, concession stands such as hot dog stalls, the bar, and so on).

At lower levels, the artist's fee will often be a fixed amount. As the artist can negotiate better deals, the fee will usually be a percentage of net receipts (in other words, after the promoter has met as many expenses as the promoter legitimately can). Depending on your clout, your booking agent may be able to negotiate an advance (often called a *guaranteed minimum*) from the promoter. Naturally, this advance will be recouped before you start to receive any share of the net profit.

When you get into the big league, a split of net profits can be in the 80% to 90% range (in the artist's favor and before the booking agent and the manager take their shares). However, you can only really expect these figures when you start selling out arenas. Before then, these figures are just a nice aspiration.

Alternatives to Booking Agents and Promoters

You don't need a booking agent, and you don't need a promoter to put on a gig. However, they can prove useful allies to have on your team because they can provide a large chunk of upfront payment as well as reducing your risks.

However, if you have your own fan base, then there are other options. The first main option is that you can put on your own gigs. This cuts the cost of the booking agent and the promoter. The downside to this approach is that you are taking the whole risk and assuming responsibility for organizing every detail. (For instance, do you know where to find security people or cleaners for the venue, if these are not provided?)

Another alternative, as noted in Chapter 9, is for you to bring your fan base to the promoter and receive a commission (from the promoter) for all sales you make.

Merchandising

As I illustrated at the start of this chapter, there are many channels you can use to make your merchandising available. Remember, merchandising is much more than just T-shirts—it can cover a range of goods, including clothing (hats, scarves, sweatshirts, hoodies, and anything else you can think of to wear), posters, programs, buttons (badges), stickers, patches, mugs, dolls, and so on.

In essence you have two choices: procure your own merchandise and sell it yourself or license someone else. If you sell the merchandise yourself, then you need to order and hold this stock (which involves investment). If you license a third party, then, in essence, all you have to do is approve the merchandise and sit back and wait for the royalties.

There are many reasons why you may wish to consider appointing a merchandising firm.

- Perhaps a compelling reason for appointing a merchandising firm is that they may pay you an advance.

- By appointing a merchandiser, you take yourself out of the whole process, so you don't need to order T-shirts, store them, and market them. That being said, if it is in your financial interest or if there is demand from the fan base, you may still want to sell your own T-shirts.

- Hopefully, even though you will be paid a royalty and will not be taking the full profit, you should be able to generate more income. There are two reasons why your income may increase. First, a firm dedicated to merchandising should be able to get the product to market for a cheaper price than you can. Second, a professional merchandising firm should be able to sell the product at many more outlets.

As a rough (and not particularly helpful) indicator, a merchandiser may pay you anything in the region of 20% to 80% of the retail price (less VAT and other sales taxes and credit card charges).

It should go without saying that you need control over copyrights in order to license other parties to produce your merchandise. For instance, if don't own the copyright to your logo, then it is likely that the copyright owner could expect to generate some income from merchandise licensing.

Record Company

In Chapter 9, I looked at the income you might be able to generate from a record company when you release a CD. Now I want to talk about some of the benefits of working with a record label beyond the fact that they will pay you. In other words, why would you want a label as part of your team?

As well as having a certain degree of financial clout, a record label is also likely to have certain strengths. These strengths include:

- Marketing. The record company will have tried most methods of marketing and is likely to have a very good idea about what will work and what won't. Also, as a regular buyer of advertising, the record company will be able to negotiate the best price. As an act working on your own, there is no way you would be able to negotiate deals as favorable as a record company can negotiate. Their marketing expertise is also likely to give a significant input into the act's strategy.

- Funding. As we have seen, a new act needs financing in a number of areas—for instance, to record a CD, to tour, and to live. Rather than borrow money from a bank, the record label can pay an advance against future earnings.

- Logistics. Record companies are well experienced at the mechanics of getting CDs pressed (for the cheapest price and at a high quality) and getting CDs distributed through any and all retail outlets. If the record company does handle the logistics, then they will involve wholesalers and distributors, both of whom will take a cut (which increases the record company's expenses and so indirectly reduces your income).

- Globalization. Many artists are able to find a level of fame in their own country. However, reaching out to an audience outside of their country can be difficult. Many record companies have the infrastructure to help artists in their global ambitions.

Clearly, different record labels are going to have different strengths and differing financial resources. As I've said for several other issues, look at what you're trying to achieve. If your aim is to get your product distributed efficiently, then a label can probably perform that task better than you. If you believe that a large-scale marketing campaign is what you need, then you probably want to find a label. However, if you're after a marketing campaign, you should perhaps ask yourself why your efforts haven't been as successful as you would have hoped before you approach a label (because the label is likely to ask itself this question).

The downsides to doing a deal with a record company are that they will take a lot of the money you earn, and they will want you to assign the copyrights of your recordings to them. As noted earlier, you don't have to sell out your copyrights; you can license the product.

There are some other apparent downsides. For instance, you will sign exclusively with a record label. However, I'm not sure this is such a problem in practice. Most record companies understand the commercial value of collaborations (especially when it helps you reach a wider market) and will not stand in the way of this sort of work (as long as it is going to make them some money).

Do also remember that record companies are commercial organizations with staff and shareholders that need to be paid. If you are intending to enter into any arrangement with a record company, then your product must be commercially viable from their perspective. To be commercially viable from the record company's perspective, a CD will need to sell enough copies to provide a large chunk of income for the record company.

If the record company takes the view that your CD will not sell sufficient numbers that it can make a profit, then it will not enter into a deal with you. However, if you are convinced about the viability of the product (and can back this conviction with a solid fan base), then your only option if you want to release a CD is to make it happen yourself (and you can then choose the on-demand or self-funded pressing route).

Publishers

If you are a songwriter, you can publish your own songs and collect all of the royalties that are due by joining the appropriate collection societies around the world. This is feasible; however, if your record is released in more than a few territories (which could be the case if you have a European hit), then it is a tedious task, and the administration will become very long-winded (not least of all because you will need to speak a lot of different foreign languages to join the foreign collection societies).

If you want to streamline this administration, it makes a lot of sense to appoint an expert to undertake this on your behalf. The experts in administering songwriters' rights are the publishers, so you could ask a publisher to administer your songs on your behalf.

Under an administration deal, you would retain the copyright of your songs, and for a fee (typically in the region of 10% to 15%), the publisher would collect your royalties and remit them back to you. You would not normally expect an advance under this sort of deal.

However, if you go for an administration deal, then the publisher will only administer your catalogue. In addition to the administration, you may want other services from your publisher, such as:

- An advance
- Covers for your songs (in other words, you want your publisher to look for other artists to record your songs)
- TV/film use (in other words, you want your publisher to find ways for your songs to be used in TV and films)

If you want the money or these sorts of services, then you will probably have to enter into a sub-publishing deal or an exclusive publishing arrangement. Both of these are likely to involve you in selling (or long-term licensing) your copyrights.

Under a sub-publishing or exclusive publishing deal, the publisher may take around 20% to 25% of your gross income (but might take more or less, depending on the deal you can cut). You should be aware that the systems in the UK and the US for calculating songwriting royalties differ. However, the end percentage that is paid may be reasonably similar at the end of the day. As always, I would refer you to Ann Harrison's and Donald Passman's books for further explanation of the legal aspects.

For further details of what you could expect from a publishing deal, check out the "Songwriting Royalties" section in Chapter 9.

11 Your Pay Packet

I'm guessing you probably didn't get into music because you wanted to hear someone talk about being sensible and saving for your pension. However, I'm also guessing that if you've read this far in the book, you are very serious about your career and you're very serious about making a living from your music.

The Cat Food Years

Unless you die young, there will come a time when your earnings from music will be reduced. This happens for all artists as they mature—almost certainly their fan base contracts. Fan bases contract for a number of reasons:

- Musical tastes change, and as the act becomes less trendy, fans lose interest in music and/or the act.

- The act may tour less and undertake less promotion. This is not unreasonable: Most people can only spend a number of years living the nomadic lifestyle of a musician on the road before they burn out. In addition, many musicians also broaden their interests, perhaps pursuing other projects that have arisen as a result of their success.

A declining fan base can, but doesn't have to, lead to a decline in income.

Although a fan base may have declined, the income expectation can become more certain and sustainable (provided the fan base is nurtured). It is not unreasonable to expect that if you have kept a fan for 20 years, that fan is not going to desert you in the short term unless you upset him or her. You may also find that each fan becomes more profitable.

Also, if your fan base is maturing, then your fans' tastes are likely to change. With a younger fan base, particularly a teenage fan base, you will be able to sell a much greater quantity of merchandise. For the more mature fan base, you are likely to sell less, but the merchandise you sell may be of a higher quality, allowing you to charge higher prices and make better profits.

The financial strategy underlying this book is to develop a long-term sustainable career that will continue to generate income over as long a period as possible. Provided you can sustain your income over a sufficiently long period, you will avoid the cat food years—those declining years when your career has gone and the money you had has gone and you are left so impoverished that all you can afford to eat is cat food.

There are many ways you can achieve this longevity. One strategy would be to make your income from the same sources that you do in the earlier part of your career, such as CDs, merchandising, and live performances. You will still be able to generate income from these sources, but to a lesser extent as you mature.

As you hit the middle stage of your career, you will probably generate less money from direct sources (CDs and live performances), but you should be able to increase the income you make from indirect sources, such as television and film licensing. Then, as you approach retirement, you can look at possibly selling off the rights to your future income in exchange for a lump-sum payment.

Of course, this is only one option. However, it does show how you can have a steady income over your whole career (or at least over a longer period than you can under a conventional music career).

The Income Stream

So will you avoid the cat food years? Let's take a look at some income streams.

"Conventional" Highly Successful Career Income Stream

Take a look at Figure 11.1. This shows the earnings pattern for very many successful, but now forgotten, artists.

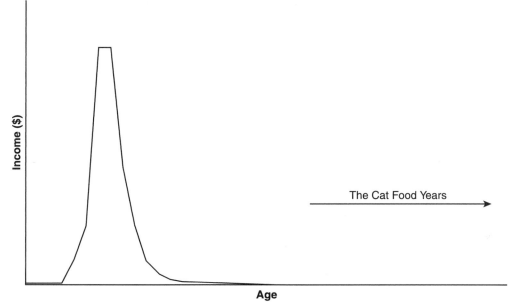

Figure 11.1 The income pattern of an archetypal successful artist. After a few years of struggle, the artist hits the big time and, after the peak, fades into obscurity around the time of his or her 30th birthday.

This graph could show the income for a guitarist in a successful band. Let me explain how his career could play out.

When the band started off it didn't generate very much income. This is normal for a band when they are paying their dues. However, this band became successful, signed a deal, and started to sell a lot of records. On the back of this success, the band toured and generated some income (primarily from the merchandising). At this point, the members of the band were starting to see quite a healthy income for the first time and were receiving figures in the high six figures or into seven figures (they were very successful).

After a few years of wild parties and a good bit of money, the band split due to musical differences. The drummer joined a cover band, and the bassist decided to become a professional surfer and moved to Australia. The singer joined another band, and that left the guitarist.

The guitarist still had some royalties coming through (mostly from overseas sources) and started to put together a solo project. The solo project was an artistic success but made a poor financial return, and on his 30th birthday, the guitarist was dropped by the label.

With no other skills and no inclination to do anything else, the guitarist survived on the last few royalty payments that trickled in over the next few years until the income from his musical career finally dwindled.

We have now reached the cat food years.

"New" Style Income Stream

Now think about the income stream you may be able to generate if you take control of your career following some of the ideas set out in this book. Have a look at Figure 11.2. Here, I have superimposed an income stream that could be generated if you follow your own course over the income stream that our unfortunate guitarist received (which was originally shown in Figure 11.1).

You will see that in this illustration, I have been far more modest about the level of income that an artist may generate. That is not because you can earn less—I just want to illustrate how the principles in this book can allow more people the opportunity to have a career in music. With the principles in this book, your career does not need to reach the stratosphere to be successful.

Now, there are a few things to notice about this alternative income stream:

- First, income is generated more quickly by this approach because you begin earning immediately. You don't wait for a record or management deal before you start generating income.

- The income stream builds more slowly. Because you are relying on (assisted) organic growth, the increase in your income will be more controlled. However, see the next bullet.

- The income stream remains at its peak for longer. With a more solid fan base, you will be able to sustain momentum over a longer period.

- The income stream then declines at a more measured rate.

- The income stream does not decline to zero—instead, it remains at a reasonable level until around the time that you are ready to retire (and even after that date, it may still provide an income).

What may not be obvious is that under this latter approach, the performer makes more income than under the first approach because the income is received at a reasonable level for the whole of the musician's career.

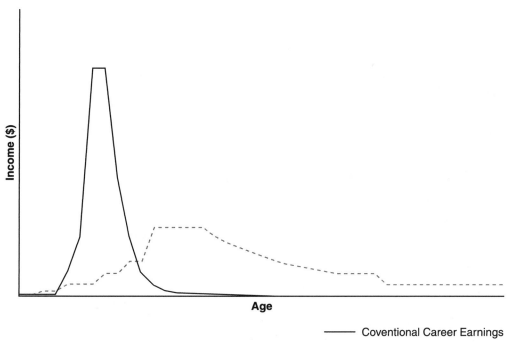

——— Coventional Career Earnings
- - - - - New Style Career Earnings

Figure 11.2 By taking advantage of the new opportunities that are available, more musicians can develop a long-term career and live on more modest earnings over a longer period. You should also remember that while very few musicians actually earn the mega-bucks (and those who do then end up spending huge amounts of this money very quickly), the more modest level of earnings is achievable by many more musicians. You should also bear in mind that while the earnings I am calling "modest" are lower than the earnings shown in Figure 11.1, they are still good earnings and would support a good lifestyle; it is only the scale used on the graph that makes these earnings look lower.

How Much Money Do You Need?

Either you are independently wealthy or you will need money in order to live. Most people have a range of expenses that include food, keeping a roof over their head (including paying for water, gas, electricity, and so on), gear for making music, and taxes (local, national, and including any social contributions). After that, most spending is on what are, in effect, luxury items.

How much money do you need? It's an interesting question, and one I propose not to answer. Instead, let me flip the issue over and give you two alternative approaches to dealing with your income.

- First, live within your means. You know how much money you have earned: Do not spend more than that. This may mean you will need to cut every possible expense—if you own a house, sell it and move somewhere cheaper; if you're renting, quit and move back with your parents; if you're in an expensive location, then move somewhere cheaper. Do everything you can do to stay afloat financially.

- Second, if the amount you *want* to spend exceeds the amount you are earning, then you are not earning enough. You (and you alone) directly control your earnings, so instead of going into debt, go out and earn more money. If that's too difficult, then you need to live within your means.

As a musician, your pay packet is not determined by the amount you earn. Rather, it is determined by how much is left after all of the deductions. We've looked at many other deductions throughout the rest of this book. I now want to look at two very specific deductions that are pertinent to you alone: taxes and pension contributions.

Tax

In most jurisdictions, you will be taxed on your earnings. Unfortunately, this is the nature of society, and there is little you can do about it (except find a smart accountant to show you the loopholes, move to a low-tax jurisdiction, or both).

Each country has its own tax regime that will affect its own citizens and foreign citizens working in the country (such as touring musicians) in different ways. Most countries have tax treaties with other countries (often called *double tax treaties*) whereby foreign nationals can avoid tax on earnings in the foreign country, provided the earnings are taxed in their own country.

Tax is a hideously complicated and dreadfully dull subject, so I don't want to go into the minutiae of double tax treaties or any of the other tax matters. However, I do want to give an indication of how tax can do really bad things to your income.

Tax systems around the world work in many different ways, and tax rates can vary greatly. However, there are a few principles that are fairly global:

- No one wants to pay tax, but people do. If people don't pay tax, then the tax authorities will pursue them and crush them merci-lessly.

- Tax for self-employed people (that is, people who are not employed by someone else—as a musician controlling your own career, you will probably be self-employed) is calculated after the deduction of expenses. So, for instance, if your tour earns $1 million but you have expenses of $900,000, then you will usually only be taxed on $100,000.

- In addition to taxes, there are often social charges at a much more modest level. These are often payable irrespective of earnings or based on a stricter calculation of earnings that discounts some expenses.

These are general principles on which you should not rely solely. You should take detailed tax advice in your own jurisdiction (and also con-sider taking tax advice in any other jurisdiction where you earn money) because each locality will have its own tax laws. For instance, in the US, self-employed people (such as musicians) pay an additional 15% self-employment tax above regular federal and state taxes. If you're not expecting this tax hit, it can be quite painful.

As I said, I want to give an example of how tax can eat up your earnings. I'm going to illustrate the loss to your pocket using the UK taxation system, looking at the situation as it applies to self-employed individuals. For this example, I will consider someone who is earning quite a reasonable amount of money: £50,000 (or roughly $100,000) after expenses. This figure may be more than many musicians earn; however, I am using it because it will show how the higher tax bands can have an effect on earnings. I should point out that all figures quoted here are for the 2006/2007 tax year.

In the UK, social contributions are called National Insurance Contributions (often known as NICs). For self-employed people, there are two components—a fixed weekly amount and a percentage based on certain earnings:

- The fixed weekly amount is £2.10 per week (or £109.20 per year).

- The percentage-based amount is 8% of earnings between £5,035 per year and £33,540 per year. So in our example, the individual would pay the maximum amount £2,280.40 (that is 8% of £28,505, which is the amount of earnings between £5,035 and £33,540).

So in this example, National Insurance Contributions of £2,389.60 are due on earnings of £50,000. National Insurance Contributions cannot be set against tax.

Under the tax system, a basic allowance of £5,035 is given. This means you can earn £5,035 before any tax is paid. So in our example, only £44,965 (in other words, £50,000 – £5,035) is taxable. There are then three tax bands:

- The first £2,150 of taxable earnings is taxed at the rate of 10%.

- The next £31,150 of taxable earnings (that is, the taxable earnings between £2,151 and £33,300) is taxed at the rate of 22%.

- Any other taxable earnings (that is, the taxable earnings over £33,300) are then taxed at the rate of 40%.

Some figures should help to illustrate. Look at Table 11.1.

Table 11.1 The Tax Paid in the UK by an Individual Earning
£50,000

Band of Earnings	Tax Rate	Earnings in Band	Amount of Tax
Earnings up to £5,035	0%		£0
First £2,150 of taxable earnings (that is, earnings between £5,035 and £7,185)	10%	£2,150	£215
Next £31,150 of taxable earnings (that is, earnings between £7,186 and £38,335)	22%	£31,150	£6,853
Taxable earnings over £38,335 (that is, earnings between £38,336 and £50,000)	40%	£11,665	£4,666
Total			£11,734

So in this example, the tax amounts to £11,734 (or 23% of earnings).

The total deduction from earnings is £14,123.6 (£11,734 tax plus £2,389.60 National Insurance Contributions), or 28% of earnings.

After deduction of tax and National Insurance Contributions, the take home pay is £35,876.40.

To illustrate the effect of tax, take a look at Figure 11.3. This shows the earnings pattern we looked at earlier in this chapter (for the new-style income stream). Against these earnings, the graph shows the elements that are taken as tax and social contributions (National Insurance Contributions).

As you can see, as earnings increase, the proportion of income that is paid in tax increases, reaching a maximum of nearly 40% of income. You can also see that because social contributions (National Insurance Contributions) are based on a limited band of earnings, the proportion of earnings paid here is limited.

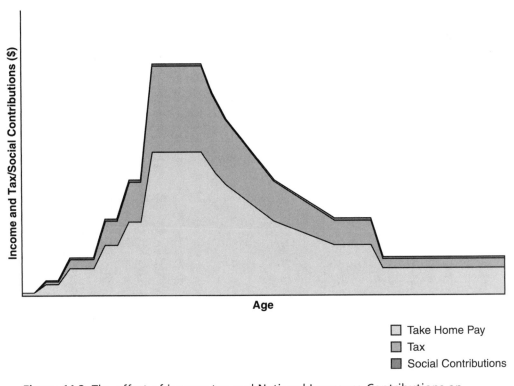

Figure 11.3 The effect of income tax and National Insurance Contributions on earnings. Note, these earnings are the same earnings shown as "New Style Career Earnings" in Figure 11.2; the scale on the axis is different, which makes the earnings look more significant.

As I mentioned at the start of this section, this example shows the effect of UK taxes. This book is about how to develop a career in music; because it is not a book about tax, I have not illustrated the tax position for every jurisdiction in which you may work. Non-UK tax laws would obviously paint a different scenario than our UK example, but the overall outcome is the same in either country: You must pay taxes, and they will eat up a significant portion of your income.

Pensions and Retirement Funds

I now want to talk about one expense that you may think is irrelevant: pensions, or as you might want to think of them, retirement funds.

Conventionally, the purpose of a pension (and a retirement fund) is to provide income when you stop working. However, under the model I am advocating in this book, you will hopefully be generating income over a much longer period. Ideally, your music will still be generating income after you retire. Throughout this chapter, don't get too hung up on any difference between pensions and retirement funds. They are essentially the same thing: a source of income when you retire.

Instead of thinking of a pension as being just for when you retire, consider it as another income stream that will come online as your earnings decrease. The idea should be that your combined earnings and pension will maintain your income at a certain level for when you decide to make the transition into retirement (see Figure 11.4). Then if (or when) the earnings from music cease, you will have another income source.

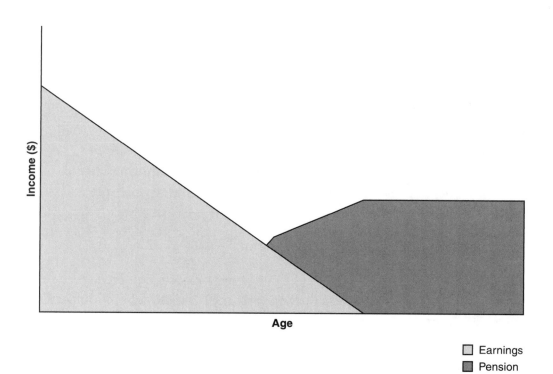

Figure 11.4 You can use the income from a pension to ease the financial transition as your earnings from music decline.

There is one problem with pensions: They cost a lot. Let me first explain how they work. Once I've done that, I'll look at some of the practical steps you can take.

Betting on Your Life

Pensions are a gamble: nothing more, nothing less. What makes them interesting is that they are a bet on your life!

Perhaps the most secure way to provide a pension for yourself is to buy an annuity. An annuity is another way of saying an income for life. Annuities are sold by financial institutions such as insurance companies. The cost of an annuity is determined by many factors, but is essentially a guess by the financial institution about how long you will live (based on statistics about the population as a whole).

If you live longer than was assumed, then you make a profit. If you don't live longer, then you won't have made a profit. You will only be able to know how long you lived after you have died, so any profit or loss will then be immaterial. However, the key factor about annuities is that they can provide you with security—they protect you against the risk of living longer than you expected.

The risk of living longer than you expected is a serious problem. Suppose your income ends when you are 60, and at that point you have savings of $500,000. You might expect to live for another 20 years. Ignoring the effects of interest and inflation, that would mean you could spend $25,000 a year (that is $500,000 ÷ 20) or roughly $2,000 per month for the rest of your life. If you then die at the age of 80, your money would be gone.

But what happens if you don't die when you expect to? If you knew you were going to live to be 90, then you could spend $17,000 a year, or $1,390 per month. If you knew you were going to live to be 100 you could spend $12,500 a year, or $1,000 per month.

Unfortunately we don't know when we are going to die, so there is a tendency to spend less and hold back some capital. However, this can never counter the effect of someone living to an unexpected old age.

Take the previous example: What would happen if the person lived to be 110? Although not many people live to be that age, can you be sure that with all of the advances in medicine and technology, you will not live to be 110? Or older?

Because of the uncertainty, annuities have a great use. However, because of the uncertainty, annuities can look very expensive (although to be fair to insurance companies, they take a very small profit on this element of their business).

As a side note, you might think that all this stuff about annuities is dull, and you can just live on the interest of your capital. Apart from tax, possibly living to be 120 years old, and fluctuations in interest rates (which could lead to wide swings in your level of income), another factor that makes this a risky strategy is inflation, which will erode the value of your capital. You would therefore need to reinvest some of your interest in order to ensure the interest level retains its buying power, whereas an annuity can have inflation protection included.

How Much Does an Annuity Cost?

The cost of an annuity varies according to a number of factors, including:

- Geographic location. Annuities are calculated in different manners in different jurisdictions.

- Age. If you are younger, an annuity may be expected to be paid for a longer period and hence will be more expensive.

- Pension increases. You can buy annuities that provide the same amount for every year. However, these annuities mean that the pensioner becomes poorer over time because prices will rise due to inflation. To counter this, you can buy an annuity that increases. The increases can be linked to inflation or can be a fixed percentage. The cost of an annuity will increase if you want pension increases (because the amount the annuity provider will pay out will increase).

- Dependants. Many people want to also provide for their spouse/significant other in the event of their death. It is common for an annuity to provide a pension for a spouse/significant other on the death of the original annuitant. Often the dependant's pension will be of a lower level, perhaps two-thirds or one-half of the original pension. A dependant's pension will increase the cost of an annuity.

- Prevailing market conditions. The financial institution will invest the money you pay to buy your annuity. If the company thinks it can do better with its investments, then it will charge you less for your annuity. However, if the company thinks the financial markets do not offer much scope for profit, then it will charge you more.

I said annuities are expensive: Let me give you a practical example. These are indicative market figures (in the UK) taken at the end of November 2006.

For this example, I have taken the following scenario:

- An individual retiring at age 60...

- ...with a spouse who is the same age...

- ...with the pension increase in line with UK price inflation, and...

- ...on the death of the annuitant, the spouse will receive a pension for the rest of his/her life of 50% of the pension that was being paid at the date of death.

Based on these assumptions, a pension will cost about 28 times the yearly amount that is to be provided. So if you wanted to provide a pension of £15,000 (roughly $30,000), that would cost £420,000 (roughly $850,000), or approaching half a million pounds.

Once you have pondered the eye-watering expense of pensions, let's move on and look at some of the practical steps you can take to ensure you secure a modest income in retirement.

How Much Do I Need to Invest?

If you want to provide a reasonable pension for yourself (and perhaps your loved ones) when you retire, then either you can hope you have a very large chunk of money when you retire (which is quite unlikely), or you can start making financial provision (in other words, saving) now.

Several factors will affect the amount of money that is available to you when you want to buy an annuity:

- The amount you invest

- When you invest

- The returns generated by your investments

Clearly, the amount you invest will have a direct effect on the amount of money available when you come to retire.

The timing of your investment also has a significant effect on your income. The earlier you invest, the longer that investment will have to grow. If you invest $10 on your 20th birthday and $10 on your 40th birthday, by the time you get to your 60th birthday, ignoring any financial disasters, the $10 you invested on your 20th birthday will be worth much more than the $10 you invested on your 40th birthday.

The statement in the last paragraph assumes that your investments always go up. As we know, depending on the nature of the investment, returns can go up and down. Broadly speaking, if you take fewer risks, then you would expect lesser returns, but those returns are more likely to be certain. However, if you take more risks, then you would expect greater returns, but there is also a much greater risk of your investment performing poorly.

The nature of your investments will vary depending on your attitude toward risk and the returns you are looking for. One thing you should always remember is that any investment returns need to be greater than the rate of inflation in order to have any real effect. For instance, if inflation stands at 3% and your investment returns 2%, then you will actually make a loss of 1%. However, if the investment returns 5%, then you would have achieved a real return of 2%.

This is a book about your music career, not about financial investment. However, your investments are important because they have such a direct impact on your living standards, so you should always take proper financial advice before making any investment decision.

I now want to illustrate how the timing of your savings can have an effect on your savings. Take a look at Figure 11.5. This shows two scenarios: first, someone who starts saving from his or her 30th birthday, and second, someone who starts saving from his or her 40th birthday. In both cases, the earnings are the same. They are based on the same new-style earnings figures that I used earlier, and therefore real earnings decline over time. This decline has a noticeable effect on the cost, as I will explain later.

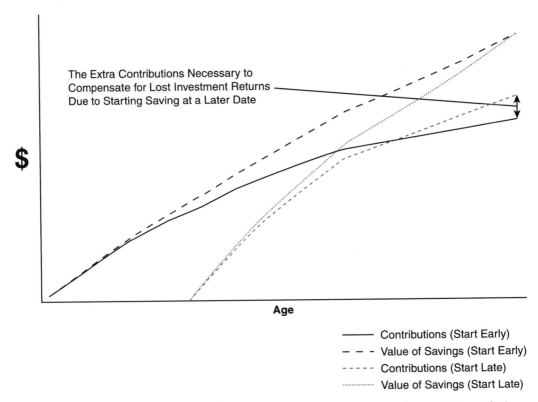

Figure 11.5 By starting to save later, you have to save more, and you will benefit less from the interest on your savings.

Let me explain what you're seeing in the graphs in a bit more detail.

For each scenario—Start Early (in other words, at age 30) and Start Late (in other words, at age 40)—there are two lines:

- The total value of the savings. The savings are made up of payments and interest.

- The total payments to date; this line takes no account of investment returns.

The difference between the two lines for each scenario is the effect of investment returns.

You will see that the total invested (including investment returns) becomes equal when the individual reaches his or her 60th birthday. However, when the individual starts saving later, the amount that has to be saved is much larger. For the two scenarios, I assumed:

- The person who started saving at age 30 paid 10% of his income throughout his 30s. When the person hit his 40s, he paid 15% of his income until retirement (at age 60).

- The person who started to save at age 40 paid 33% of his income until retirement.

The 33% is not a random figure—this is the figure that the person would have to pay from age 40 to make up the same level of savings as the person who started at age 30. In other words, by starting later, the amount of income that has to be saved (as a percentage of income) is tripled at certain times.

You will see that for the individual who started earlier, the investment has more effect (the difference between the two lines is greater). The person who starts later pays more in real terms, and his or her retirement fund has a lesser proportion of investment returns.

As I noted, the progressive decline of the earnings has an effect on the amount that is being paid. For this illustration, I have assumed that a level percentage of earnings is paid (for the person who starts earlier, there is a step up in the level savings amount at age 40, when the contribution is increased from 10% to 15%). Through keeping a level percentage contribution, the pain of funding the pension is spread evenly throughout the career.

For the person who starts paying at age 30, his earnings are much higher than they are at age 40 (at 30, he's just about to hit his highest earnings period—by his 40th birthday, the glory days are gone, but there is still a good living to be had). This means that there is a doubling effect: A lower contribution can be paid because it will be worth more due to the extended investment period, and a lower percentage gives a higher amount. This is why the amount of contributions appears to grow at a similar rate when they first start to be paid.

If the person who started paying at 30 wanted to be really sensible, then he would put away huge amounts of savings during those years of high earnings. He would then not need to make any further pension contributions for the rest of his career, and he could still end up with a similar level of pension provision.

You might still be left speechless by the notion of paying 33% of your earnings for 20 years and expecting a massive retirement fund for that sacrifice. Let me put this into context. The fund that will be built up by the contributions suggested here will provide a pension of roughly 50% of the annual earnings at retirement. The earnings at retirement are roughly 16% of the level of earnings at the peak of the career. This means that after paying 33% of your earnings for 20 years, you could end up with a pension equal to 8% of your highest years' earnings.

As I started this section by saying, pensions are eye-wateringly expensive.

Taxes and Savings as a Proportion of Earnings

However, there is a small bit of silver in this cloud of tax and pensions. In most jurisdictions, pension contributions can be set against tax. You should take advice in your jurisdiction to confirm whether these contributions are allowable for tax purposes and, if so, what conditions apply.

I'm now going to show two graphs that use the same figures we've been using throughout this chapter. Each graph illustrates a similar point: It shows the artist's income and the proportion of that income that is swallowed by tax, social contributions (in this case, National Insurance Contributions), and pension contributions. In each case, note that when the pension contributions kick in, the tax bill goes down because pension contributions are tax-deductible.

Figure 11.6 shows the position when the pension contribution kicks in at age 30. You can see that when the percentage that is paid is increased (from 10% to 15%) at age 40, there is not a noticeable increase, and the take-home proportion remains broadly consistent.

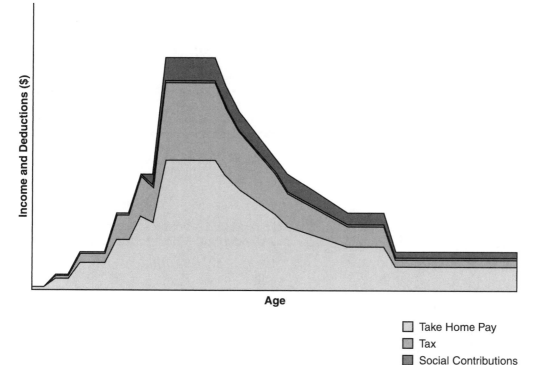

Figure 11.6 By starting to save early in your career, you will maximize the tax-efficiency of your savings, but your savings will only reduce your take-home pay by a comparatively modest amount.

By contrast, if you look at Figure 11.7, when the pension contribution kicks in, although there is a considerable drop in the tax bill, the take-home pay amount is noticeably reduced.

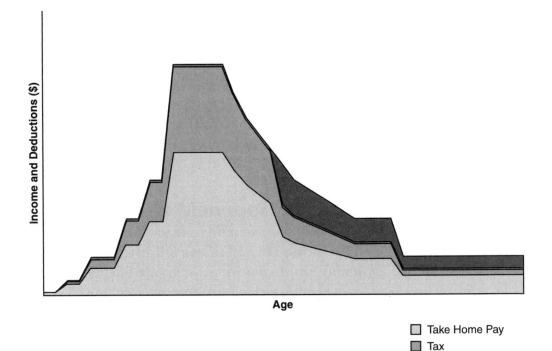

Figure 11.7 When savings start late, they can represent a significant chunk of income if the aim of saving is to retain a reasonable standard of living into old age.

Some People Just Earn Less than Others

I've thrown a lot of figures at you. I make no apologies for this: The factors affecting your take-home pay and your financial well-being are complicated.

Whatever your personal situation, you need to understand what will affect your earnings and how much money you need in order to be able to live your life at a reasonable standard. You then need to make some serious decisions about how you make money from music. Those decisions may be uncomfortable because two of the factors you will have to consider are:

- Does the music I am producing have sufficient commercial potential? Remember my example earlier about poets—a highly successful book of poetry may sell around 800 copies in a year. If the poet does really well and makes $3 for each book of poetry sold, that still only works out to $2,400 income, which really isn't enough to live on. Are you just being a musical poet, condemned to live your existence in poverty?

- Am I/are we really good enough? Or is the reason for your lack of income simply that you are rubbish?

If your music has sufficient commercial appeal and you're good, then you stand a fair chance of making a living, provided you cultivate and nurture your fan base.

Putting the Theory into Practice

12 Putting All the Pieces Together

I hope by now that you've realized that the strategy I am outlining in the book is really quite simple; there are essentially two strands:

- First, find a fan base. Once you have got the fan base, cherish these people so that you can nurture and grow your fan base.

- Second, collect lots of small (and perhaps less small) pieces of income from lots of different sources. Whatever you do, ensure that you don't miss any small piece of income. If you are running an efficient and low-cost-base business, then all of these small pieces of income will form a significant stream of earnings that can easily get lost if you have a large overhead.

This is a robust and scalable business model that allows for great flexibility—for instance, if you want to sign up with a major record label for part of your career, you can. The principles are also applicable to any musician, irrespective of genre.

The Jigsaw Puzzle of Your Career

Before we look at the issue of scalability of your business, I want to draw out a few points about this chapter. First, let me state a few blunt truths that I hope are self-evident:

- Just because you have produced a CD, that does not mean you have a career.

- Just because you are the most talented musician that has ever walked the earth, that does not mean you will have a career making music.

To have a career, you need to focus on strategy. The success of your career, like a successful military operation, is based on logistics. Once you have the basics (that is, you can actually create music that people want to listen to), then it's all about what you do and when. The only differentiating factor between those who succeed and those who do not is implementation.

If you can't implement a strategy to achieve your goals, then you will fail.

This chapter is about putting together all of those pieces that are necessary for a successful career, to create a cohesive strategy. To think about it another way, this chapter is about defining your own roadmap to success.

A Question of Scale

The issue of scalability is important, and I've already briefly mentioned the topic in Chapter 1. In many ways it is very easy to run a one-person business. The difficulty with one-person businesses is that they can only generate so much income—there are only 24 hours in a day, and the person running the business needs to sleep and so on. Therefore, in order to generate more income, the business needs to grow.

To a certain extent, anyone working in the music business has scale constraints. For instance, you may find it hard to play more than 365 gigs in a year. (In fact, if you play 200 gigs a year without burning out, then you're doing well.) You cannot play more shows than you are physically able to.

Simply growing your business is not enough: You need to increase the revenue and increase the profitability while reducing the risks that your business is taking. If you can't grow your business, you can always look at ways to make it more profitable. The ways to make a business more profitable are to cut expenses (which you can achieve by a number of means, including cutting staff numbers and using cheaper suppliers) and to increase your prices (see Figure 12.1). These are both quite drastic actions—the better solution is not to spend money you don't need to spend in the first place.

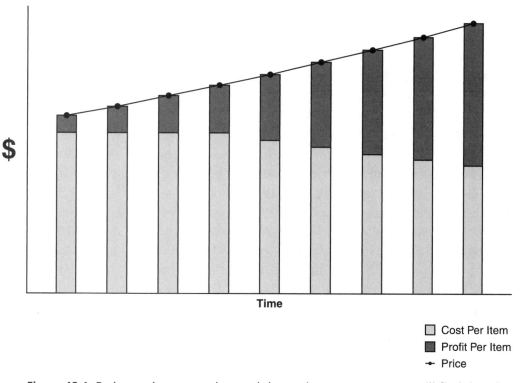

$

Time

☐ Cost Per Item
■ Profit Per Item
← Price

Figure 12.1 By increasing your prices and decreasing your costs, you will find that the combined effect leads to a rapid increase in the profit you generate on each item.

There are several ways to scale up your business. Here are a few examples:

■ Create more (profitable) products. There is probably a practical limit to the number of songs you can write and therefore the number of CDs you can release. Also, there is a limit to the number of CDs you can market that your fan base will buy. However, you can increase your range of products by producing DVDs and merchandise.

■ Take on staff (whom you can pay lower wages) to undertake functions you had previously carried out. This works if you can then use your free time to create more income. If you take on new staff and don't create more income, then all you have done is increase your costs.

- Play bigger gigs. As I have already mentioned, there is probably a limit to the number of gigs you can play, and this limit is probably determined by the physical stresses that gigging will place on all of the musicians' bodies. Therefore, to generate more income from touring, you can play bigger gigs. Bigger gigs are more expensive to stage and hence may increase risk. However, they do offer the potential to generate more revenue. If you feel like grabbing even more money from your fan base, then you can also look at increasing the price of tickets at gigs as another way to increase your income still further!!

Figure 12.2 shows how you can significantly increase your profits by scaling up your business. In this figure, the increasing profitability shown in Figure 12.1 is multiplied by increasing sales. The combination allows for profitability to grow by a considerable amount.

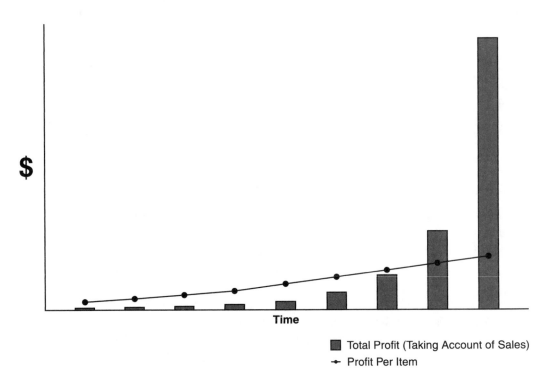

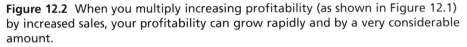

Figure 12.2 When you multiply increasing profitability (as shown in Figure 12.1) by increased sales, your profitability can grow rapidly and by a very considerable amount.

However, as you scale up your business (that is, as your business grows because you are more successful), there is danger that you will be less efficient as your costs grow. In particular, you are going to need to build a team around you, and with a group of people, as well as the wage bill, there is an inherent inefficiency. However, that inefficiency can be managed, and you should be able to counteract it with a greatly increased income due to the increased sales (which is the reason why you would have needed to hire people in the first place).

In scaling up your business, as well as retaining the efficiency, you must make sure you continue to exploit the foundations of your business. So make sure you continue to take advantage of the speed with which you can create and release products; the direct link to, and communication with, your fan base; and your low-cost operation. The easiest way to lose these advantages is to get swept up with an entourage and a bunch of hangers-on who will drain the life out of your business and bleed its finances dry.

Reducing Risks and Increasing the Certainty of a Sustained Career

You can generate income without a fan base (for instance, you can license your music for use with TV, video, or film, or you might find a patron to sponsor you). However, it is far riskier to focus your long-term career on a single source (or a few sources of income) than it is to put in the time to build a broad fan base. You can afford to lose one or two fans, although I would recommend that you try not to. However, if you only have (say) two sources of income and you lose both of them, then you're in trouble.

It may take longer, and it may be slower, to build a career on a solid fan base when compared to the apparent quick buck of getting a recording contract. However, when you build your own fan base, you start to get results sooner because you can earn money immediately, rather than having to wait until you have repaid all of your record company advances. Also, with the more solid foundation, as well as reducing your risks, you are increasing your chances of having a long-term career.

You've probably heard the old saying that it's not about *what* you know, it's *who* you know that matters in the music industry. This is true, but many people misinterpret this idea. Many people think this means that all you need to do is become acquainted with a senior person at a record label (or a well-known producer or similar) and you will have a career for life.

This couldn't be further from the truth. In reality, the person you need to know is each one of your fans, individually. Once you understand these people and know what they want, then you will produce product that they will buy. Once you have a stream of income flowing from your fans, you have the basis of a career.

Now that I've reinforced the messages of this book, I want to do several things with this chapter:

- Pull together all of the various strands that were discussed in the earlier chapters

- Look at how the elements can then be developed into a strategy

- Talk about how to start implementing this theoretical strategy in practice

In short, this chapter is about your business strategy; the next chapter will deal with your personal career strategy. You need a business strategy for several reasons:

- First, you and your collaborators need to agree upon how you will proceed together.

- Second, if you are going to borrow money or look for an investor, you will need a business plan. Your business strategy will form the basis of a business plan, which you can present to a lender or an investor. Without a coherent business strategy, you will find that no one else (apart from family, friends, and fools) will give you any of his or her money.

The Arc of Your Career

Without wishing to sound like a tearful Hollywood actress, grasping an award and mindlessly blubbering about the wonderful arc of her character, let me talk about the arc of your career.

First, let me explain what I mean by the arc of your career.

When you start out, you will start from nothing. Over time you will gradually build a fan base until you reach the point at which you can be self-supporting. As you progress further (providing everything goes well), you will reach the point where you are making a good living from your career. If you reach superstar status, this is the point at which you will be thinking about a Rolls Royce; a Ferrari; properties in London, Paris, New York, and your own private island in the South Pacific; a boat or two; a plane or two; and any other dreams that may come to mind.

From this peak, your career is then likely to decline over time. This happens to all artists and is quite natural. It doesn't mean your career is over; it's simply the case that you are not at the peak you once were. For examples of this, look at Sir Paul McCartney or the Rolling Stones. These two are no longer at their peak, but they still have highly lucrative careers. (As you saw earlier in this book, the Stones earned a lot of money last year.)

The arc of your career is the pattern by which your success rises, reaches a peak (which will hopefully be a long peak), and then falls. Your career may not necessarily follow a perfect arc—for instance, you may have several peaks (or several troughs if you are of a less optimistic frame of mind); however, it is likely to follow this general pattern. Perhaps the most unknowable factor is how high the peak will be.

That being said, the idea of going from nothing to being a superstar overnight (a hero from zero) may be appealing. However, it may not be the best course. One of the key advantages of measured and managed growth is that you can gain hands-on experience about how your business works (and from a performing point of view, you don't do your growing up in public). This knowledge will be invaluable when your business grows, especially when you need to hire other people to help you, because you will know what to expect from the business because you have already run it yourself.

The reason I am introducing the notion of the arc of your career is that I want to give some context around the strategies I am going to outline. Different business strategies may be appropriate at different points in your career. As well as defining your strategy at certain points, you have to find a way to transition seamlessly from one strategy to another as your business grows. If you can't manage change, then you will find that your career may not evolve in the way you hope.

The points I am going to identify on the career arc are, by their nature, very generic points. Please don't see this as a career map, but rather as an indication of points that your business may pass through. If you are looking for more thoughts about career planning, then check out Chapter 13, "Career Templates."

Figure 12.3 shows a typical arc of a career and highlights the main points through which your career will pass.

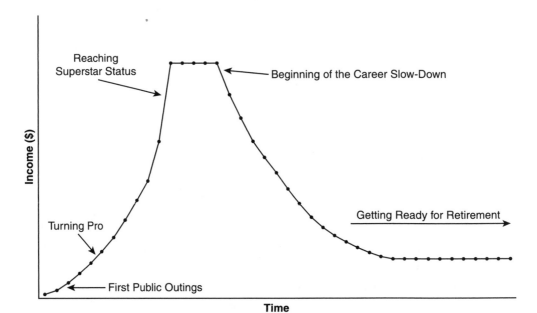

Figure 12.3 A typical career arc. The illustrative earnings are the same used to illustrate the "new style" income in Chapter 11, but have been adjusted slightly to give a smoother curve.

Preparation for Your Career

When you are starting, the only finances that your business is likely to have on hand are the money in your bank account and any loose change you can find down the back of the sofa.

This lack of money is a good thing: It means you can't go and spend money on stupid things such as recording your first CD in the most expensive recording studio in town. One recommendation I would make (and this is about as far from rock and roll as it is possible to be) is to start saving. It doesn't matter how or where, just start saving. If you're smart, you'll put your money somewhere where you can get interest (ideally tax free). As this section develops, you will see that you are going to need investment in your career—this is where your savings will help you.

When you start out you should have one focus: to create some good music. There's little point in trying to reach out and find a fan base if you've got no music for them to listen to, or all you've got is a really poor recording of a few turgid songs.

You need to take time to learn your craft and to improve your skills. As part of that you need to ensure that your songwriting skills are as good as your skills as a musician if you are intending to create an act that will be performing songs you have written. Learn as much as you can and, if possible, learn from the experts.

It may seem that this apparent lack of action goes against everything I have said so far in that I'm not saying get out and gig on the day after you first pick up a guitar. However, it is a smarter strategy: If you start before you are ready, then you will just look like a fool in public. As well as losing credibility you never really had, all you will do is land your business in debt. Once you're in debt, your expenses will double: You will have to pay interest on your debts as well as paying living expenses. That being said, please learn to distinguish between preparation and procrastination.

First Public Outings: Accelerated Learning

When you are more confident of your skills as a musician, performer, and songwriter, you are ready to take the next step. You can now start reaching out and looking for a fan base.

At this stage of your career, you will probably find that you have a lot of time between public outings. This is a good thing—it gives you more opportunity to practice your craft and to create new music. Think of this as being your research and development stage for the next part of your career.

To reach this point, you don't need to be as skilled as you could ever hope to be. You can still have a lot of room to develop. (In fact, if you don't have room to develop, then your career is going to be very short.) You just mustn't be embarrassing or so excruciating that you will lose your audience before they have found you.

Your initial public outings—whether they be virtual outings by putting music on the internet or real outings, such as live performances—should have one purpose: to seek out fans. If you can make any money to offset your costs, that is good. However, you should ensure that your focus is on finding an audience and not on making money.

Soliciting Feedback

One thing you will find when people hear your music is that they will give you their opinions.

Take the time to listen to these opinions, especially the negative comments. If possible, try to ask people about their opinions and find out exactly what it is they like and don't like. Often a comment such as, "You're just rubbish" (which may be phrased in slightly harsher terms) will tend to show that actually people don't like specific songs or don't like your style, and not that they think you are a talentless waster who should be deported to Siberia to live out the rest of your natural musical life in the frozen wastelands.

Also, take some time to find what people like. There may only be a few elements that appeal; however, it is important to find what you are doing well so that you can build upon it. I'm not suggesting that you should simply become a populist outfit driven by what you perceive people want. Instead, I am suggesting that you should understand what it is that you do that people like. I am presuming that what you do is credible, so giving your growing fan base more of the stuff they like (without repetition) should be a good thing.

Now, I'm sure we've all seen the graffiti: Just because no one understands you, it doesn't mean you're an artist. Unfortunately, this is true. If no one "gets you," then you're going to have a really hard time forging a career. Artistic freedom may be great; however, absolute freedom also gives you the freedom to fail, absolutely.

(Not) Building a Career on the Web

For many people, it will be much easier to put music on the web than it would to get out and play live. This is especially so for people who are creating music on their own. If you are looking to build a fan base solely on the internet, then you are going to have a really tough time, not least because there are thousands (if not millions) of people trying to do this too.

There are several key challenges that you will encounter with this strategy:

- First, you have to draw attention to yourself with a lot of people. There are several strategies you can adopt at the start of the process. For instance, you may be able to draw some attention to yourself if you hit every music-related forum and get people talking about you. However, if you follow this option, you are likely to spend more time on the internet than on making music.

- Once you've drawn attention to yourself, you have to stand out from the crowd. Given the numbers this is nearly impossible. If you're putting your music out on the internet, then it is going to have to be as good as or better than anything that's around at the moment (including music on the charts). After all, you are in competition with every other artist who has released a CD of music that covers your genre.

- There's also a question about your motivation if your only intention is to share your music on the internet. Music is an inherently social activity. If you are looking for a career in music, then it would not be unreasonable to assume you are trying to communicate with a wide group of people. Why, therefore, would you shy away from opportunities to communicate directly on a face-to-face basis? The best way to communicate on a face-to-face basis is through a live performance, not anonymously through cyberspace.

- If you do create any sort of following on the internet, then it may be hard to capitalize on it. First, the internet creates a very temporary, easy-come-easy-go type of loyalty. Second, the internet is likely to give you a very widely spread fan base (in this context, widespread on a geographical basis). You may have thousands of fans, but if the closest one fan lives to another is 100 miles, then pulling these people together for a gig (or other publicity/revenue-generating exercise) will be nearly impossible.

- As a purely internet-based act, one of the biggest difficulties you will have is that you will have little or nothing to say. If you're not gigging or getting your music out there in any other way, then this greatly reduces the story you can tell your potential fans. Essentially the only story you are going to be able to tell is, "Sat in my bedroom today making music." That looks like a sad and tedious existence that is unlikely to draw people to you.

That's the downside of the internet. However, there are many upsides. One of the best uses of the internet is to solicit opinions from your peers, which may be a sensible idea before you start trying to get your music to a wider public. This is where one of the social networks, such as MySpace or SoundClick (www.soundclick.com), that has a large music community could be useful to you.

Although there are stories of people breaking into the mainstream based on their MySpace offering, don't misunderstand these sites and see them as a quick way to fame. Instead, think of these sites as ways to get some feedback from your peers and perhaps to get one or two initial fans.

Setting Up Your Own Website

Whatever you do with cyberspace, I would suggest that you establish your own website at a comparatively early stage. This may be a very simple affair, or you may want something more sophisticated.

Although you may have little to say, I suggest you establish some form of presence. This will give people a chance to sign up for your mailing list and will also give the search engines an opportunity to start indexing your pages. By the time you move on to the next stage, you will need a fully functioning website and a substantial mailing list.

At this stage you can afford to experiment with your website. Ideally it will become a conduit for communication with your fan base and a place to involve fans and show them how much they matter to you. You can do this in simple ways—for instance, you could put up lots of photos of the people who come to your gigs. As well as involving fans in this way, hopefully the site will encourage others to come along and see what all the fuss is about.

Live Performances

If you are looking to interact with a real audience, then to a certain extent you will have to take whatever opportunities arise. However, not all opportunities will be suitable. If possible, try to match the forum for your live performance to your potential audience. So for instance, if you're a rock band, then a gig in a bar may be suitable. However, if you're a bubblegum pop act, then you might want to try and arrange some shows at a school. If you're a dance act, it is always going to be difficult to build a following; however, perhaps a series of nightclub appearances would be a suitable place to start building a fan base.

These are the obvious starting points. If you are to stand any chance at working in a creative industry (which the music industry is), then you will have to be creative in finding venues and looking for outlets where you can connect with people.

Any gathering will do; you just have to find a way to set up the gig. For instance, if you are a progressive rock act with a whole bunch of songs about sorcerers and goblins, then maybe the ideal forum for you to try to connect with your fan base would be at a convention for people with an interest in fantasy comics. This could be a very profitable option because you may find that many of these people have never seen live music before (let alone daylight), and so you could find a whole new audience. Added to which, these people are on the whole very loyal (remember, they go to fantasy comic conventions) and so are likely to stay with you as you build your career.

Your first public performances present you with a great opportunity to sell product. At this stage, don't!! You will still be growing as an act. Instead, make sure you use all of your public performances as an opportunity to get to know your audience (and get to know their contact details). Seek their feedback and find out what they like. As you can align your output with your potential fan base's tastes, you will increase your chances of success.

Releasing a CD

There will be one temptation that you may find irresistible: the desire to release a CD. You may find this desire is particularly hard to resist if you have recorded some tracks that you have made available on the internet. However, I would still counsel you against releasing a CD.

My main reason for cautioning against releasing a CD is that it will be bad (and in this context, bad means of poor quality, not good). At this early stage, unless you are a modern-day Mozart, you will not have the talent to put together an album of sufficient quality, although you may have one or two good songs. Everything will be wrong: The songs will be poor, the arrangements will be dubious, the playing will be weak, and the recording will be second rate. You are still growing and still learning—don't record your mistakes for posterity.

If you really, really, really have to release a CD from captivity, then please do it this way. First, find a local producer: You need someone who is prepared to tell you that you are useless. If they tell you that you're good, they're just flattering you to get your money.

Your choice of producer is going to be quite difficult. Unless you are exceptionally lucky, there will be a very limited number of people to choose from, if you can find anyone. Also, you are unlikely to have many contacts to ask for a recommendation. However, although this may be difficult, you do still need a producer.

With the producer in place, hire a local studio and record your best song...and only your best song. Get the song mixed and mastered so it is of the highest possible quality.

At this point, do nothing. Wait a week and then listen to the song. Either this will be the best thing you have heard or it will be a disappointment. If it is a disappointment, that is good: You will have learned something about the process. Wait at least six months and then repeat the process, and hopefully the six months will give you the opportunity to write some new songs that are better than the one you recorded.

If the song really is the best thing you have ever heard, then create some CDs. Burning a few CDs on your computer will be fine. On the CD label, you want to include the name of the act, the name of the song, and your web address. Anything else is superfluous and will distract from the music. (However, I won't argue if you want to add a copyright notice.)

Now, if against my suggestions you have reached the point of releasing a CD, then I assume you have a website, and on that website you have:

- A list of forthcoming gigs
- A way for people to sign up for your mailing list

If not, then you should.

Assuming your website is up and running as intended, give your CDs away. Don't just give the CDs to anyone, give them to people who really dig your music and give them to people who care about music. What you are looking to do is to use word of mouth to create a buzz. Don't give the CDs to your mom/dad/uncle/friend who is into origami—give them to people who can act as your ambassadors.

At this point I can sense you're trying to say to me, "But why only one song? We've got two/three/seven/twenty-five etc. great songs!" My reasoning here is simple: If you give away two songs, then you are doubling the chance of disappointing the listener. Give away three songs, and you triple the chance of disappointment.

You will also find that if you give away one song and someone loves it, that is great. You may have found a new fan. If you give away one song, and someone is so-so about it, then they will probably give you the benefit of the doubt and may turn up at a gig, which gives you an opportunity to really wow that person. However, if you give someone two songs and he or she loves one but is so-so about the second, that person may see you as only having one good song and not bother coming to the gig.

Remember, the only reason you would give away a CD is to create buzz that will encourage people to find out more about you. Hopefully, this will help you to get some more names onto your mailing list. You are not trying to create something for posterity at the moment, nor are you trying to generate any income from CD sales.

I suggest you hire a studio and a producer for several reasons. First, as I have already explained, I think you will get a better end product and will gain some useful feedback, hopefully learning a lot from an experienced person.

The second reason is that it will test your commitment to your career and test whether you can behave like a professional. If you are not prepared to make a comparatively small investment in your career at this stage (and remember, this will pretty much be your first "major" investment), then you should be hearing alarm bells ringing. Not only will a reluctance to invest in your career graphically illustrate your lack of commitment, it will also demonstrate to anyone else whom you want to invest in you that you don't have commitment and belief in what you are doing.

Another reason for going into a proper studio with a producer is to check out your ego. You may well have the technology to be able to record at home. However, you may also be too arrogant to make a good recording. Take some time in a studio and with a producer, and show a bit of humility by allowing yourself to change. You will be surprised by the improvement.

Funding

Clearly you will not be generating much, if any, income. If you need a source of income at this stage, I would recommend you follow the age-old tradition of getting a job. You don't need a glamorous job—in fact, the less glamorous it is, the easier it will be to turn your back and walk away—you just need a job where you have sufficient flexibility to be able to get out and play gigs and write new material.

The lack of money should also teach you financial discipline. It is crucial that you maintain this discipline once the money starts to come in. Remember, you will be dealing with lots of very small amounts of money. Spending large amounts will rapidly wipe out many months' hard work.

Accelerated Learning

I headed this section "Accelerated Learning," and I haven't detailed any sort of education so far. So why did I call this accelerated learning?

You have seen that in this section (as with the next section), you are going to have to do a lot of new and different things. Essentially, I am advocating a learning-by-doing strategy or, if you prefer, on-the-job training.

You will make a lot of mistakes through this strategy. However, your learning will be far deeper than could be achieved by simply reading a book or theorizing about a strategy. Through this approach, you will find your own path (if you don't, then you won't have a career), and most importantly, you will find what works and what doesn't work for your career.

You've seen that I advocate you limit your activities. For instance, I have suggested that you don't release a CD. I have set out my reasoning for the courses I have suggested. One other reason for focusing on what you are doing is to limit the scope of your mistakes. This will help to limit the financial risks you will be taking by making mistakes.

I'm also keen that you don't start with something until you are able to take full advantage of each situation. Staying with the example of a CD release, you may happen to release an acceptable-quality CD;

however, if you don't have the skills to exploit this product and generate income from the release, then you have wasted an opportunity.

In the next section ("Turning Pro"), we will go from accelerated learning to turbo-charged learning.

Turning Pro

The next stage in your career is often seen as the pinnacle for many musicians: turning pro. However, this is really just the beginning. Anyone can turn professional—generating an income, continuing to work as a professional musician, and creating a sustainable career are the hard parts.

This stage may come one or two years after you start interacting with the public. It may (and probably will) take longer. It depends how good you are and how hard you work (the real hard work being building up your fan base).

How Do You Know When You're Ready to Turn Professional?

There are certain key indicators that will tell you that you are ready to turn professional.

- Great songs. Not good songs or all right songs, but great songs. Not only do you need great songs, but you need lots of them— enough to fill a set and/or a CD with some left over. Having enough truly great songs is a real challenge, and it will probably take years to reach the stage of having enough great songs.

  One way to check that you have a lot of really good songs is to count the number of songs you have rejected and thrown off of your set list. The number of songs that you once thought were good enough but obviously you now don't should greatly outnumber the included songs. If it doesn't, then you are probably not being sufficiently discerning, and you need to get back and write some more. Alternatively, you are just not creating enough new (great) songs.

- Your stage craft should be perfected. By this point you should be able to put on a really good show. You should know how to work an audience, how to structure a set, and how to make sure that there is always a lot of energy on stage. In short, your show should be as good as any professional act that you might go and see.

- A mailing list with thousands of names.

- The ability to hustle. You will know how to get gigs, and you will have gig dates set for up to a year in advance. More than that, you will know how much you can earn from gigging and you will have cut your gigging expenses to the bone so you stand a chance of making a profit.

Hopefully, this won't be all you have achieved; however, it is the absolute minimum before you move to become professional.

Making the Transition

The transition to being a professional music maker should be an organic change. You won't wake up one morning with the realization that you are at this point; it will probably be something that comes to you gradually over time.

You will probably initially keep your day job (if you have one) and work as a musician, but then drop the day job when you can afford to. However, I would caution against burning all of your bridges and generating your income solely from music until you are convinced that you have enough great songs, your stage craft is sufficiently developed, and your fan base is sufficiently well established.

That being said, while you keep your day job, you are likely to find excuses not to force yourself to be successful in your music career—there's nothing quite like the prospect of poverty and starvation to force you to go and find work. There are many advantages to having a "proper" job—for example, regular pay. You will find many options for self-sabotage that will keep you doing the sensible thing and staying employed (even if, as I suggested, you took a scummy job so it would be easy to quit and you would be motivated to quit).

There are many other reasons why you may be unwilling to let go of a regular, secure income. For instance, you may have financial responsibilities (such as a mortgage), or you may have family responsibilities. Without wishing to sound harsh, if these are concerns for you, then the unsettled existence of a working musician is probably not a career you should follow. By all means keep music as a hobby, perhaps even a hobby that makes some money, but don't kid yourself that you're going to make it a career.

Once you are convinced you want to be a professional musician and you are ready to be, then go for it! There's no need to go wild; you can build your income and career steadily. However, it is imperative that you do start to build your career and stop making excuses for not being successful.

Marketing

If you have read the rest of the book, you will have seen that I am pretty skeptical about marketing because I feel it has little tangible, measurable value.

That being said, you will need to do some marketing at this stage in your career, largely to help you get in touch with the people who will help you build your career. In other words, you need to raise your profile so that people who may hire you for gigs will hear about you or, if you contact these people directly, you will have some materials to support you.

At this stage in your career, you need a fully functioning website. When I say "fully functioning," your website should perform the following functions for you:

- Tell people a bit about the act. This doesn't need to be anything too extensive, just enough to be interesting and encourage people to keep looking at the website.

- Capture interest. In other words, there should be a way to record the details of anyone who is interested so you can contact them to tell them about upcoming gigs, new products, and so on.

- Give details of how you can be contacted. There's nothing worse than knowing that someone wanted to book you for a gig but didn't know how to get in touch.

- Sell product. I'll talk more about your product range in a moment (for now, just accept that you need some, but you will need a very limited range). You will also see that I am fairly cautious about selling online at too early a stage.

- List all of your gigs (and includes details of how to get to each venue).

- Interact with fans. You don't need to do much to interact with fans—for instance, you don't need to set up a chat forum (although your fans may appreciate it). However, you do need to demonstrate that the relationship between you the artist and your newly acquired fan base is a two-way thing. You can do this in small ways. To extend an example I've used before, perhaps you could include pictures fans have taken at your gigs.

- Carry clips of your music and perhaps even video clips.

Added to this, your website should be capable of being (and should be) picked up by the search engine spiders.

If your website does all of these things, then it will be working both as a marketing tool and as a support for your business.

You may also seek out some press reviews around this time. As I've said before, I'm not convinced that reviews will increase your fan base. However, reviews are useful if you want to include comments on your flyers and other publicity. If a recognized music magazine calls you the next big thing (or some other similar cliché), this will help to add an element of credibility.

Anyone who hires you for a gig can then put this sort of comment on posters advertising the gig. Think of it from the perspective of the person hiring an act for a gig: If there are two acts that look fairly similar, what could sway you to choose one over the other? One influence would be favorable comments by a trustworthy source.

Keep On Keeping On

Although this will be a period of huge change in your life, there are certain things you need to keep doing:

- The most important thing is to keep learning. As you progress you will find what works and what doesn't. You will find new ways to generate income that you can exploit to your advantage. You will also continue to grow as a human being, and this will influence your creative output. In parallel, your fan base will grow (as individuals), and their tastes will change. You need to learn and understand how this affects their relationship with you.

- The second most important thing is to keep creating new material. Each new song is a possible new source of income. Once you stop creating new material (and thinking about new ways to exploit that material), you career will start to decline. If it starts to decline at this stage in your career, then it won't take long before you have nothing.

- The one thing you should be cherishing and protecting with your life is your fan base. This needs to be nurtured so it will continue to grow. If it does not grow, then you stand little chance of growing your income to sustain a successful career.

Generating Income

It is at this stage in your career that your income becomes serious.

Hopefully by now you will be generating a reasonable income from your live shows. That is not to say you will be generating a profit, just that you're not making too much of a loss. Obviously, your aim should be to generate a profit, and if you are doing so, then I congratulate your hard work and business acumen.

Unless you are performing every day, then you probably need to perform more shows and make more money/less losses from each show.

As well as gigging, now that you're a professional musician, it is time to start developing a range of products. If nothing else, you should now be at a stage that you are ready to record your first CD and you should have a sufficiently large fan base to ensure some sales. With any products you may want to create, and irrespective of what stage your career is at, if you don't have people to buy your product, then don't create it. Find an audience and then create a product to sell to these people, not the other way around.

Your first CD may be your first really big project. It could therefore be your first really big opportunity to lose a lot of money in one go. Due to the risks involved, your budgeting needs to be very tight. However, against this you must balance the need to create a first-rate product.

You may be tempted to cut costs and record the whole CD at home. In the same way that I advocated the involvement of an external studio/producer if you wanted to release a single track, I would advocate external involvement in any album-type project. However, given the costs and your additional development by this stage, I would not suggest this in such strong terms here.

Indeed, you may find that you can combine approaches. For instance, you might make some recordings in your home facility and some in a commercial studio. You could then pass the recordings over to someone else to mix the tracks. In this manner you can keep the costs to the minimum and produce a professional result. However, I still believe you will achieve the very best product that you can by using a professional producer from the start to the end of the project.

Before you begin a project such as this, it is worth drawing up a budget. As you probably already know, budgets are nearly always exceeded, so make sure you include a contingency for overspends. The minimum contingency you should include is 20% of the budget. If you're inexperienced or have had overspends before, then perhaps think about something more realistic, in the 40% to 50% range.

When drawing up your budget, try to be realistic about all of the costs involved. For instance, think about how much it is going to cost to get CDs pressed. It's pointless to spend all of the money on recording a project to then run out of money before you can produce the product that will generate income.

Try to balance your projected sales against the costs. It is incredibly hard to estimate how many CDs you are going to sell, and when making this projection, you need to be very wary about over-optimism. Just because you have 50,000 people on your mailing list, that doesn't mean you're going to sell 50,000 CDs. In reality, you will probably be doing well if you can sell to between 4% and 5% of the people on your mailing list. That being said, if you have 50,000 on your mailing list and you sell a CD priced at $15 to 5% of the list (that is 2,500 people), then you will generate $37,500 income, which is not bad. It should certainly cover the pressing costs and may even cover a chunk of the recording costs.

On a tangent, in case it doesn't go without saying, I hope you will ensure that your music is available for sale at iTunes and all of the other major (paid) download sites.

The two staples of most gigging acts are CDs and T-shirts, so you should think about T-shirts too. Remember, that as well as generating income, a T-shirt will also work as advertising for you, so it is worth taking a lot of time to get the design right.

Once you have got the design, there are many other areas where you can easily make silly decisions. To repeat a few of the examples I have mentioned throughout the book:

- Initially, you will have no clue about how many T-shirts will sell.

- While you will get a better unit price for ordering more T-shirts, you then have the problem of storing your stock.

- When thinking about T-shirts, it's very easy to think about getting shirts in small, medium, large, and extra-large sizes. However, this only increases the stock you have to carry. Perhaps for your first order you could get shirts in large only. If these are successful, then you can consider getting a wider range of sizes. Alternatively, take orders for other sizes (and print the shirts when you have enough orders to cover your costs).

The way to minimize your losses due to stupidity is to keep your orders for T-shirts to the minimum and to place an order only when your stock has nearly all been sold. Although this may mean that you are not getting the best prices when you buy your stock, it will mean that you will not be left with huge amounts of stock that cannot be sold, and the losses due to theft and so on will be reduced.

The easiest way to sell your CDs and T-shirts will be at gigs. You will have a ready audience who (provided the gig has been good) will be receptive to buying whatever you can sell. If you limit the range of goods on offer, then you will increase the chances of selling the individual items you are offering (since there are few other options).

One advantage to selling at gigs is that you can readily take cash, which means you don't have to deal with credit cards if you don't want to. (In fact, dealing with credit cards at a gig could be a pain.) The disadvantage to taking cash is that you have to trust the people who are selling your merchandise—it is very easy to pilfer cash and then claim the products have been stolen.

You can sell your products on your website; however, I would suggest you don't rush in here because there are several logistical challenges to overcome:

- First, you need to set up a way to receive credit card payments. This isn't overly difficult; however, it will take some time (especially if you want to set up a merchant account).

- When you can receive payment, then you need to find a way to fulfill the orders. This is unlikely to be more complicated than packing the products and putting them in the mail; however, you will need to ensure that the packaging is suitable, the correct postage is paid, and the packages are picked up for onward delivery. (You may find that with the number of packages, you can't fit everything into your local mailbox.)

- You'll also need to figure out who will send out the orders. Initially, it will probably be you. However, if you're going to be out of town (which hopefully you will be, because hopefully you will be gigging), then who will send out the orders for you? This is another area of risk for you. If you delegate the task and someone gets it wrong (for instance, they send the product to the wrong place or they send a product when a credit card has been declined), then you will start taking a loss on your operation.

None of these issues is insurmountable, and indeed, you will have to address all of them at some point if you are to have a successful career. You will also find that these issues are much easier to sort out if you have kept a very narrow product range.

Non-Performing Artists

If you are a non-performing artist (for instance a composer, a "pure" songwriter, or a studio-bound musician) who hasn't created some sort of act that can go out and perform (thereby transforming yourself into, and giving yourself the advantage of, a performing artist), then life will be tough at this stage. Your options to build a fan base will be severely limited, and without a fan base, there will be no one to whom your product can be sold.

In Chapter 7, when looking at the options if you don't have a fan base, I mentioned the possibility of event-type performances of your music, with the example of people who make spacey-type music arranging an event at a planetarium where their music could be played to accompany a show of some sort. If you can't find these sorts of outlets (or you can't create a suitable event yourself), then it will be really hard to kick start your career.

Life will also be tougher for the non-performing musician because you will reach the stage that you feel you want to (and are ready to) release a CD much sooner than a conventional performing act that is out gradually building up its fan base. You will find that you pressurize yourself to record and release a CD: Your logic is likely to follow the argument that if you don't release a CD, then what are you doing that could constitute calling yourself a musician, let alone a professional musician?

If you're a non-performing musician who is approaching this stage, and you can't find an outlet for your music, then please try harder. Recording and releasing a CD may make you feel good (at least temporarily), but if you don't have a fan base to buy your CD, it will ultimately be a fairly fruitless exercise, and you'll be left with a lot of CDs cluttering up your home.

Building the Business: Opening an Office

You will ready to move on and start building your business when you are:

- Working as a professional musician. (You probably dispensed with any collaborators who did not share your level of commitment to progress their career.)

- Gigging regularly (or putting on some other form of performance regularly) with the necessary equipment to get to gigs and put on a good show and so on.

- Selling a limited range of products (and these products sell well).

At this stage in your career, you will be building the foundations so that you can grow from a musician scratching out a hand-to-mouth existence to one making a reasonable living.

Raising Money for Investment

This may be the point in your career at which you need to invest money. If you have been working as a professional musician for the last few years, then you are unlikely to have much cash (even if you saved your money as I recommended earlier in this chapter). Most of your money is likely to have been spent meeting the expenses of promoting your act.

There are several sources of finance. The main choices will be bank loans and business partners (such as a manager). I will discuss your relationship with a manager later in this section.

If you borrow money from a bank, then you are opening yourself up to a whole new scale of debt (see Figure 12.4). So far in your career, most of your losses (or potential losses) have been containable and/or limited. For instance, if you take a loss on a gig, it is usually a comparatively small loss. Typically the most you would lose would be the cost of hiring the venue (if you hired it), the cost of promotion, the cost of staffing for the gig, other expenses (such as insurance), and the cost of transportation to the gig.

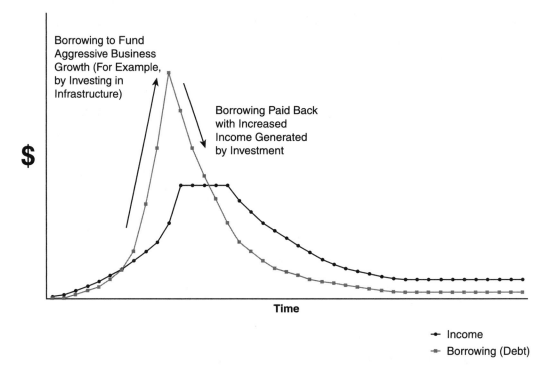

Figure 12.4 To grow your business, you will probably need to borrow money, and this borrowing will be a debt to your business. When you are borrowing in order to invest to grow your business aggressively, your total level of debt is likely to exceed your income. At this stage in your career, a large proportion of your income will therefore be spent on servicing your debt (that is, paying interest on the money you owe).

That is not to say that you couldn't lose a chunk of money with a gig; however, you would usually not expect to lose that much. For instance, if you lost $1,000 on a gig, that may seem like a lot to lose. Typically, if you are looking at a gig with a promoter, then the most you are likely to lose would be your own expenses traveling to, and in connection with, the gig.

Losses of this level are usually an amount you can walk away from. However, it is still possible to get into serious debt just by gigging.

In contrast, if you borrow money, then you are getting a large chunk of cash that has to be repaid. You will borrow money because you need to invest it. Investment is a euphemism for spending with the hope that you will generate income. If you spend money you have borrowed and you don't generate enough income to repay the loan and the interest, then you will owe money to the bank (or whoever has lent you money).

If you owe money to a bank, they will usually be reasonable initially. However, after a while they will get bored and will stop being patient. At this stage they will ask for the money in an unpleasant manner, usually by making you (personally) bankrupt. You're far more likely to face financial ruin at this stage, when you appear to be becoming successful, than you will when you are at the starving, struggling musician stage.

However, if you don't invest, then you won't be able to grow your career. If you are not willing to invest, then it is probably best that you walk away from your career now.

You are likely to need money to invest in three things:

- People
- Places
- Processes

In short, you are going to invest in the infrastructure of your business. You will need people to run the business for you, a place for those people to work, and processes to get your products to your fan base.

You're likely to find yourself in a bit of a "chicken and egg" situation, wondering whether to sort your infrastructure before you grow your product range. Unfortunately, there is no simple answer here, and you will have to find a pragmatic solution (as I will discuss).

People

I talked about hiring people in Chapter 9. Finding the right people to work with you is one of the toughest tasks. However, the joy of finding the right people to work with you and benefit the business is amazing.

The first people you hire are going to have to be very flexible and be prepared to undertake a wide range of tasks. (You certainly don't want an overly rigid attitude toward their tasks.) For instance, your first hire's job description could include many of the following tasks:

- Answering the phone
- Chasing up and booking gigs (as well as hustling for gigs)
- Processing orders to merchandise and sending out the products
- Ordering goods for sale
- Webmaster/mistress as well as moderator on any internet forums
- Looking after your paperwork (orders, receipts, and so on)
- Fixing the plumbing and feeding the office cat

In short, your first hire will do all those tiresome but crucially important things that you should be doing. This will be the person who runs your business, so make sure you treat him or her right!

Places

Your person (or people) will need somewhere to work. If they are flexible enough to take on all of the tasks I have outlined, then they will probably be fairly flexible with their work environment, provided it is warm and dry and there is somewhere to get a cup of coffee. In addition to housing your staff, you will need property to house your stuff (which could include the business's paperwork and your stock).

Buying or renting property is a very expensive business, so if you can (at least initially), borrow space. This may mean you (or more importantly, your staff) have to put up with a slightly less than ideal workspace. For instance, you may find a shed, a garage, or a cheap industrial unit. Whatever you find, make sure it is secure—it will be no fun trying to complete your tax return if all of your records get eaten by mice or shredded during a break-in.

Processes: Getting Your Product to Your Customers

"Process" is one of those nasty management-speak words, so let me turn it into English in the context of this part of the chapter. Your processes are the means by which you get your products to your customers. This is not simply a matter of fulfillment, but it also includes getting your stock in the first place, holding the stock, as well as sending out orders after first having made sure that the appropriate money has been received (and checks cleared, if appropriate).

I mentioned the chicken-and-egg situation about whether processes or products come first. To my mind, processes equate to the egg and therefore come first. When you first start, your process (such as it will be) will probably be to sell CDs at gigs. However, when you grow, and especially when you want to sell products from your website and you're not there to send out the orders, then you need a solid process in place.

There are probably two ways to get your processes in place. One is to sit down and agree on the processes between all of the shareholders. The second option is to get your office person to sort things out.

I favor the second option. If you trust this person and he or she is competent, then he or she should be perfectly capable of undertaking this sort of task (although you may find your office person gets bored very quickly if this is all he or she does all day every day).

And by the way, if you don't trust your office person, or if he or she is not competent, then fire that person immediately—remember, that person is looking after your business. For your own peace of mind, you may want to check the processes he or she has put in place, just to make sure your office person is thinking about the task from the perspective of your fans' experience (rather than trying to make life easy for himself or herself).

When you start thinking about fulfillment, you have three main options:

- Send out the product yourself.

- Use a third party to send out your orders.

- Use an on-demand service.

These three options can be integrated into your processes, and you can, of course, mix and match these options. So for instance, you could start off by getting your office person to send out products, but as you grow, you could outsource this function to a specialized fulfillment service.

When you start scaling up your business, particularly when you start finding new fans who are based overseas (in relation to you), you may find that an on-demand service offers many advantages to your business. As I have said before, these on-demand services may not generate the biggest profits; however, they do allow you to expand your business while minimizing your business risks, and you can always use them for a very short period of time.

Manager

Many of the challenges associated with people, places, and processes can be readily addressed if you have a manager. Indeed, it would not be unreasonable to expect a manager to supervise these tasks on your behalf and to provide premises (since any manager should already have premises).

However, if your manager is going to help, then you should ensure that he or she does not charge twice. So for instance, the manager shouldn't charge you for staff he or she might "lend" you to help run your business but not allow the cost of those people against the fee you pay for management services.

Increasing Income: Increasing Profitability

When you have your infrastructure in place (or at least a basis for your infrastructure to become operational), then you can look to grow the business. To grow the business you need a healthy, active, and growing fan base, and you need a wide range of products to sell to your fan base. You need both elements (the product and purchaser); one without the other will mean you can't generate income.

Under the previous step, I suggested that you should get your infrastructure sorted before you start to expand your range of products. I stand by this view: You can have all the products in the world, but if you don't have the wherewithal to get them out to people who are paying you money, then you will find lots of very unhappy people, and you will spend your life dealing with complaints rather than making music. (And it will be you dealing with the problems, because you won't have hired someone to run your office as I suggested.)

Anyway, let me now slightly qualify that view. It is pointless to have an infrastructure if you don't have anything to sell (or anyone to sell it to).

Building an infrastructure will cost you money, and as I have already suggested, you may want to borrow money to finance that exercise. Although I have separated the two steps (building your infrastructure and building your products), you should make sure that in practice the two steps are linked so that you can generate some income to repay your investment.

The sensible approach is to build part of the infrastructure and grow the product line. Once that small expansion has been incorporated, you can build your infrastructure a bit more and grow the product line to a greater extent. An example of this step-by-step growth was shown earlier with the illustration of outsourcing order fulfillment.

Anyway, once you have your products and processes in place, then you can start aggressively scaling up your business. Earlier in your career, it is harder to scale up in a meaningful way. If you have five fans, then you may be able to triple the size of your fan base by gaining another ten people. Fifteen people will not generate sufficient income to sustain a career. When you have a wide range of products and a fan base into the hundreds of thousands, then scale becomes a significant issue.

To really increase your earnings (which, after all, is the point of scaling), you will have to:

- Earn more money from each fan. (You can do this by offering more products, increasing your prices, or both.)

- Increase the size of the fan base. To be worthwhile, you need to ensure that this increase is permanent. There's no point in gaining fans and then losing them quickly or alienating your existing fans because all you will do is create a large number of dissatisfied individuals. That's one of the problems with growing in scale—you can upset many people. When you're small, you can only upset a few people!

- Take advantage of the size of your fan base. Anything you do is much more likely to become an "event."

I'll touch on some of these themes through the rest of this section.

Increasing the Product Range

So far I haven't advocated expanding your product range beyond a CD and a T-shirt. Before I go any further and talk about your product range, let me give you some examples of how other businesses make their money. (These are both examples from the UK. Even if the conditions don't directly apply in your market, I am sure you can find a product for which a similar principle does.)

If you purchase a new car in the UK, you can almost always negotiate a discount on the manufacturer's price. It may not be much of a discount (perhaps only 5%), but you will be able to get a discount. This isn't because there is a huge profit margin on cars. In fact, the contrary is true—the margins are wafer thin, and having given a discount, there may be not profit for the dealer. Instead, the reason for the discount is that the dealer wants to secure you as a customer.

Once the dealer has secured you as a customer, then it will make money from you in two places: first, by offering finance for the (discounted) car that you will be buying, and second, from the servicing costs. Arranging the financing will give the dealer a lump sum commission payment (which can compensate for the cost of selling the car as well as providing some profit), and the servicing will provide a stream of income for the dealer over the lifetime of the car.

The other example I want to give you is printers. If you go to a PC store, printers are dirt cheap. However, when you buy an ink/toner cartridge, you need to spend a small fortune. To illustrate this, I could buy a Hewlett-Packard LaserJet 1018 today for £49.99 (roughly $100). A print cartridge (from the same store) will then cost me £39.95 (roughly $80). In other words, every time I want a new toner cartridge, I would have to spend almost as much as I paid for the printer.

So what's the point I am trying to make here? My point is twofold:

- First, don't expect to earn money from those parts of your business that you may see as being your core business. (That is, don't expect that your music will be what sustains your income.)

■ Second, don't get too precious about your pricing strategies. You need to bring people in so that you can convert them to becoming fans. In the world of the internet, music is becoming increasingly commoditized, so in the end, you may find that your music (whether as a CD or a download) is sold very cheaply or even, in certain circumstances, given away.

It is very hard for a musician to accept that the activity that defines him or her (the making of music) can be ascribed a lower value than a transitory piece of merchandising. However, while I share your pain, this is unfortunately the nature of the world today. I don't like saying this, but you're just going to have to get over it and get on with your career.

After that introduction, my thoughts about your product range are quite straightforward: Progressively build your product range. Check back in Chapter 8, when I discussed the range of products you could consider. The challenge in building your product range is to introduce products progressively and to offer the right products.

If you go from offering only a CD and a T-shirt to offering a whole wardrobe, posters, mugs, dolls, and everything else you can think of, then you will look like you have sold out. You will also find that it takes time to design and order your products.

If you only have one T-shirt for sale, then a much more sensible approach is to offer two T-shirts, perhaps in different sizes, and maybe a sweatshirt. Once you have got those items and they are selling, then (and only then) think about something else.

Record labels often stipulate a minimum and a maximum number of CDs that an artist must produce over a certain timeframe. The minimum number is obvious. The maximum number restriction is quite sensible. If an artist produces several CDs, then it is very hard to market them all. It is much easier to market one CD, and then market another CD a year later. If you are producing CDs (or DVDs) or any other product that needs to be highlighted as a specific product, then it makes sense to limit your output.

Also, as a working musician, you are unlikely to be able to produce several CDs in a year with the time it takes to write and record an album.

As you are looking to expand your product range, remember that I included gigs within the scope of products. You should be looking to increase your income from gigs. There are two main ways to do this:

- Play more gigs. As an established artist who is looking to grow, you should be playing as many gigs as you are physically able to do. There should be no problems organizing gigs, and you should be increasing the territories in which you are playing.

- Play bigger gigs. Larger venues will allow you to make more money, which will come from several sources:
  - The greater number of people coming to see you
  - Enhanced sponsorship opportunities
  - More merchandise sales (as there will be more people at your gigs)

You will also find many other opportunities to generate income from live performances—for instance, support bands will pay to join your tour (or rather, their record labels will pay).

Licensing Deals

I'll talk about the risks associated with running an expanding business later in this section (under the heading "Increased Risks"). Licensing deals can generate income and help you manage the risks in your business. Once you have reached this stage in your career, you are likely to be sufficiently interesting for potential licensees to consider a deal with you. You are also likely to have enough clout to negotiate a reasonable deal.

The main advantages of licensing deals are:

- Risk management. The licensee will have the cash-flow challenges and will have to make the difficult commercial decisions (such as how much stock to order).

- Logistics. The licensee will deal with ordering and fulfillment. If you want to include sales from your website to make life easy for your fan base or generate some commission from referred sales, then you may need to arrange some clever programming, but once that is working, life should be simple.

- Administrative ease. At a stroke, all of the paperwork associated with the licensed merchandise will be passed to your licensee.

- Increased sales. The licensee should be an expert in selling merchandise and will have an incentive to sell as much product as possible.

- Advances. The licensee may be prepared to agree to pay an advance. This may ease cash-flow problems for you in other areas.

There will be additional work in choosing and appointing the licensee that would not arise if you undertake the work yourself. Also, you are likely to have to agree on and approve merchandise (which you would do in any case if you were looking after your own merchandising). However, on the whole, the appointment of a licensee can be very beneficial, reducing your costs and risks while increasing your income.

Expanding the Fan Base

If you've been paying attention, you will have picked up on my many references to my skepticism about marketing. This is where things change....

You should still keep nurturing your fan base. (You're really going to need them on the way down.) However, you may find at this stage of your career that advertising can be effective (although it will never be as effective as word-of-mouth recommendations).

Instead of just paying for advertisements in the press, you will have the opportunity to generate far more buzz through your activities—for instance, your gigs will provide an opportunity to gather a lot of press coverage.

If you play a gig to 1,000 people, then no one really cares. (Well, your mother will, and I'm sure you will love it.) If you a play a gig to 10,000 people, that is interesting, and the music press will probably cover the event. However, if you play a gig to 100,000 people, you're going to be making the evening news.

I've said it before, but it is worth repeating: At the stage when you have a range of products to sell, then each new fan is more valuable to you because each one can buy a lot of product. At the stage when you only have a CD and a T-shirt for sale, the amount of money you can generate from each fan from non-gigging activities is highly limited.

Getting Serious about Web/Mail Order

If you haven't done so already, it is now time to get serious about your web/mail order activities.

One of the reasons I particularly favor word-of-mouth marketing is because it gives you the opportunity to (metaphorically) cross borders. People have friends and family overseas and "chat" with "friends" from around the globe on the internet.

With a highly geographically scattered fan base, one of the best ways to connect with people is to give them the opportunity to get hold of your CDs and merchandise. This is where you need to have a slick operation that is ready to deal with the international postal systems. For this, you will need to be able to charge the appropriate postage and comply with any restrictions (such as the declaration of any duties to be paid) of the destination country.

You also need to understand that there are some countries where there are enormous challenges with the postal system. For instance, some systems are incompetent; others are just plain corrupt, and any goods sent to these countries will simply be stolen.

Let me just quickly mention the non-performing musician. At this point you may be thinking that a highly scattered fan base that could never expect to see you gig is ideal (and for some, it may be). However, to get this sort of fan base you need to rely on word-of-mouth marketing. This isn't something that happens with conventional marketing.

Word of mouth mostly works for acts that can create a buzz. Unfortunately for you, it is very hard to create a real buzz unless you perform live.

As part of your selling activities, you should capture as much information as you can about your fan base. This will give you useful information such as an indication of where all your fans are based. If you then find that enough fans are located in one city or country, this gives you a very strong hint about where you should be performing.

For instance, if you're an act based in Romania, and you find that you've got one million fans in New York, then you should go to New York. You may not have the necessary skills to put on your own gig in New York; however, if you can find a reputable promoter in New York, then you should be able to make the case for the promoter to hire you for a gig, given that you have a strong fan base in the city.

Increased Risks

As you expand your business operations, you are going to be increasing your risks considerably.

When you look at individual items—for instance, the cost to order 1,000 T-shirts—the costs may seem manageable. However, if you look at ordering 1,000 small T-shirts, 1,000 medium T-shirts, 1,000 large T-shirts, 1,000 extra-large T-shirts, 2,000 sweatshirts, 500 hoodies, 5,000 posters, 2,500 baseball caps, 500 mugs, as well as 50,000 CDs, then your cost will increase greatly. However, this is not the only issue to consider:

- First, you will be holding stock. This stock has a value that can be reduced or wiped out if the stock is damaged or stolen. To guard against these risks, you may want to think about insurance (which is yet another cost). If you are using a fulfillment service, you should check who has the risk for your stock. I would guess you would be quite upset is someone else let your assets be stolen and then told you that they're not insured.

- Until the stock is sold, its purchase represents a loss to your business. There will be a timing difference between when you order your stock and when you sell it. You therefore need to ensure it is available for sale at the very earliest opportunity. You've probably heard businesses talking about their cash-low problems—this is the situation to which they are referring. In extreme circumstances, buying too much stock without selling it quickly enough can make you technically insolvent.

- With ordering and selling stock, you will have lots of bits of money moving around, and often you will be dealing with a large number of small sums. If you are not on top of the situation, there is a significant risk that some of the sums will not reach your bank account (whether by mistake or by criminal intent).

Superstar Status

I've used the term superstar because I knew it would catch your attention. For the purpose of this section, superstar status is a misnomer—by the term all I mean is that you have reached the peak (or hopefully the plateau) of your career. This isn't to suggest that your business cannot get better once you've reached this point; it's just that it will be at a very good level, and you will be making a good living.

When you reach this status, you won't do many new things, but you are likely to do some of the things you already do somewhat differently. Here are a few pointers:

- You're probably likely to gig less. There are several reasons for this (in no particular order):
    - There will be more opportunities for other forms of publicity and income generation (for instance, from television or offers to write music for films).
    - You will do bigger shows. It is simply not practical to do too many shows. (Generally you can't do mega shows year after year in the same city.)
    - There will be larger geographical distances between shows. Travel and time zones will militate against too many performances.

- ❑ You will probably want more time for yourself, whether to spend with your family or to write new songs or to get involved with other projects.

- ❑ Your health. By the time you reach this stage you may be past the very first flush of youth. (In other words, like me, you may be out of your twenties.) Common sense alone may dictate that you slow down (even if only slightly).

- You will probably take a more global approach and will be keen to ensure you are selling in as many geographical markets as possible.

- To maximize your penetration of global markets, you may well partner with other businesses. In English, this means that you may enter into an agreement with a record label.

- With your increased earning power/fan base, you may want to renegotiate your existing deals. If you don't renegotiate now, you may not get another chance. You will also find that licensees and business partners will seek to maximize their earnings from their business they carry out with you—in short, they will increase their prices to your fans as far as they possibly can.

As I said, these are just a few pointers. How, when, and whether these are practical will depend on a range of situations, and to be frank, by the time you get to this stage in your career, you need highly specialized advice that will be unique to your situation and is therefore beyond the scope of this book.

You should not regard this list as being possibilities only when you reach superstar status. You can do many of them at an earlier stage; however, for some, this is the optimum point to adopt them into strategy.

Managing the Downward Path

At some point your career will move off its plateau. It is probably overdramatic to call this the beginning of your career descent, and it also has all sorts of negative connotations that I do not wish you to associate with a downward trend. However, we must accept that you cannot stay at the very top of your game forever.

It might seem out of place to think about managing the decline of your career, especially if it has yet to start. However, I think it is worth considering because many of the decisions you make on your way up will have a far greater impact on your way down. For instance, if you sell off all your rights, then you won't have any continuing income from your music. If you get enough money for selling your rights, then you may not care. However, if you don't earn sufficient income, you may spend your retirement years in comparative poverty.

The Start of the Downward Path

There is probably one key characteristic by which you will be able to recognize that the peak/plateau of your career has ended, and you have begun the downward path. Your fan base will stop growing—in other words, the number of new people who become fans will be less than the number of people who drift away from you.

Clearly, it is difficult to measure this point because you are unlikely to be able to accurately measure the number of fans you have lost (which could include fans who have simply drifted away or with whom you have lost contact). However, there are two measures that you can look at:

- The rate of growth of new fans
- The rate of growth of the income of the business

When either of these measures slows, it is likely to be indicative that you're entering the next phase of your career.

You should note that for both of these factors, I suggest you look at the rate of growth, not just the growth. The difference is important: If you add one fan, then your fan base is still growing. However, if you only add one fan in a year, then you're probably in trouble. Take a look at Table 12.1, which gives an example set of figures for income.

These figures look impressive and show year-on-year growth. Now look at Table 12.2, which shows the same figures but has added in the figures for the income growth and the rate of growth. Although income is growing, the rate at which it is growing is starting to fall. This is often an early indicator that the income is going to start falling.

Table 12.1 An Apparently Healthily Growing Income Stream

Year	Income
Year 1	$1,000,000
Year 2	$1,100,000
Year 3	$1,210,000
Year 4	$1,320,000
Year 5	$1,420,000

Table 12.2 A Healthy Income, but a Declining Rate of Growth

Year	Income	Income Growth	Rate of Growth
Year 1	$1,000,000	–	–
Year 2	$1,100,000	$100,000	10%
Year 3	$1,210,000	$110,000	10%
Year 4	$1,320,000	$110,000	9%
Year 5	$1,420,000	$100,000	7.5%

As you can see, although the growth is still good when expressed in dollar amounts, in this example, between Years 3 and 5 the rate of growth falls by 25%. If this is your business, then this sort of fall is probably indicative that you are entering the mature phase of your career.

Take a look at Figure 12.5 and you will see that I have shown the figures in Table 12.2 graphically. Instead of showing the rate of growth figures, I have shown the change in the rate of growth because this more clearly illustrates when a career may have started its downward path, even though the increases in income (when taken in isolation) suggest that everything is fine.

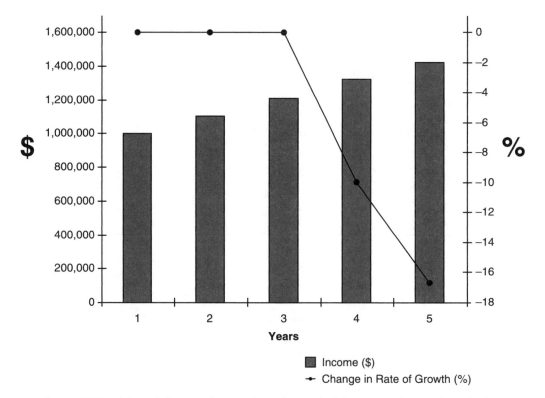

Figure 12.5 Although income is growing, the underlying rate of growth is declining. This is an indication that income may soon start to reduce.

Maintenance, Not Growth

There are a lot of things you can do when you have reached superstar status that cost of lot of money. These massive investments can usually be rewarded with even larger inflows of income. When your income starts slowing, you need to stop spending money (or at least reduce your spending habit); otherwise, you will find yourself taking losses very quickly.

The main expenses you should start cutting and the main costs you should take control of are:

- Advertising. When you are growing your career and at the peak of your career, advertising can be cost effective. However, advertising loses much of its effectiveness when you are on the downhill slope because you will largely be appealing to an existing fan base (who want direct contact, not flashy public advertising).

Cutting your advertising because you're in a declining market will work as something of a self-fulfilling prophecy, so if you cut all public visibility, you will simply drop off the radar as far as many people are concerned. Therefore, you should aim to maximize your media coverage but minimize your spending.

- Record label costs. If you enter into a deal with a record label, then the label will take a large chunk of the income. This is not unreasonable, provided the record label is selling lots of CDs for you. However, when sales start to slow, you may find it becomes more efficient to change the nature of your deal or to release your own CDs (subject to any deal with the label being negotiable or expiring).

- People. Superstars tend to surround themselves with lots of "people." Unless these people have a function that directly contributes to your income, you should end their employment relationship with you.

- Infrastructure. While you are growing it is logical to include some slack in your infrastructure to allow some growth. This is a prudent business practice. When the business is contracting, slack equates to waste, so the efficiency of the infrastructure should be improved.

Publishing Income

You will notice that so far in this chapter I have not mentioned one significant source of income: publishing. There are several reasons for this, but the main reason is that the time to get a publishing deal (if you are going to get one) will be very dependent on your business and your personal needs.

If you are a death-metal band, then it is unlikely that you would expect many other people to cover your songs, so you may feel that it is not worth the expense of paying someone to search out covers. For this reason, you may want to keep your publishing. That being said, there are probably many opportunities for a death-metal band to have their music synchronized to video, and a publisher may be able to seek out these opportunities.

By the time you reach the end of your career peak, you should have created a large body of work. When you are on your way down, you need to look for as many opportunities as possible to keep exploiting this music. One of the best ways is through publishing, in terms of both of covers and synchronization to various media.

You could find there will be many more opportunities to synchronize your music to video. For instance:

- There will be times when your style/sound fits the time period covered by the video (in the same way that sometimes you need a track from the Sixties).

- There will be programs about you, your generation, and your genre.

- There will be times when a particular track is thematically right. (For instance, there are some times when the only track that is right is Elton John's "Sorry Seems to Be the Hardest Word.") With a larger catalog, you will have many more chances of hitting these "everyman"-type themes.

When you're past your career peak, the discipline of the early years and the ruthless focus on picking up all of the small amounts of money should come back to you. (Indeed, I hope it never goes away.) These synchronization opportunities may not earn much money when looked at in isolation, but if you add them all together—particularly if you are taking a global approach—you will see that they can generate a healthy income.

Other Sources of Income

As well as looking at publishing, you'll have to find ways to make your assets (that is, your existing recordings) work harder for you. Most of these options are likely to have been followed by any record company (if you signed to one). You should still consider these options if possible:

- Reissue the back catalog at a cut price.

- Issue a "Best Of" or other retrospective-type CD.

- Include your music on compilation CDs.

- Mine the archives for interesting but previously unreleased recordings.

You should be careful not to ignore the other sources of income that are open to you:

- You can still release new CDs. However, at this stage in your career, you are likely to sell less than you did at your peak. This doesn't mean you have to make less profit; it just means you have to manage your costs more closely.

- New CDs usually create an opportunity to tour. At this stage in your career, you should have a large, loyal following who still want to see you, provided you are making your gigs a real event. Remember, when you reach this stage of your career, your fan base is likely to have aged in the same way that you have. With age, most people get more discerning and so will have higher expectations from a gig. They will also be prepared to pay more money, so you will probably find that gigs can become incredibly profitable.

- Unless you have a really strong brand image, merchandise may become less of a significant source of income, but you should still look after this source because it could continue to generate healthy chunks of income.

Reinventing the Record Label (and the Rest of the Music Industry)

I could write a whole book about reinventing the record label and the rest of the music industry. In fact, that might be my next book....

Anyway, I'm being slightly melodramatic here, but the opportunities for artists also present new and different challenges and opportunities for record companies whose businesses are being bent out of shape by the changes in the market. (See Chapter 3 for a discussion of some of these issues.)

This section sets out some thoughts about how record companies (and others in the established music business) may change in light of the new opportunities. These thoughts may also be useful if you are looking to cut a deal with an established label or management company, or they may be particularly pertinent if you're looking to set up your own label or get into management.

Structural Weaknesses of the Recording Industry

Record companies have two main problems: the inherent weakness of their brand and their lack of relationship with the record-buying public. Let me explain each point in turn:

- Record companies do not have recognizable brands any more. By which I mean that if you go to a record store and see a CD on the Universal label or the Sony BMG label (for instance), that doesn't give you any indication about what the music on the CD might be. I'm not suggesting there was a golden age of record company brands; however, there certainly was a time when you knew what to expect from, say, a Motown or an Atlantic record.

- Record companies do not have a relationship with the record-buying public. This is not surprising. After all, why would anyone care about one particular label? There are two main conduits through which the record company and the public communicate:
  - Advertising (especially television advertising), which is the label's opportunity to disseminate its message to the public
  - Sales, which is the only form of communication where record companies really listen to the public

One of the reasons why you don't have any expectations of a particular musical style from a particular label is that they tend to sign a wide variety of acts. This is not a bad thing. There are labels that specialize in particular genres (for instance, there are several labels that specialize in metal), but these labels don't necessarily exploit this specialization to their maximum financial advantage.

Record labels have other systemic difficulties with their conventional business model. In particular:

- Ninety-five percent of acts do not recoup their advances.
  This doesn't mean that 95% of acts create a loss for record labels; this simply means that there are a lot of shattered dreams (and for a fair chunk of that 95%, the record company won't make any profit).

- Most signings involve huge amounts of risk for labels. The label will sign an act, and when they release their CD, the label will market the product like crazy in the hope of generating sales. The only way that record labels address this problem is by becoming more risk adverse (that is, by adopting more conservative signing policies). This conservatism leads to a view that the music industry is homogenized with all artists looking the same.

On a side note, just because I can identify a few weaknesses, please don't think for a moment that I am suggesting the recording industry is in crisis or will topple if my thoughts are not adopted immediately. The recording industry is owned by many very large corporations who will squeeze every last drop of income out of their investments and will ensure the business carries on in some form or another.

A New Business Model for Record Companies

That's enough criticism about record companies. How about something positive? How about something radical (and cheaper than the current system)? Here's an outline of a business model a record company could adopt to use some of the techniques outlined in this book.

- Focus on a particular genre. (Pop would be a good starting point.)

- Forget the notion of being a record company in the current sense. Instead, think about becoming a magazine or an internet portal. I'm not saying a label should *be* an internet portal, just think about acting like one. (I will explain later.)

- Stop any artist development. (Some people may suggest this happened a long time ago.) Instead, look to managers and production companies to bring you fully developed artists (in your genre) that are ready to go. An artist who is ready to go has:

  - An image

  - A number of songs (recorded and ready to be released)

  - Most importantly, an established fan base that is desperate to buy that act's CD

- Sign a number of acts, maybe 10—certainly more than a label would sign if it were to operate in a conventional manner. Make the deals on the following basis:

  - No advances. Instead, pay to purchase the fan base. (Note: Depending on the jurisdiction in which a label operates, there may be data protection legislation implications. Also, both the label and the act will need to ensure that this action does not alienate the fan base.)

  - No royalties. Instead, profit sharing.

  - The record company has an interest in all income sources (CDs, DVDs, merchandise, touring, and so on).

- Release lots of singles (in other words, single strong songs rather than albums with variable-quality content) if practical, given the chart requirements in a particular location and the buying patterns of the fan base. Aim to reach a stage, as soon as possible, where no physical product is sold (in other words, the label only sells digital downloads and so cuts cost of business).

- Undertake all of the logistics (such as getting CDs pressed and distributed, getting music onto iTunes, and so on). Do this at a lower cost and better than any act could perform this function independently.

- Develop a relationship with the fan base (in other words, develop a fan base for the label). Develop the label's own brand of merchandise (as well as merchandise for the label's acts).

- For live performances, put several of the label's acts on the same bill. Depending on the nature of the acts, it may be possible to share the backing band between acts. For a pop label this may work, but for a rock label, this will be impractical. However, with a rock label, instead of putting on a simple gig, the label could (for instance) organize a touring festival of its acts (much like, say, the Ozzfest festival).

I have a feeling that this may be a bit too radical at the moment, but let's see what happens. Remember, you read it here first....

Why Adopt This New Business Model?

As a record company, there are many reasons to adopt this model:

- First, the label has outsourced the development risk for new acts. This means that at the point of signing, the label will know and understand what it is signing and will already have a first single and video produced by the management/production company. This also means that the label can focus on its strengths: marketing and distribution. By reducing its risks and its ridiculous cost base, the label can sign more acts (and therefore generate more income).

- By thinking as a magazine/internet portal, the label will be thinking about how it presents a cohesive and integrated front to its own growing fan base over a sustained period (rather than just trying to flog one solitary single). By behaving in this way, the record company can start to develop its own brand-based fan base that commands loyalty independently of its acts.

- Once the label has built up its own community, it won't need to be so concerned about advertising (although that doesn't mean that advertising has no place). The label will already have a list of all the people with whom it wants to communicate. This has other advantages—for instance, by using its fan base it will be much cheaper and faster to launch/build new acts.

- A greater focus on singles and digital downloads will cut costs because the label won't have to deal with stock (both holding stock and dealing with returned stock). That being said, if the label enters the merchandise market, there are stock implications unless merchandising is licensed out.

- Through cutting costs, the label can take a longer-term view. Keeping an act that isn't performing so well in the short term won't hit the label financially.

- Through direct involvement with the fan base, with greater reliance on download sales and live performances providing income, the effects of piracy will be greatly reduced.

- Back catalogues will never be deleted. Instead, they can be made available from download services and CD on-demand services, thereby giving a much longer timeframe over which income can be generated.

- Record labels will truly be able to operate as global organizations and not headquarters organizations with lots of bickering satellite companies over which the local label has no control.

Changes to the Role of Managers

Clearly, if any of these ideas is adopted, then the role of the manager will change considerably and probably for the better.

It would be likely that managers would morph into production companies, taking a range of talents (such as performers, writers, producers, and video makers) under their wing. In this way, the manager could become a one-stop production shop that then gets its product to market through the conduit of the record label.

13 Career Templates

In the previous chapter I talked about how you could put the pieces together to develop your own career to make a living from music. In this chapter I am going to take that theme further with a range of career templates for artists in various situations in order to demonstrate how the various themes discussed in this book can be applied in practice. For all of the templates, I have started from near the beginning of the career. For two of the templates I end at the career plateau, but for one I continue and look at how the career decline can be managed too.

The templates in this chapter do not detail every step when building a career; instead, they focus on different aspects, although there will always be certain similarities (for instance, I'm never going to recommend that you don't gig). Any artist will have lots of options when developing his or her career; these templates illustrate how certain choices can be made. The choices I have put forward are what I feel would help an artist achieve a sustainable career in the quickest manner. Of course, in the real world, each career step would have to be reviewed in light of experience and current conditions.

You will also see that I haven't sought to slavishly follow the principles set out in this book. In developing your own career plan, you need to apply the ideas in light of your own situation: You will need to figure out what works for you. It is pointless to try to do anything that will not give you results (unless you want to be an expert in things that help your career to fail).

You will see that of the three templates, two are for non-US options. My reason for doing this is not that I am advocating a Eurocentric career; however, it is possible to have a career in the US without ever having to leave the country (although, if you have a very niche audience, you may need to look outside of the US). By contrast, the countries in Europe are all much smaller, and so it will usually be necessary to cross national borders to go in search of your audience.

Singer/Songwriter

For this first template, I'm going to look at a US-based female singer/songwriter performing with a guitar—a 21st-century take on Joni Mitchell or Tracy Chapman (not that either of these artists is not valid in the 21st century).

One of the great advantages of guitar-based singer/songwriters is that they can perform anywhere at any time—all that is needed is a guitar (which they can carry). There is no complicated or heavy gear that needs to accompany the artist. This means that the artist can perform in a wide variety of venues and can travel to gigs very easily and fairly inexpensively (it is the cost of a ticket for the artist).

Equipment costs are equally low. All the artist needs is a good guitar (which has a built-in pickup/microphone to make amplification easy) and a sturdy flight case. Clearly the guitar should be good, but it shouldn't be too precious because it may get damaged or lost during the artist's travels.

This simplicity is one factor that will encourage people to hire someone in this situation. All that is needed is a microphone and a PA, and the act will be ready to go. There will be no expensive equipment for the promoter to worry about. Equally, the cost of hiring a single person can be much lower than the cost of hiring a whole band.

Sources of Income

Typically, for a singer/songwriter in this genre, the two main sources of income will be CD sales and live performances. Merchandise will be a less significant income stream, although it should still be taken seriously. Typical merchandise may include some clothing (T-shirts, sweatshirts, and perhaps baseball caps) and may also include souvenir programs. Items that would be unlikely to sell would be those more associated with the teen/pre-teen market (such as fluffy pencil cases and the like).

To my mind, for this sort of artist, the key to success is to build a credible live reputation. This sort of artist should be able to progress well into her career before thinking about a CD release and even further before thinking about any merchandising in a significant way.

Added to this from a logistical perspective, if we are just thinking about a "girl with guitar" act, then traveling with a stock of T-shirts and CDs to sell is likely to be impractical.

I will look at other sources of income later in this section.

Figure 13.1 shows the likely career path of a singer/songwriter. The rest of this section describes this path in greater detail.

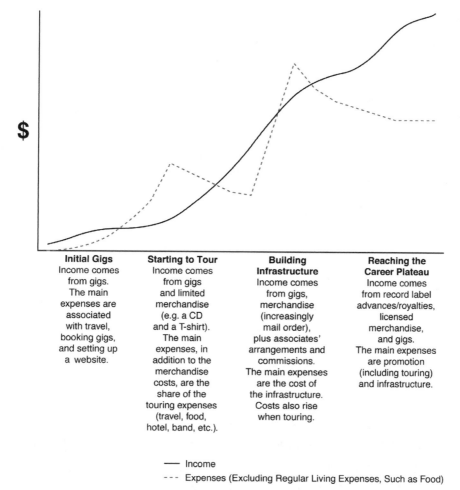

Figure 13.1 The career path of a singer/songwriter.

Initial Gigs

The obvious way to start building a small following and to polish the artist's act is by gigging. I would expect that contact details would be collected from the start and that a suitable website would be set up and maintained, so I will not mention these further.

As a single performer, many avenues may be open for an acoustic singer/songwriter—the clichéd example is a coffeehouse performance. This venue would clearly not be suitable for a rock band or a symphony orchestra, but it is nearly perfect for a solo performer. Equally, arranging small gigs where you invite a few friends who bring along a few friends (and so start the word-of-mouth marketing campaign) is a very simple task. You may even find that you could borrow a friend's front room to perform.

There are many other outlets you can consider beyond the traditional gig circuit and singer/songwriter nights—for instance, fairs and shows. Alternatively, again taking advantage of the "can play anywhere/no setup time" message, you could perform between acts at a concert. One of the most significant pieces of exposure that Tracy Chapman received was when she came on at Nelson Mandela's 70th birthday gig in 1988: This catapulted her into the consciousness of the global record-buying public, and she hasn't looked back since. Although you may not be able to organize this level of exposure, getting in front of larger audiences will help you to find more potential fans.

For the singer/songwriter who has some good songs and is quite dogged about chasing down gigging opportunities, the transition to full-time professional musician should be relatively smooth.

Building an Audience/Starting to Tour

Fans of this genre tend to be fairly broadminded, so they will consider seeing other similar acts. This provides a great opportunity for gig swapping and audience sharing. If you can find enough people to swap gigs with (say five or six other acts with fan bases in different geographical locations than yours), then you have the basis for a tour. This may be quite a small-scale tour—perhaps a tour of only one coast. However, it still provides an opportunity to get your music in front of more people and to expand your fan base.

Bringing together several solo singer/songwriters gives each artist some new options:

- First, you could hire a band. The same band could be used for all of the artists. If there are five artists on the bill, this would mean that the cost of the band would be split five ways, so you could have a band for 20% of the regular cost.

- A tour of singer/songwriters is quite a unique event—this sort of event has happened before, but it is still not an everyday occurrence. This unique factor should make it much easier to generate some press interest. Added to which, instead of just generating your own publicity, you have four other acts promoting a show with which you are involved.

Building Infrastructure

If you are going to tour, then it would seem daft not to have at least some products to sell. Hopefully, as part of the shared tour facilities, you will be able to share the selling of merchandise. Initially, I would suggest you start with just a CD and a limited amount of clothing, perhaps just a T-shirt.

Once you're into a world of having goods to sell, then you need to think about your infrastructure. This is another area where you can think about collaborating with others, perhaps with the people with whom you have swapped gigs or toured. Again, this will help you to share the costs with a number of people.

However, you may have a few disagreements about who should do what and take which risks and responsibilities. In the end you may find that one person sets up his own infrastructure and will sell your goods/fulfill your orders for a charge.

Once you have goods to sell, you can look at ways to generate income from your website. Clearly you will want to sell (or facilitate the sale of) your goods from your website. There are other sources of income that can be generated from the website:

- First, you can use an associates-type arrangement (such as Amazon Associates) to generate commission for yourself on the sale of goods that may interest your fan base. For instance, you might want to recommend some poetry anthologies to your fan base.

- Second, you could refer people to the websites of the people with whom you are sharing (or have shared) a tour or with whom you have swapped gigs, and generate some commission on these sales.

Although I would expect you to have a fairly healthy career, at this stage you may still be essentially a one-person band, perhaps with a friend or family member answering the phone and dealing with office-type issues. Accordingly, if you are going to need an infrastructure, then you may find it easier to get someone else to do everything for you. In this case, you could:

- Sell CDs through CD Baby (or another fulfillment service)

- Sell merchandise through one of the on-demand services

You could also license your merchandise; however, with this arrangement you will come under pressure to allow a wider range of goods to be produced.

Career Peak/Plateau

As a singer/songwriter, you are likely to be able to hit the peak of your career comparatively soon, perhaps around the time you will be thinking about a second CD. You should also expect to be able to maintain the peak/plateau for a number of years, provided you don't get too overexposed.

While you are at the career plateau stage, there will be a number of changes to the way you work.

CD Releases

Given the small nature of your operation, you may find that the best way to get your CD released is to work with a major record label. Maybe you could sign a full exclusive recording contract, or perhaps some form of manufacturing and distribution deal would more suit your needs.

However, record labels like to release lots of product and repackage old material. (It's not uncommon to see acts who only released two or three CDs during their career having seven or eight variants of Greatest Hits/Best Of CDs.) Most singer/songwriters would be unhappy with their material being treated in such an overtly commercial manner and would therefore look to keep some sort of control. This may mean that you work with a smaller label that gives more personal service and has less of a "sell at all costs" attitude.

Live Performances

As you grow in popularity, there are likely to be two groups of fans:

- Those who have followed you for years and wish you would go back to your solo acoustic roots. (These are probably the people who complained when Bob Dylan went electric.)

- Those who love what you do now.

There is scope to please both of these fan groups; however, you must approach them in different ways.

For those who love what you are doing now, you should put on big shows (as would any major act). Obviously, for this level of show you would need your own band—it wouldn't really be practical to tour with other singer/songwriters and share a backing band once you have reached this level (unless you could find someone of a similar stature).

For those people who yearn for the intimate solo gigs, you can give them that. Hire specialist venues—perhaps theatres where the stage is in the round (rather than having a proscenium arch)—instead of using conventional gig venues.

Ironically, these smaller, more intimate gigs may be viewed by the press as being more newsworthy. However, these gigs will generate far less income, so you need to extract the maximum income from each performance. One way is to push up prices (certainly these gigs should be priced higher than the front-row seats at your big shows). In addition, this sort of show would make a great basis for a live DVD.

Other Products

When looking to broaden your portfolio of products, it isn't necessary to go down the standard merchandising routes. For instance, your fan base may be interested if you wrote a collection of poems or a book. These products may not be as commercial as items of clothing, but your position may give you an outlet for your creative endeavors beyond your music.

Personal Development

When you reach your career plateau, it is important that you don't stagnate personally or artistically. Your audience will be developing as individuals and will expect your songs to reflect their changing hopes and concerns. They will also expect your songs to remain relevant to the prevailing political situation. For you as an artist, this is good: Your audience not only gives you permission to change, it expects you to change. The challenge is to ensure you stay in tune (metaphorically) with their concerns and don't get too far ahead of your audience.

Rock Band

For my second template, I am going to take the example of a hypothetical rock band from Luxembourg (which does sound like a great basis for a spoof movie). I've chosen Luxembourg for this fictitious example because it is a very small country: The population is around 500,000. To survive, this band will have to cross national borders, which is lucky because the members are very international in their outlook.

Figure 13.2 and Figure 13.3 show how this rock band could kick-start their career and grow to be an act on the international stage. Please note that these graphs show the main trends and are not drawn to scale. The remainder of this section explains this career plan in greater detail.

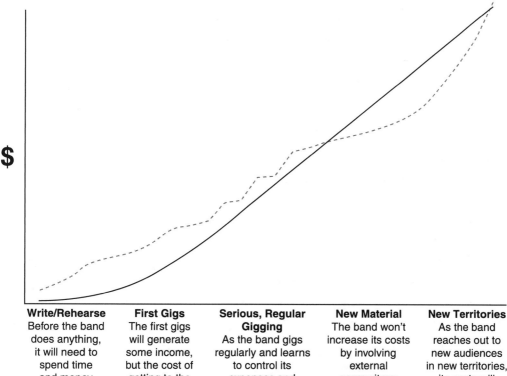

Write/Rehearse	**First Gigs**	**Serious, Regular Gigging**	**New Material**	**New Territories**
Before the band does anything, it will need to spend time and money creating an act.	The first gigs will generate some income, but the cost of getting to the gigs is likely to exceed the income generated by the performance.	As the band gigs regularly and learns to control its expenses and increases its income, it can start to make a profit. There will be jumps in the expenditure when the band purchases a van, T-shirts, etc. and hires a producer in connection with the production of its CD.	The band won't increase its costs by involving external songwriters; however, this involvement will help to increase the band's income (through offering a better product).	As the band reaches out to new audiences in new territories, its costs will increase. This additional expense will be offset by increased income from the band's existing markets.

——— Income

- - - Expenditure

Figure 13.2 The career arc of a rock band in its growth phase.

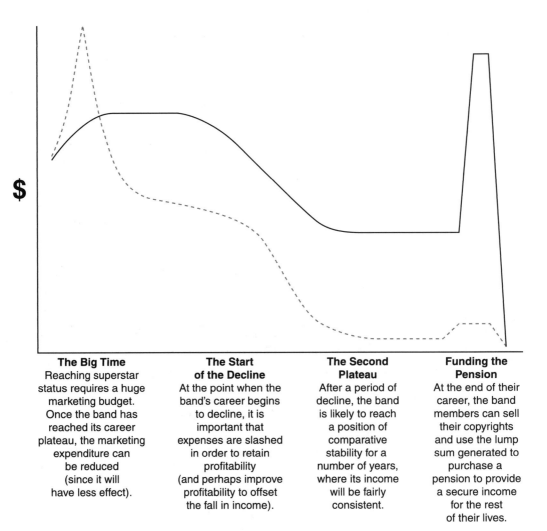

$

The Big Time	The Start of the Decline	The Second Plateau	Funding the Pension
Reaching superstar status requires a huge marketing budget. Once the band has reached its career plateau, the marketing expenditure can be reduced (since it will have less effect).	At the point when the band's career begins to decline, it is important that expenses are slashed in order to retain profitability (and perhaps improve profitability to offset the fall in income).	After a period of decline, the band is likely to reach a position of comparative stability for a number of years, where its income will be fairly consistent.	At the end of their career, the band members can sell their copyrights and use the lump sum generated to purchase a pension to provide a secure income for the rest of their lives.

—— Income from Music
--- Expenditure

Figure 13.3
The career arc of a rock band as it reaches its career plateau and then declines.

Before Anything Else Happens

Clearly, the first step for any ambitious rock band is to write some songs, rehearse those songs, rewrite the songs, and then rehearse some more. This refining process should carry on until the band feels it is really hot. At this stage, it will probably be average at best.

The next step would be to perform a few informal/low-key gigs and learn from that experience so the material can be honed and the performance refined.

An important factor for any band with international ambitions is their fluency with non-domestic languages, in particular English if English is not their mother tongue. While many within the English-speaking world can only speak one language (English), English-only speakers are sometimes intolerant of others who are not able to get by in English (and this double-standard does not seem to concern them). Fortunately, most Europeans speak three of four languages (including English) well.

This band should ensure that (at the very least) their lead singer is fluent in English and as many other languages as possible. French and German are spoken in Luxembourg. As well as the UK and US, there are well-developed rock markets in Northern Europe (Germany, Belgium, Denmark, Finland, and Norway) and Japan, so the band should try to become acquainted with these (if only to say "Thank you very much... the next song is called..."). The more languages that can be spoken, the more chances this band will have to find an audience, and the more chances they will have to organize gigs outside of Luxembourg.

First Serious Steps

After a year or so, the band should have a set of songs and be able to put on a show that lasts around an hour. This is when the serious gigging should begin.

Luxembourg is approximately 20 miles wide and 30 miles long. To give you some idea of scale, Luxembourg is smaller than London (if you assume London is the area within the M25) and has a population that is approximately 5% of the size of London's. Therefore, if this band is going to get anywhere with its career, it needs to get out of Luxembourg.

One of the advantages of Luxembourg is that it is located very centrally in Europe, so traveling to Belgium, Germany, Denmark, or even the UK is comparatively easy. If you include Russia (with the former Soviet republics) as well as the European Union candidate countries, there may be around one billion people in Europe. This is a huge potential audience. Most of those people can be reached with a drive of less than 24 hours from Luxembourg.

At this stage, the band should get out and play wherever and whenever possible. All the usual tricks should be used to find gigs: calling up friends, asking other bands, calling venues, calling promoters, swapping gigs, and so on.

At each gig the band should collect email addresses (or other contact details) from everyone who turns up. Each month the band should send an email (or a flyer in the mail) to let their fans know about their upcoming gig schedule. Naturally, all of these details should be included on the band's website (which, at this stage, should be a fairly simple site).

During this period, the band will need to ensure it keeps writing new material and improving its stage performance.

Regular Gigging

It may take a year, or it may take longer, but at some point the band should be in a state of permanent gigging. At this stage, the band may need someone to help coordinate its activities and to ensure that the money is all accounted for. This help could come from a manager, an accountant, or an office administrator with an eye for detail.

My preference would be for the administrator, who could then also coordinate gig bookings. I would expect the role of this person to be crucial as you grow as a band—indeed, it may become the role of several people. On the assumption this is something that the band would be happy to look after, I will not mention the role of the administrator again in this section.

At this stage, if it hasn't done so already, the band should make an investment in a reliable van (ideally one with low running costs).

The band might want to think about getting some T-shirts to sell at gigs. To keep costs down, the band could start by only ordering one size. If this initial order sells well, it can fund more T-shirts in more sizes.

The key issue with these gigs is for the band to stay afloat financially.

The gigs may not create huge profits for the band, but as long as the gigs do not suffer an overall loss, the band will probably be doing well financially.

A First CD Release

At some point when the band has been gigging constantly for a year or so, they are likely to want to release a CD. This first release should serve three purposes:

- To create something to sell to the fans and so generate income

- To create something to sell to the fans to cement the relationship with them and so that they can play the band's music for their friends (potential new fans)

- To promote the band (in other words, something you can send to the media)

At this stage, the band probably won't have enough topnotch material, so a prudent course would be to record a five-track CD. Limiting the number of tracks means that only the very best material can be selected.

Recording a rock band is a specialized job that requires people with experience working in this genre. It is not something that can usually be successfully accomplished by using a home computer. If the band is serious, then even though the CD is its first professional recording, they will go into a first-rate professional studio to record these songs. To ensure an internationally acceptable commercial sound, the band will also hire a producer who has experience working with their genre.

Make no mistake; this is a big step forward for the band and probably one that will cost a fair chunk of money. Not to mention, it can be quite a challenge to persuade a recognized producer to work with an unknown band. However, if the band is serious about carving out an international career, then this is the action it needs to take.

To meet this expense, the band may have to take out a loan. To ensure this loan can be repaid, the band must have a strategy to generate enough sales to raise the money to repay the loan and make a profit that can go to partially finance the next project.

There are two obvious places to sell the five-track CD:

- At gigs. (The band should, of course, keep gigging as much as possible before and after the CD is recorded.)

- From the band's website. (When the CD is ready, the band can email its whole mailing list to let them know about the new CD.)

If the band is going to the expense of recording the CD, then it should spend a bit more money and get a professional website created.

It is important that the CD is not released until the band has some really good songs and the fan base has sufficient critical mass that the band can be fairly sure that sales of the CD will, at a minimum, cover the expenses of the project. Until that critical buying mass has been achieved, the band should stay away from the studio and continue to gig and build its fan base.

Opening More Doors

As well as generating income, the process of producing the CD should also be used to open doors. Associating a "name" producer with the band will generate more buzz within the industry, and if the band develops a good working relationship with the producer, he or she will be able to make contacts for the band to further their career. One contact that may be worth pursuing is a songwriting partner.

Working with outside songwriters could have many advantages for the band. In particular, it will help them to:

- Create a range of commercial songs.

- Hone their songwriting skills.

- Improve their marketability. (Again, the association with hit writers can create a buzz around the band.)

However, while outside songwriters are important if the band is going to improve the quality of its material (and therefore stand a better chance of making it to superstar status), do not get too distracted by this route. Remember, the band's income comes from its fan base. The purpose of generating credibility within the industry is to find people who can help the band and will want to work with them. The credibility won't bring any income on its own—it is only useful if it leads to an expanded fan base and converts those new fans into a stream of income.

The band should be taking its new songs and playing them to their audience. This will give them some instant feedback about the quality of the new material and the direction being taken (if there is a change). Bringing in an outside songwriter doesn't necessitate a change of style; however, it does mean that something will be different. If there is no change, then there's no point in working with other people. It is up to the band to ensure the new material is the sort of stuff to which the fan base will want to listen.

The other advantage of performing your new material live is that the co-writers will receive some payment (through performance royalty collection agencies). This is only likely to amount to a few cents for the songwriter, and although this won't represent everything the writer could hope to receive, it will be a start. Hopefully over time, the co-written songs will generate a good income for the band and the co-writers.

More Live Performances, a Second CD, and More Merchandise

Assuming the new material is going down well, the band should now start adopting a new strategy.

At this stage, the band will probably have been gigging for several years. Often there may have only been a few months to separate gigs in a city. This presents a danger of overexposure, which could mean that gigs will not be seen as "events," so fans won't bother to turn up.

To guard against this, the band should start to play less frequently in its established locations, and these less-frequent gigs should be played in larger venues (ideally more than 1,000 seats and maybe even aiming for up to 5,000 seats). Typically, the locations where there is a fan base of sufficient size will be the major cities: It is unlikely that the band will be popular throughout a whole country (except, perhaps, for some of the smaller countries). Larger venues will also help to generate larger income and provide a better forum for selling merchandise.

The band should still continue to play as many gigs as it can in locations where it is less popular at the moment. Remember, the potential audience in Europe is around 1 billion people—in other words, about three times the potential audience that the band could reach in the US. That's not to say the band shouldn't try to reach an audience in the US (and the Far East, too). Adding the US, Japan, and South Korea would give an increased potential audience of around another 500 million people.

The band should consider a second five-track CD. There will be the temptation to go for a full album, but that again risks too much substandard material being included. The same strategy should be adopted as with the first five-track CD: Hire a professional studio and an experienced producer and make the best recording possible.

As a side note, the band shouldn't get too worried about releasing two five-track CDs rather than an album. At some point in the future, these two CDs can be combined (maybe with the addition of one or two tracks) and released as an album. When the two CDs are finally released as one album, they will provide far more income than they did when they were released individually (and far more income than would have been generated if a whole album was released in the first place).

By creating two five-track CDs, the quality of the included material will have been enhanced. It's much harder to include substandard tracks when you only have five tracks to think about. If both of the CDs are made available on iTunes (and the other download services), then there will be an album's worth of material available at this point. However, unlike conventional albums on which the first three tracks are great, the next two are good, and the rest are weak, all of the material will be topnotch.

As well as having a second CD to sell, the band should think about expanding its range of merchandise. In particular, it could think about one or two additional T-shirt designs and perhaps a poster. More merchandise may be appropriate, depending on the attitude (and buying preferences) of the fan base.

The band should also make efforts to build relations with the rock press. The rock press is important because it has a number of specialized magazines that reach the target audience the band will be looking to attract.

There are some comparatively cheap ways to build a good relationship with the press. Perhaps one of the most appealing (from the journalist's perspective) is to take a journalist on the road for a few days. This tends to make journalists think they have lived the rock-and-roll lifestyle and are part of the gang. This may not be true, but it does usually encourage favorable comments.

Stepping Up to the Big Time

By this point, the band should have:

- A loyal following spread over several European countries (and the band will know how to contact these people)

- A lot of gigging experience and the ability to put on a first-class show in any size venue—the band should be playing some fair-sized gigs

- At least five products to sell (two CDs, two T-shirts, and a poster)

Now the band can take that bold step and record and release its first album.

Albums are expensive and time-consuming to record. Added to this, they need a video or two to accompany the singles (or the tracks that are being promoted). There are then the logistical aspects of production and distribution to be considered, and a marketing plan will be needed. All of these aspects should be coordinated by one person: This is where a manager would be useful.

However, any manager may balk at the strategy I am about to propose. Added to that, a manager is likely to suggest that the band sign with a record company (in part because this addresses many of the challenges in producing an album and will generate an advance, which means that the manager gets paid). The other alternative for the band is to consider whether their administrative person is up to the task.

Anyway, I'll leave the issue of whether to find a manager just hanging for the time being. Whatever happens, unless the band has generated significant profits from its gigging over the last few years, it will need some source of finance to pay for the album project. The money could come from a number of sources, including:

- A publishing deal. With the imminent release of an album, a publisher may well be happy to put up an advance. However, this is unlikely to be enough money to finance the album.

- A manager. An entrepreneurial manager may put up some of his or her money to help finance an album. However, managers who will take this sort of risk will be few and far between (and will expect a hefty payback for this risk).

- A record label.

- Borrowing.

Only the last two are likely to provide sufficient funds. Borrowing by the band is a riskier strategy but is also the course that could lead to much higher rewards if the project is successful.

Because this is only a hypothetical situation, I'll leave you to ponder the course you would take, and I will move on to talk about the album.

I prefaced this part with the assumption that the band should be a great live act and playing some significant gigs. Therefore, the band's first album should be a live album, again recorded with a producer.

By recording a live gig, the band will cut their studio and recording costs and the accommodation and living expenses associated with recording an album. By involving a producer, the band can ensure that the album will be of the very highest quality. If the gigs are recorded on video, this will create the videos that can be seen on music TV channels, and the band also has the option of releasing a DVD.

For the recording, it is crucial that the venue and audience are carefully selected. The venue should be big enough to ensure the band looks like a force to be reckoned with, but not so large that it looks as if they are playing in an aircraft hanger. A smaller venue will also mean a smaller stage, which will help the band to physically dominate their environment—with a larger stage, they could look like dots onstage when the camera pans out. Also, it is good if the venue is small enough that the band can play several nights—this will give them a chance to record each track several times.

Choosing the right audience is also a challenge. Perhaps the band could try to make more of an event out of the recording and encourage fans to come along. Given a reasonably central European location with good transportation links, there should be a good number of people ready to make the journey. The band could also organize hotel accommodations (and, of course, take a commission here too).

At the time of recording, the band will have been on the road fairly constantly for a few years and so should be as hot as it is possible for a band to be. A live album with accompanying video will demonstrate that the band is a force to be reckoned with on the live circuit.

The live album/DVD combination will be able to generate a lot of buzz. With this buzz, the areas the band should capitalize on are:

- Finding more fans. These potential fans need to be converted to fans who will spend money. Perhaps the best way to convert these people is to play in front of them, so the band had better get back on the road very soon after releasing the album.

- Finding promoters. Promoters will help the band to get more gigs, bigger gigs, and gigs in different territories. Working with a promoter will also help to reduce the financial risks of touring for the band.

The album is also likely to generate some record company interest.

Reaching the Career Peak/Plateau

It will probably take somewhere between five and ten years for the band to reach its career peak/plateau, and as the band starts to reach this stage, it will be working like crazy. If the band decided not to get a manager earlier in their career, this is the point to reappraise that decision and to find a manager they can trust. The success of the live album will mean that the band has enough clout to find a top-rate manager who will be able to take the band's career to the next level and ensure they stay at the top for as long as possible.

The manager should be charged with the following tasks:

- Taking control of all of the business activities of the band. The administrator should be kept on and could perhaps step up to act as a business manager (if the administrator became the manager, then perhaps it is time to hire a business manager). The manager should take a strategic view of the band's activities and should look at creating additional sources of income. For instance, so far the merchandising income has been restricted to a few T-shirts and a poster. Perhaps the first deal the manager can find for the band is a licensing deal for merchandise.

- Finding a record company to work with. The band may want to enter into an exclusive recording contract, license their material, or enter a production and distribution deal. All of these options should be open to the band, and given the band's global ambitions, it is probably not practical to try to operate with a homemade solution. This is a time when the band needs to get their product into brick-and-mortar stores (even though this reduces many of the immediate possibilities for direct communication with their new fans).

  With their manager looking out for their best interests, the band can probably negotiate a good deal. Let us assume they negotiate an exclusive recording contract with their royalties being calculated as a share of profits.

- Sorting out the band's first world tour. This should not simply be a dream for the band. A manager should make a world tour happen and find ways to open up international markets for the act. Organizing a world tour is a logistical nightmare and is an area where a manager will prove his or her skill.

Reaching this stage, the band will follow the well-worn path of releasing an album every two or three years and then going on a world tour to support the album. Clearly, this will be a financially rewarding period for the band (and anyone else who takes a cut). During this time it is important that the band keeps collecting contact details from as many people as possible. This group of people will form the core fan base that sustains the band until their retirement.

The Beginning of the Descent

After a certain period at the top, times will change: The band members may get tired of each other, or they may get tired of the constant merry-go-round of being on the road. Alternatively, the public may just become less keen on their style of music, which may have ceased to have any currency against the prevailing trends. Whatever the reason, at a certain time, the descent will begin for our fictitious band.

For the sake of argument, let's suppose that this begins around the time the band hit their 40s. (This will make it easier to delineate the next career periods.)

The first step on the downward path (if the band wants a slow, steady descent and they don't want to plummet like a stone) is to renegotiate their record deal. A profit-sharing deal can be good when you're at the top of your career. At some point on the way down, it will start to operate against the band's financial interest. If they negotiate now, then there is some advantage for the record company in changing the financial terms (because the band will give away a greater share of their current earnings). If the band negotiates later, it will be in a much weaker position because it will be generating less income with which it can negotiate.

The band will have many options, assuming they are negotiating a new contract rather than renegotiating terms with their existing label. They can stay with a major (and negotiate different terms), go with an independent label, or revert back to a self-release strategy in the same way that they self-released their five-track CDs at the start of their career. Whatever they choose, it is important (if possible) to retain as many copyrights as possible. The reasoning for this will become clear later.

Let's assume the band goes with a production and distribution deal with a major. Depending on the nature of the contracts that the band entered into, it may have a range of options for its back catalogue. The main options will be:

- Repackage back catalogue (and perhaps re-master too). These could then be sold through the band's website. Alternatively, the band could include these reissues as part of their production and distribution deal. The advantage of direct websales is that the band may generate more income on each sale than will be the case for sales from brick-and-mortar stores.

- Re-record the band's classic songs (perhaps with a unique modern twist) and release the recordings as a new album. This offering would mostly appeal to existing fans.

- Make serious efforts to license out the back catalogue for use with video (particularly for use with television programs).

There will be two other significant changes. First, the nature of gigs will change. In particular, they will become smaller and less frequent. This gives the band the opportunity to choose to play more intimate, discreet gigs. They can also perform unique reinterpretations of their material—for instance, they could perform a series of acoustic gigs. Although these smaller gigs will generate less income overall, they can generate more income on a per-audience-member basis.

The other main change will be to merchandising. The sales will fall, particularly if there are fewer gigs and fewer people turning up at the gigs. However, if the band is still happy to license a merchandising firm to produce this gear, then they can continue to generate an income with little financial risk.

Age 50: Taking It Easy

After a decade of decline, the band members will be in their 50s. At this stage, CDs of original music and gigs will be less frequent occurrences. The prime new income source will be from licensing their music.

Age 60 and Onward: Pension

At the age of 60, the band members may want to convert their uncertain musical income into a certain stream of income. They can do this in two steps. First, they can sell all of the rights that they own. (This is why I suggested earlier in this section that the band retain as many copyrights as it can as it moves off the peak of its career. Clearly, without owning the rights, the band wouldn't be able to sell them to generate a lump sum.)

With the cash lump sum generated by selling the rights, the band members can then purchase an annuity, which will provide a far more stable income source.

This may appear to be a strategic about-face: The band kept many rights during their career, but are now selling everything. This also appears to go against all the principles of owning a copyright. These comments are true; however, this sale is one way to ensure a financially secure retirement (especially when the band has spent many years partying).

Boy Band

The boy-band format is a pretty tired idea, so let me tell you what I would do if I were a London-based manager looking to create a male-voice, close-harmony, pop group with five members.

The first thing I would do is totally ignore the US market. This is not because the US market is a bad place, but simply because UK/European boy bands don't have a great history of success in crossing the Atlantic. Instead, I would focus on the markets where these bands have historically been more successful: Europe and the Far East.

As far as the band goes, I would recruit members from around the European Union. The intention would be to get a mix of looks, musical influences, and languages. I would not choose more than one person from any one country.

The members of the band would be aged between 16 and 21. As the members reach 21, they will "retire" from the band. New members will be found (again bringing new and diverse European cultural influences).

Through this approach, the band will never age. This is good because the age of the fan base for this sort of band is fairly set: The audience tends to be preteen and young teenage girls who will grow out of these types of bands.

The "retired" members will hopefully stay with the management stable, and many will go on to have solo careers, which can be launched on the back of their career in the band. The solo careers will give the artists the chance to grow and hopefully keep an audience with them who have grown out of the band. In this way, the existing fan base will be retained for its economic value. However, it should go without saying that not everyone who leaves the band will have a successful solo career.

Another aspiration of making an ageless band is that mothers will introduce their daughters to the band and so the audience will go full circle. Added to this, because a fan is likely to be interested in the band for five years (at most), the hit songs can be recycled (or should that be reinterpreted?) from time to time. This will help the parent-to-child continuum.

That's the basic concept; let's look at some of the details. You will see that this template covers the establishment of the band and its launch on the road to fame and fortune. I'll leave you to think about some of the practicalities, such as what sort of arrangements should be made to release CDs.

Getting Started

Unlike the previous examples, this sort of band would find it very hard to earn money on the traditional club circuit because there is little potential audience at these venues. Added to this, given the expenses of running this band (which I will discuss), the income from gigging is unlikely to be sufficient. However, the clichéd venues for boy band personal appearances are still likely to be popular: schools and gay clubs. The twist I would add is to use these appearances as opportunities to collect contact details and rely heavily on word of mouth to spread interest.

To capitalize on the word-of-mouth interest, it would be necessary to have a very well-developed website that is up and running from day one.

In addition to the appearances, I would look for as many television and other media appearances as possible. I would keep a publicity person on the staff whose salary would be partly determined by the amount of media coverage that the band received.

Preparing the Act

One of the difficulties of not having a conventional gig circuit for the band to join is that they will not have an opportunity to learn their craft the traditional (hard) way. Another issue for this band is that due to the investment that is being made (as will become clear), the backers would be looking to make profits more quickly than would be the case in the two previous example career templates. To make bigger and quicker profits, the band will have to be at the professional level from the moment it is launched on the public.

This will have an effect in two areas:

- Songs for boy bands must be highly commercial, and the production must be very current. To get both of these factors right, outside songwriters/producers would be approached. These writers would be approached from the start of the project (maybe before the band members have been selected). For a unique twist, instead of the regular ballads, I would go for something more blues-based (which I think would end up giving more of a soulful feel).

- The band's stage show and public perception (during interviews and the like) must be topnotch from the onset: There is no scope to grow in public. To get to this level of professionalism, the band will need to be groomed. Essentially, a singing tutor, dance tutor, and media advisers will be necessary to build the perfect beast of a ready-to-launch professional boy band.

Website

The band's website is of crucial importance because it is the tool that will capture the interest generated by word of mouth and convert that interest into fans (and into an income stream). It is also the conduit through which the band will make their fan base aware of their activities and sell much of their merchandise. In short, it is the focus of all of the band's activities.

The website will have several unique features:

- The site will be open to the public; however, the real content of the website will only be open to a select few (that is, those who pay money and will in essence form the band's official fan club). There will be other benefits of fan club membership (including a discount on merchandise to offset the membership fee).

- Although not a feature of the site itself, a full-time journalist will be retained by the band to provide a constant source of news. The journalist will also be responsible for the content of the site and will ensure that the site is updated regularly. (In this context, regularly means at least weekly: The site will be very much like a weekly magazine.)

- Because of their age, most of the fans will not have credit cards. Without a credit card these people will not be able to spend money very easily. This problem will be addressed by two main solutions:
  - Fan club members will be able to set up wish lists for merchandise. They can then grant (password-protected/identity-checked) access to this wish list to certain individuals (typically friends and family looking to buy gifts for the fan club member).
  - There will be an arrangement where credits that can be spent in the web store can be given to the individual. These credits can be purchased directly (in the same way that other merchandise is purchased) and can then be given as a gift. The real advantage of this approach for the band is that they get the cash before it is spent, and the longer before it is spent, the more interest the band will accrue.

- There will be a forum on the website; this will only be open to fan club members. Given the typical age of the fan base, this will be heavily moderated. In all matters, the safety of the individual fans will be paramount—particularly because it will be hard to verify the identities of people who join the fan club (usual credit card–type checks will be difficult).

Naturally, members of the band will drop in from time to time to say "hi" on the forums (usually one member, once a week).

From Zeroes to Heroes

I've mentioned a few times that at launch the band must be totally professional—in other words, ready for their first album launch and ready to become stars. They should expect their competition to be all of the other acts on the charts. If they are anything less than brilliant, then they will fail and fail very quickly. Not only will this cause the demise of the band, but it will associate the management company with a failure, which is never a good thing.

In the pop music world of boy bands, it is possible to get success comparatively swiftly after a public launch. One of the key influencing factors of success is the marketing campaign, and this will require a lot of money. You may notice that this approach smacks of conventional record company behavior. However, there are a few differences here.

First, the band has already done quite a lot of publicity work (with the low-key gigs at schools and gay clubs). There has also been a lot of word-of-mouth publicity and the facility to suck in a lot of new fans. Having a list of fans means that the management can assess whether the band had achieved sufficient critical mass before it begins its marketing campaign. Although this doesn't guarantee success, it does at least allow a picture of the possible interest in the band to be developed.

You will also remember that the band has a full-time journalist on staff who will be able to spend his or her time creating many stories about the band, which will be great publicity.

Perhaps the biggest difference from the conventional approach is what happens when the fans have found the band. For this situation, there is then the direct relationship between the band and the fans, which will cement the relationship, adding more permanence. Although it is understood and acknowledged that a relationship with a boy band will never be permanent, it does give an expectation of a longer relationship and builds a solid basis on which the solo careers can be built.

Figure 13.4 illustrates the career path of the band.

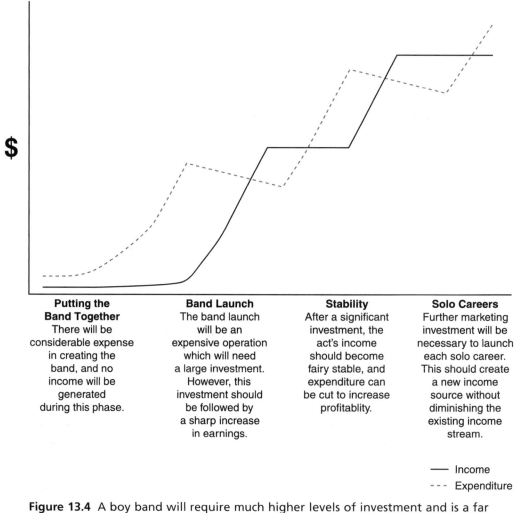

Putting the Band Together	Band Launch	Stability	Solo Careers
There will be considerable expense in creating the band, and no income will be generated during this phase.	The band launch will be an expensive operation which will need a large investment. However, this investment should be followed by a sharp increase in earnings.	After a significant investment, the act's income should become fairy stable, and expenditure can be cut to increase profitablity.	Further marketing investment will be necessary to launch each solo career. This should create a new income source without diminishing the existing income stream.

——— Income

--- Expenditure

Figure 13.4 A boy band will require much higher levels of investment and is a far riskier proposition.

Fan Club Membership

Fan club membership is another device for cementing the relationship between the individual fans and the band. There will be many benefits for the fan (in return for the joining fee):

- Access to the fan club–only area of the website. In addition to the forum, the website will include:
  - Short video and audio clips of songs (including previews of forthcoming singles) and interviews with the band—this may become a band diary as a video podcast
  - Competitions

- A quarterly DVD, which will feature:
  - Video clips of songs and interviews with the band—these will be longer versions of the material that is available on the website.
  - Band members telling fan club members about the cool new merchandise that is available.

- Discounts on merchandise
- Priority booking for concert tickets

Fans will also be given the opportunity to earn more credits (which can be spent at the web store) for each new fan club member that they recruit.

Product Range

The product range will be broad and deep and will have every conceivable piece of merchandise.

One staple of the product range will be DVDs. With the constant turnover of band members, there will be many opportunities to show the process of recruiting new members, and the DVDs could be made comparatively cheaply. If part of the audition process is the submission of a video audition, highlights of some of these videos may be included.

There will also be a frequent number of films produced. These will be low-budget, quickly made films, which—as well as providing a source of income—will also provide a possible path into an acting career for some of the retired band members.

Financing

This option for creating and building a band is a far more high-risk strategy than the two earlier templates. It also requires much greater levels of investment. As a rough guess, perhaps an investment of between £500,000 and £1 million ($1 million and $2 million) would be necessary, although there could be many higher- or lower-cost options.

However, this strategy seeks to rapidly establish a cash cow (a business that generates a reliable stream of income), and in this context, the investment may not be so onerous. That being said, even a highly successful manager would think twice about investing $1 million or $2 million of his or her own money.

There will be several sources of income open to a management company establishing this sort of boy band. These include:

- Personal assets. The management company could fund the exercise.

- Business loans. The band could be established as a separate business. (Indeed, this is likely to be a wise route to take.) The business could then take out a loan (for which the management company may have to act as a guarantor, at least for part of the liability).

- Joint venture with a production company. One of the production companies that would be involved in providing material may be interested in taking a larger piece of the action and putting some cash up front. The only downside to this source of income is that the production company may expect to do all of the songwriting, and this could dilute the overall standard of the songs.

- Collaboration with a record company. Any nature of deal could be entered into with a record company. This would have the added advantage of providing a production and distribution partner.

Clearly, the financing is not all needed at once, and more than one of these financing options could be adopted.

14 Tales from the Sharp End

So far in this book there have been a lot of ideas put forward—that is rather the nature of a book that intends to show a range of different ways to do things. For this closing chapter, I want to look at two real-life examples of people who have made a living from music by doing their own thing.

The first example looks at the band Marillion, which has already been mentioned several times. Marillion has adopted a business model that has allowed them to make a living and create the sort of music that they want to make. For those of you who don't know Marillion, their music is not obviously commercial; however, it does appeal to their highly loyal fan base. If you've never heard their music (or if it's been a long time since you heard anything by them), you should check them out. Several other bands (for instance, Simply Red) have since adopted similar strategies, and according to press reports, many other bands are also considering managing their careers in a similar manner.

The second piece comes from Derek Sivers, the president of CD Baby. Before founding CD Baby, Derek made his living as a musician. Derek has been kind enough to give his insights into how musicians can make a living on the US college circuit.

MARILLION

If you want some measure of the influence Marillion (see Figure 14.1) has had on popular culture, check out how many girls born after 1985 have been named Kayleigh. Although parents may not have consciously named their daughters after Marillion's 1985 hit single, there has certainly been an increase in the incidence of the name since then. If you don't believe me, check out the number of baby girls named Kayleigh born in 1984 and 1986—there's quite a difference.

Figure 14.1
Marillion: A band that has achieved musical longevity by running their own business.

A Bit of Marillion's History

Marillion can trace their roots back to the late 1970s. At the start of 1982 they were gigging regularly, and before the release of their first album, the band had played several high-profile London gigs, helped in no small part by the band's ability to hustle and their hiring of a publicity agent. The band signed with EMI at the end of 1982, and their first album (*Script for a Jester's Tear*) was released in 1983.

The band had some modest success with their initial releases. However, it was the single "Kayleigh" from their album *Misplaced Childhood* that propelled them to the big time.

In 1988, the lead singer, Fish, suddenly left the band. Rather than split, the band recruited a new singer, Steve Hogarth, and since then both Marillion and Fish have continued to make their living by making music.

By the late 1990s, although they still continued to work, Marillion's glory days were apparently behind them. When their deal with EMI came to an end, despite selling more than 10 million records, the band was still in debt to the label. With the split from EMI, the band set up their own record label and in 1997 released what was to be their ninth album, *This Strange Engine*.

A New Relationship with the Marillion Fan Base

In 1997 the seeds of a new business strategy were sown when the band explained to fans in North America that they did not have sufficient finances to afford to tour the territory. The fans' reaction was surprising, but the reaction demonstrates the loyalty of the band's fan base. Instead of moaning, the fans raised around $60,000, which was enough to fund the tour.

In 1999, the band released its next album on its record label, Marillion.com, which highlighted the band's website. At this stage, the website was becoming an increasingly important tool in maintaining the band's relationship with its fan base. As you would expect, the website also provided an opportunity to purchase a wide range of merchandise. I probably don't need to tell you the URL, but in case I do, it's http://marillion.com. If for no other reason, you should check out Marillion's website as an excellent example of its kind—it should give you lots of ideas for your own website.

The band's approach to funding their 2001 album *Anoraknophobia* was unique: They asked fans to pre-order the album more than 12 months before release. More than 12,000 fans were happy to prepay for the album. For their 2004 album *Marbles*, they took this concept further and adopted the same pre-ordering arrangement, although this time they raised money to fund the album's marketing campaign.

Ironically, despite the marketing budget, one of the smartest moves the band made was to encourage their fans to buy the single (or several copies of the single) during a specific week. The fans happily bought "You're Gone," and the single entered the charts. Indeed, the band encouraged their fans to help with their marketing by supporting street teams who would put up posters, distribute flyers, and request radio play of their music in the teams' local areas.

Even the large number of pre-orders only constitutes a small percentage of Marillion's sales, so the band also makes their CDs available in brick-and-mortar shops through conventional distribution means.

Marillion now has a small organization that runs their business. There are five band members and five members of staff. Instead of a conventional manager, the band and their communications and marketing manager, Lucy Jordache, manage the band. This small organization is responsible for all of the band's output (including CDs, which are then distributed by a distribution company—there is no outside record label). As you would expect, the main expenses are staff (including a wage for the band members), rent, producer costs, electricity, and equipment.

As well as running the office, Lucy Jordache also works as the band's tour agent (and as the gig promoter in the UK), so the expenses of gigs can be kept down. This means that all tours can make a profit—sales of merchandise are then an added bonus. In addition, with the relationship between the band and its fan base, the band has a much better idea about the numbers that are likely to attend their gigs, so they can cut better deals with promoters when they gig outside of the UK.

At the time of writing this book, Marillion was about to release its fourteenth album, *Somewhere Else*. This album further demonstrates a band that has been able to keep artistic control and make a living from its music.

The continued success of Marillion is founded on its incredibly loyal fan base spread over at least 80 countries. One way the band rewards its fans is by giving away a CD to fan club members around the Christmas season. These CDs include a mixture of previously unreleased tracks, unused recordings, and other snippets that would be unlikely to see the light of day in any other format.

There are two other moneymaking activities that Marillion undertakes that I want to highlight: the Marillion Weekend and the Front Row Club.

Marillion Weekend

Every other year Marillion hosts what may best be described as a Marillion convention. The band hires a holiday camp for an entire weekend and is joined by 2,500 of their fans. This year, they were joined by fans from 38 countries.

Over the course of the event, the band will usually play three separate sets of a wide range of material—for instance, over the most recent Marillion Weekend (at the start of February 2007), the band played:

- On the first night, a complete performance of their album *This Strange Engine*, together with some songs from their new album, *Somewhere Else*.

- On the second night, a collection of covers and some band songs that either have never been played live before or are only played rarely.

- On the third night, a selection of the band members' own favorite Marillion songs.

For the fans, the weekend is highly rewarding, providing a unique opportunity to see the band. For the band, the weekend is a great opportunity to meet their fans and to play material that may not normally be heard. Also for the band, the weekend provides a good source of income—typically, a weekend will generate more income than a four-month tour.

You can read more about the Marillion Weekend at http://marillionweekend.com.

Front Row Club

The Front Row Club was set up to provide fans with access to archives, rarities, and other recordings that could not or would not be released otherwise. It is a membership club for collectors and anyone with a keen interest in Marillion.

Selected recordings are pressed to CD. These recordings are a mixture of live recordings, but they are intended to be of much higher quality than an average bootleg recording, and are not on sale anywhere else. Each CD is then professionally packaged before it is released.

Each member will receive four releases during his or her membership period. The member has the option of which CDs he or she wants to receive.

One of the downsides of CD releases is the potential for duplication of tracks. Therefore, from the start of 2008, the band intends to make this service available as a download-only service.

A Musician's Advice about the College Market by Derek Sivers from CD Baby

Derek Sivers is president and programmer at CD Baby. Here, in his own words, is his advice to musicians about earning a living by playing the college market in the US. Although the advice relates to the US market, the principles can apply to anywhere there is a sufficient number of venues within a geographical area that can be readily reached.

Figure 14.2
Derek Sivers from CD Baby.

From 1995 to 1998 I made my full-time living playing at colleges. I got hired by over 350 schools for about $300,000 (gross, not net) on the East coast (from Florida to Maine, as far west as Arkansas).

I'll try to put into one article, here, every bit of advice or wisdom I could share with my fellow musicians, from my experience. (Disclaimer: These are my opinions and observations from my unique experience only! Others may disagree.)

Who Does the Hiring at Colleges?

One thing to get straight: Don't confuse college radio with college gigs. The kids that run college radio are the real music fans. The ones deeply into music for music's sake. But the ones with the big budgets for entertainment and activities are called the "Student Activities Office."

These are usually made up of the girls in pink sweaters who won the election for class treasurer in high school. (Think Reese Witherspoon in the movie *Election*.) It's a very play-it-safe environment because they want everyone (yes, every last person) to be happy, so they can get re-elected.

This means that the Student Activities Office wants to hire the most fun, safe, lively, crowd-pleasing entertainment possible. Whether it's a hypnotist, comedian, rubber sumo-wrestling suits, the guy that brings the exotic lizards, a famous talk-show host, hot-wax hands, a magician, or musician—they just want entertainment.

When approaching them, you need to emphasize what a safe bet you are. Your marketing should be filled with testimonial quotes like:

"One of the finest performances we've had here all year!"
—The College of St. Angus

"The crowd couldn't stop laughing at his lyrics!"
—The Thirsty Whale

"A real joy to work with—we can't wait to have her back!"
—Siberian Sunbathers' Convention

Your bio should mention all the awards you've won and what big mainstream media sources have also recognized your talent.

It's Not Glamorous

Ask anyone who's done over a dozen college gigs without a big track record. You often play at lunchtime for a depressing cafeteria of stressed-out students who are trying to study and scowl at you for disturbing them. But at least you get paid afterward. Some actual situations I've had:

- Their contract said they had an adequate PA system, but it turned out to be a tiny microphone that plugged into the wall for the principal to address all classrooms. (I did the gig anyway and sang into it.)

- We drove 22 hours for a $4,500 gig in Arkansas, but they forgot we were coming, so we played to eight people in a backyard in 40-degree weather. (Fingers numb.)

- In a big echoey gymnasium, having to set up next to the noisy cotton-candy machine because that was the only power outlet in the room.

An Example

Here's my diary from two typical weeks on the road:

Friday, August 22, 1998	Salem-Teikyo University; Salem, West Virginia
Saturday, August 23, 1998	Longwood College; Farmville, Virginia
Sunday, August 24, 1998	St. Bonaventure University; Olean, New York
Thursday, August 27, 1998	Alfred State College; Alfred, New York
Saturday, August 29, 1998	Franklin Pierce College; Rindge, New Hampshire
Sunday, August 30, 1998	Worcester State College; Worcester, Massachusetts
Wednesday, September 2, 1998	Douglass College – Rutgers University; New Brunswick, New Jersey
Wednesday, September 9, 1998	Greenfield Community College; Greenfield, Massachusetts

Wednesday, September 9, 1998   Lasell College; Newton, Massachusetts

Thursday, September 10, 1998   University of Maine; Orono, Maine

Friday, September 11, 1998   University of New England –
Westbook Campus; Portland, Maine

Friday, September 11, 1998   University of Maine Machias;
Machias, Maine

It's not a perfectly scheduled tour. The idea of a real "tour," where you cross the country in a perfect line, rarely happens. The way I was able to make a full-time living out of it was by saying yes to everything.

Ohio on April 8th.

Connecticut on April 9th.

Michigan on April 10th.

Maine on April 11th. No problem!

Play for 2 hours. Drive for 14. Play for 2. Drive for 16. Repeat and fade....

Another scenario: You live in New York. You mail your flyer to colleges from Florida to Maine, imagining a nice, long tour. Instead, you only book two gigs: one from South Carolina, one from New Hampshire.

Because of this, doing the college circuit on the East Coast is a lot easier than doing the West Coast. There are 500 colleges within an eight-hour drive of New York City.

But You're a Road Dog, Right?

- You can perform in any situation, right?

- Your guitarist quits the night before a gig, and you've got another guitarist to take her place, right?

- You've got enough money to pay for your own transportation and hotel both ways, in case something goes wrong, right?

- After driving 14 hours, you're clean, lively, and friendly, right?

- When they change their mind at the last minute and want you to perform at 11 a.m. instead of 11 p.m., you roll with it, right?

- When the drunk frat boys heckle you and run their "Play some Skynyrd!" joke into the ground, you keep your cool and do your best show possible anyway, right?

- You know plenty of crowd-pleasing cover songs for emergencies, right?

- You've played in the cold with numb fingers, sang full-voice at 9 a.m., and can do three two-hour shows with no break in one day, right?

If not, prima donna, this is not for you.

They Usually Book Long in Advance

Rule of thumb: They book the spring semester in the fall and the fall semester in the spring.

Exceptions: I always booked a lot of April shows in February and December shows in October. But these are usually the smaller "last-minute" shows.

Secret: June is a great month to contact the colleges. The staff-employee, the Director of Student Activities, is there working for the summer when things are quiet. This is a good time for her to book some "Welcome Week" entertainment for the end of August and the beginning of September.

Consider Being Flexible in Your Size

I mainly got into the college market to promote my five-piece funk band (Hit Me). But I figured since I was going to spend all that money on membership fees and marketing, I might as well make some other ways to book me, too. So I made:

- For $1,000, the five-piece funk band.

- For $600, the acoustic two-person version (me and one other band member).

- For $450, me alone.

- And as an afterthought, I made the Professional Pests, where I would run around campus in a black fabric bag, bothering people. Price? $1,500. (Of course, the Professional Pests got as many bookings as my musical acts.)

Point being, I was able to work with any budget they had. Of course, I wished they could always book my $1,000 full band. But if not, I could always sell them on the scaled-down version.

About NACA and Their Conferences

There's an organization called the National Association for Campus Activities (NACA) that puts on conferences where all the Student Activities buyers can get together to check out showcasing talent. Their website is http://www.naca.org.

It's *very* hard to get a showcase spot there. You're up against the best of the best that are spending thousands on making a super-professional video submission. Artists on the Billboard charts, performers with 20 years of college experience, comedians from *Saturday Night Live*, etc. Everyone puts together a great three- to five-minute video of their live performance sampler. Quality matters. Edits matter. That's a whole 'nother subject, though. In short: Your video needs to be amazing. Once a year (summer) you can submit it for showcase consideration. Out of approximately 250 submissions, they pick approximately 20.

And it's expensive to get involved! First, you have to be a NACA member (approximately $300), then buy a booth (approximately $200), then a registration (approximately $125), then a submission fee (approximately $50), and after all that, the odds are 19 out of 20 that you'll be rejected. But if you get accepted, there's a showcase-acceptance fee (approximately $150), then the cost of going and playing (approximately $500). Now, I'm not complaining. I don't think NACA is getting rich. This is just what it costs to do everything they do.

For my band, I submitted for three years (and spent $20,000 doing it!), until I finally got a showcase spot. But once my band played on that main-stage showcase on the opening night, we booked 30 gigs at about $1,000 each, right there on the spot. (Another 100 or so over the next year.) So it *can* all be worth it if you're really going to commit to this and really think it's your thing.

On the other hand, some people spend years trying to get a showcase, finally get one, and don't get any gigs from it. My band was a *very* fun/party/crowd-pleasing band. I think that's why we did so well.

NACA or no NACA?

Every month, I would send out flyers to the Student Activities buyer at every college in my area. My advice on making a good college flyer is here: http://cdbaby.org/collegeflyer.

Out of the 350 schools that hired me, I think over 200 of them came because of my flyers. Which made me think if I had to do it all over again, I might just skip the NACA conference completely and save the money to spend on marketing methods that go directly to the college buyer.

You can see that in my older article, here: http://cdbaby.net/college.

My advice: If you are considering doing the college scene, start with the mailing list and sending flyers. Get a few shows that way and see what you think. If you love it and want to commit years to doing it, no matter what the startup expense, then either join NACA or get a NACA-friendly booking agent.

Index

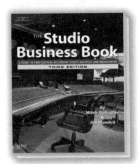

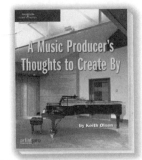